IMPORTANT INFORMATION ABOUT

The information in this manual is not copyrighted and may be reproduced or trans... ...needed.

Every effort has been made to provide, in this publication, the most current and accurate information as of July 1, 2022.

Misprints or outdated information that may appear within these pages will not override or supersede changes that have occurred in the law, promulgated rules and regulations or policy that has been initiated since the printing date.

Where You Can Obtain a Copy of this Publication
This publication is available at every Driver Service Center location across the state.

This publication is also available online at the Tennessee Department of Safety and Homeland Security website:
tn.gov/safety

Written comments/concerns about this publication should be sent to:

> Tennessee Department of Safety and Homeland Security
> Driver Services Division
> PO Box 945
> Nashville, Tennessee 37202

Service Locations to Obtain or Renew Your License:
The Department of Safety and Homeland Security has Driver Service Centers located throughout the state. Our centers are normally open 8:30 a.m. to 5:00 p.m. and closed on official state holidays. Our centers will typically have an increased volume after being closed for a holiday so please plan your visit accordingly.

To find the nearest location that best fit your needs, go to our website at tn.gov/safety or by calling toll-free 1-866-849-3548.

TDD assistance for the hearing impaired can be provided by dialing 615-532-2281 (Telecommunications Device for the Hearing Impaired).

The Tennessee Department of Safety and Homeland Security (TDOSHS) is now issuing more secure driver licenses and identification cards. These new licenses will be produced using an improved production and issuing process resulting in a more temper-proof construction. This will make it much more difficult to alter or counterfeit, protecting private information even more effectively. This process will also help protect you by combating identity theft by allowing TDOSHS to verify photographs stored in the system with customers presenting themselves for new documents.

Interim Documents
A new security practice has been implemented with the issuance of an interim license or ID for customers who are getting a driver license for the first time or renewing their license. This interim license is valid for up to 20 days, and the

permanent license or ID will be mailed to the customer's address. All interim licenses are printed on special security paper and include a photo and signature for identification purposes. The information on the front of the card can be validated by reading the 2D barcode. Many other security features have been incorporated to protect you in preventing driver license fraud and identity theft.

REAL ID

The Real ID Act of 2005 establishes minimum security standards for license issuance and production. It prohibits Federal agencies from accepting for certain purposes driver licenses and identification cards from states not meeting Act's minimum standards. Beginning **May 7, 2025**, all persons must have a REAL ID license or a valid non-expired US Passport, or other forms of TSA acceptable identification to board a commercial airline flight within the United States, entry on to certain Federal properties such as military bases and federal buildings, as well as nuclear facilities. Please visit our website at **TN.gov/safety** for the latest information on REAL ID.

Tennesseans are not required to obtain a REAL ID compliant license or ID. The decision to obtain a REAL ID credential is completely up to you. A REAL ID driver license or identification license is not for any other reason than to allow you to board a domestic commercial aircraft within the US and access certain federal facilities including Military bases and nuclear facilities. The currently scheduled effective date is May 7, 2025.

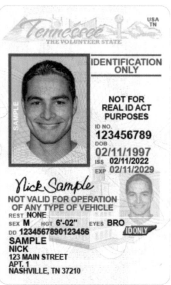

REAL ID COMPLIANT CREDENTIAL EXAMPLE   **NON-COMPLIANT ID EXAMPLE**

For the latest information on REAL ID, please visit the Department of Safety website at:
https://www.tn.gov/tnrealid/

Additional information from the Transportation Security Administration's website can be found at:
https://www.tsa.gov/travel/security-screening/identification for additional acceptable forms of identification.

REAL ID

You DO NOT need a REAL ID compliant credential to:
- Drive a Motor Vehicle
- Vote
- Access federal court buildings
- Visit the post office
- Apply for or receive federal benefits such as Social Security or Veterans' benefits
- Purchase alcohol or cigarettes
- Access hospitals

There is no difference in cost to obtain a REAL ID compliant credential and a non-compliant REAL ID Tennessee license or ID. If it is time to renew your license, the cost to obtain a REAL ID driver license or identification credential will be the standard renewal fee of an 8 year credential. If you are not renewing your license and wish to obtain a REAL ID credential will be the cost of a duplicate license.

Persons under 18 years of age are eligible to obtain a REAL ID compliant license or ID credential. If you are under 18, and have a current driver license or ID credential, you have the same choice as existing license holders and can obtain a REAL ID compliant credential by following the same process as adult credential holders.

Any REAL ID compliant credential issued from another state can be transferred into the state of Tennessee, however you must present and meet all the documentation requirements to obtain a Tennessee REAL ID credential.

You can schedule an appointment to obtain a REAL ID credential at any Driver Service Center. Scheduling an appointment will allow you to be served on a specific day and time. To make an appointment use the QR code below or visit our website at: https://www.tn.gov/content/tn/safety/driver-services/online.html#Appointments

DISTRACTED DRIVING

Every employee of the Department of Safety and Homeland Security is committed to your safety to ensure you get from point A to point B safely anytime you are driving a motor vehicle or using other forms of travel. With the information located throughout this manual, we want to make every effort possible, we reduce your chance of being involved in a crash in Tennessee as well as becoming a fatality.

For just a minute, can you ask yourself as a driver of a motor vehicle, what do you consider as distracted driving? Anything that takes your hands off the wheel, your eyes off the road and your visual, mental, and physical focus away from your driving is distracted driving. Distracted driving comes in many different forms. It could be cognitive, it could be visual, or it could be manual. It can be a combination of all three forms of distraction, but anything that a person does that takes their mind off of what they need to be doing while operating a motor vehicle is distracted driving. It is any activity that diverts attention from driving, including talking or texting on your phone, eating and drinking, talking to people in your vehicle, putting on make-up, shaving, finding your favorite radio station, as well as make adjustments to your stereo, entertainment or navigation system — anything that takes your attention away from the task of safe driving.

The most common form of distracted driving is cell phone usage and it can be extremely dangerous. It has caused death and destruction across our nation with the severe consequences of fatalities and serious bodily injuries in Tennessee. Texting is the most alarming distraction. Sending or reading a text takes your eyes off the road for a minimum of 5 seconds. Driving at 55 mph, that's like driving the length of an entire football field with your eyes closed.

Distracted driving is a serious problem in Tennessee. According to the National Highway Traffic Safety Administration, 3,142 people were killed by distracted driving in 2019. One out of every four car crashes in the United States is caused by texting and driving. Cell phone use while driving leads to 1.6 million crashes every year. According to Tennessee's integrated traffic analysis network "also known as Titan," a crash involving a distracted driver in Tennessee occurs every 26 minutes and 13 seconds. As a result of poor driving habits, there are approximately 191,065 crashes reported annually to the Department of Safety

It's quite simple, just put your phone down and pay attention to your driving when you get behind the wheel of your vehicle. Having access to the World Wide Web on our mobile devices is great too, however it's not meant to be used while operating a motor vehicle. Taking your hands of the wheel to look at that text you received or replying by sending a text, or just using your phone to call back, is distracted driving as it only takes a few seconds of distraction to result in a crash.

Tennessee implemented a hands-free law in 2019. According to Public Chapter No. 412, it is illegal for a driver to:
(a) hold a cellphone or mobile device with any part of their body,
(b) write, send, or read any text-based communication,
(c) reach for a cellphone or mobile device in a manner that requires the driver to no longer be in a seated driving position or properly restrained by a seat belt,
(d) watch a video or movie on a cellphone or mobile device, and
(e) record or broadcast video on a cellphone or mobile device.

Technology is being adding to our vehicles with each new model. However, in some instances it can potentially contribute to distracted driving if not used properly. GPS is great in place of a paper map however if you are trying to use it while operating a motor vehicle, you are still taking your eyes of the road. You are not allowed to touch your phone in order to use GPS. If you need to access GPS or to use your phone, you must find a safe place to pull over such as in a parking lot, bring your vehicle to a full stop and operate your phone or GPS technology.

We encourage you to plan your travel and travel your plan. You need to set your navigation before you begin your drive. If you have to change or make trip adjustments, please pull your vehicle safely off the roadway. Please don't try to do handle your GPS while you're driving as this is a very easy and deadly way to be distracted.

Attempting to video record from your phone or other devices while driving, is also very dangerous to do, as often seen and evidenced by persons posting on social media. It's very dangerous and it is a violation of law to video while you're driving. Please commit to yourself and your loved ones to not use your phone while driving and that you will keep your eyes on the road and hands on the steering wheel.

One of the hardest jobs for any law enforcement officer is having to notify a family that a loved one has been killed in an auto crash. If you will commit to these simple practices to prevent distracted driving, you can save a life and that life you save, may be your own. Help us help you arrive alive!

INTRODUCTION

This Tennessee Comprehensive manual has been divided into three (3) separate sections. The purpose of this manual is to provide a general understanding of the safe and lawful operation of a motor vehicle. Mastering these skills can only be achieved with practice and being mindful of Tennessee laws and safe driving practices.

Section A.

This section is designed for all current and potential drivers in Tennessee. It provides information that all drivers will find useful. Section A consists of pages 1 through 24. This section will help new and experienced drivers alike get ready for initial, renewal, and other license applications by explaining:

- the different types of licenses available

- the documentation and other requirements for license applications

- details on Intermediate Driver Licenses and how this graduated driver license works for driver license applicants under age 18

- basic descriptions of the tests required to obtain a Driver License

Section B.

This section is designed to help new drivers study and prepare for the required knowledge and skills for an operator license. It includes helpful practice test questions at the end of each chapter. Section B consists of pages 25 through 90.

This section of the manual provides information related to:

- Examination requirements for the vision, knowledge and road tests

- Traffic signs, signals, and lane markings

- Basic Rules of the Road

- Being a responsible driver and knowing the dangers and penalties of Driving Under the Influence of alcohol and drugs.

Section C.

This section provides information and safety tips to improve the knowledge of all highway users to minimize the likelihood of a crash and the consequences of those that do occur. This section consists of pages 91-117. It also provides information about sharing the road with other methods of transportation, which have certain rights and privileges on the highways which drivers must be aware of and respect.

It is important to read this information and learn what you can do to stay safe, and keep your family safe, on the streets, roads and highways of our great state.

TABLE OF CONTENTS

TABLE OF CONTENTS

TABLE OF CONTENTS

TABLE OF CONTENTS

TABLE OF CONTENTS

TABLE OF CONTENTS

SECTION A

Determining Which Class Of License You Need

CLASS OF LICENSE	If you want to get a license to drive this type of vehicle or a similar tank vehicle	Special endorsement may also be needed
A • Combination vehicles • GCWR over 26,000 lbs. • Towed vehicle(s) over 10,000 lbs. • Used for commercial purposes		**ENDORSEMENTS** **N** Tanks 1,000 gallons or greater **H** Hazardous materials (Haz Mat) **X** Tanks and Haz Mat **T** Double/triple trailers **P** Designed to seat 16 or more passengers including Driver **S** School bus **GCWR** Gross Combination Weight Rating **GVWR** Gross Vehicle Weight Rating
B • Trucks or buses over 26,000 lbs. GVWR used for commercial purposes • Any such vehicle towing a vehicle not in excess of 10,000 lbs. GVWR used for commercial purposes		
C • Vehicles weighing 26,000 lbs. GVWR or less, used for commercial purposes: – Placarded for hazardous materials – Designed to seat 16 or more passengers including Driver OR –Used as a school bus		
D • Generally, all passenger vehicles, not used for commercial purposes, excluding vehicle in Classes A, B, C, or M		**F For Hire** When a Class D vehicle is operated by a person employed for the principal purpose of driving, and used as a public or common carrier of persons or property
H • Hardship license for drivers between the ages of 14 & 16 in special hardship cases		SPECIAL RESTRICTIONS MAY APPLY
M • Motorcycles and motor-driven cycles		SPECIAL RESTRICTIONS MAY APPLY
P • Issued as an instructional permit for a Class A, B, C, D, and M license	SPECIAL RESTRICTIONS APPLY DEPENDING UPON THE PARTICULAR CLASS	

Section A-1 **YOUR LICENSE**

Who Needs a Tennessee Driver License?

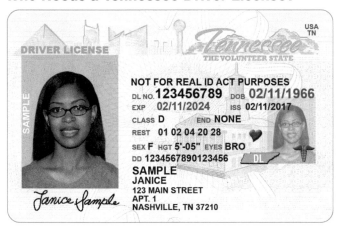

If you live in Tennessee and want to drive a motor vehicle, you must have a valid Tennessee driver license or Temporary Driver License (TDL).

A person who moves to Tennessee and has a valid driver license from another state or country must apply for a Tennessee driver license (or TDL) if they:
- live in Tennessee longer than 30 days OR
- are working in Tennessee OR
- would otherwise qualify as a registered Tennessee voter.

WHAT CLASS OF LICENSE DO YOU NEED?

In Tennessee, driver licenses and Temporary Driver Licenses are issued specifically for the class and type of vehicle you operate. The class of license you need depends on the type of vehicle you operate and why you use your vehicle.

The chart on page A1 and the discussion below should help determine which class of driver license is needed, as well as whether or not any special endorsements are needed.

Class D License

Driver license applicants who will be operators of regular passenger vehicles, pick-up trucks, or vans need a Class D license. This handbook provides the information you need to get a Class D license.

- A Class D license is required to operate any vehicle, up to a maximum weight of 26,000 pounds. Vehicles that are under 26,000 pounds cannot be operated with a Class D license if the vehicle is (a) transporting hazardous materials, (b) transporting sixteen (16 or more passengers (including the driver), or (c) used as a school bus. (If the vehicle is used for any of these purposes, a Class C license is required.)

To qualify for a Class D license, you must be at least 16 years of age, and must pass a vision screening, knowledge test, and driving test. If you are under age 18, you must also

meet special qualifications for the Intermediate Class D license. (Graduated Driver License Program - See Chapter A3.)

Class D with F (For-Hire Endorsement)

If a person's main job is to drive or transport persons, or transport property in a Class D vehicle, a For Hire endorsement must be added to the Class D license.

The Class D license with a For-Hire endorsement serves as a bridge between the regular driver license required for private transportation and the commercial driver license required for tractor-trailers, large trucks, buses and the like. Examples of persons whose job requires them to have the For-Hire endorsement include:
- **Persons**   Taxi, shuttle service drivers, ambulance drivers, etc.
- **Property**   Couriers, delivery services (flowers, pizza, etc.)

The chart on page 1 and the discussion below should help determine which class of driver license is needed, as well as whether or not any special endorsements are needed.

Persons hired for some purpose other than driving but drive in the course of doing their job, generally do not need this endorsement. Examples of persons that normally do not need a for-hire endorsement are plumbers, meter readers, and engineers. While they are driving in the course of their business, their main job is not to drive or transport people or property.

NOTE: Although you may not be required by law to have the For-Hire endorsement, your employer may require you to obtain this endorsement for insurance or safety requirements.

To add the For-Hire endorsement, drivers must meet the eligibility requirements, pass the appropriate tests, and pay a fee of $4.50. Applicants are eligible to apply for this endorsement if:
- They are at least 18 years of age, or 16 years of age if the vehicle the applicant is hired to drive is owned by the applicant's family business to conduct deliveries of goods and products exclusively for the family business.
- They will be operating a Class D vehicle.
- They have 2 years of unrestricted driving experience.

For-Hire endorsement applicants must pass a vision screening, and a knowledge test designed specifically for the For-Hire Endorsement. The knowledge test uses information from Section B of this manual.

CLASS M (MOTORCYCLE)

The operator of a motorcycle, motor-driven cycle, or motorized bicycle/scooter will need to apply for a Class M license. These two and three-wheeled vehicles are categorized by cylinder capacity and other design features. Generally, if the vehicle is over 125 cubic centimeters, a Class M license is needed; if the vehicle is under 125 cubic centimeters, a Class M limited license is needed.

Class M licenses may be issued as a single license, or along with another primary class. For example, if a driver wishes to be able to operate both a motorcycle and a Class D vehicle, Class DM license is required.

Applicants wishing to apply for a Class M license should obtain and read the **Motorcycle Operator Manual** in addition to this manual. The Commercial Driver License manual is online at: tn.gov/safety.

"Off-road" motor vehicles cannot be used for the road test. In fact, "off-road" motor vehicles or All-terrain Vehicles (ATVs) may not be driven on any Tennessee/Federal highways/interstate roads. Legally this type of vehicle can only cross roadways by taking ninety-degree (90 degree) angles and must not directly cross any road/highway/interstate.

Class A, B, or C - Commercial Driver Licenses -
Operators of larger and more complex vehicles weighing 26,001 or more pounds will need to apply for a Commercial Driver License (CDL). These licenses include Class A, B, and C depending upon the Gross Vehicle Weight Rating (GVWR), Gross Combination Weight Rating (GCWR), and what is being transported.

Drivers of commercial motor vehicles (CMV) require a CDL. A CMV is a vehicle or combination of vehicles weighing 26,001 pounds. Smaller vehicles require a CDL if they are used to transport hazardous materials; to transport sixteen (16) or more passengers including the driver, or used as a school bus.

Drivers who need a CDL should obtain the Commercial Driver License Manual which contains detailed information necessary to prepare for the tests. These manuals are available at all Driver Service Centers or online at: tn.gov/safety

NOTE: If a person holds a valid commercial driver license (Class A, B, or C license), this license is also valid for operating a Class D vehicle. No separate Class D license is required. A Class M license would be needed, if a commercial driver also wanted to operate a motorcycle. (Example: Class AM for class A vehicles and Class M for motorcycle vehicles)

Class PD - Learner Permit
Instructional permits are issued with another class of license, indicating the class of vehicle which the operator is legally entitled to drive. For example, the Class PD license allows drivers to learn how to drive Class D vehicles.

To obtain a Class PD license, you must have reached the age of 15 and pass the written knowledge test and vision screening for a class D license. A driver with a Class PD license may operate an automobile only when accompanied by a licensed driver who is at least 21 years old and is sitting in the seat beside the driver.

To exchange your Class PD license for a class D license, you are required to take a road skills driving test. If you are younger than 18 years old, you must have held a valid Class PD for 180 days and abide by all the requirements of the Graduated Driver License law as outlined in Section A-3, of this manual.

When Class PD drivers apply for an Intermediate Class D license, they do not need to repeat the knowledge test unless the license permit expired more than 12 months prior to the driving skills test.

Class H-Hardship
A hardship license (Class H) may be issued to a minor who is 14 years old to operate either a Class D passenger vehicle or Class M motorcycle or both. This license is only issued in cases of family hardship and are limited to specific needs.

Proof of hardship must be mailed with a Hardship License application to the Driver Services Administrative Office for evaluation. Each application is reviewed and evaluated on an individual basis. Less than one percent of all licenses issued to minors are hardship licenses. If approved, the applicant will receive a letter authorizing application for a hardship license.

Applicants who are approved to apply for a Class H hardship license must pass a vision screening, knowledge test, and road test to operate a Class D passenger vehicle. However, to drive a Class M vehicle, the applicant will also be required to take the Class M knowledge and driving test in addition to the Class D knowledge test. Upon being licensed, operation of the Class M vehicle is limited to 125 cc.

The Class H license is valid only for daylight hours and for travel to authorized locations as specified in the approval letter.

Drivers with a hardship license who are at least 15 years of age are extended the same privileges as those holding a Class PD license, when they are accompanied by any of the responsible adults listed for the Class PD.

Regardless of age at time of approval, a Hardship License will expire when the applicant reaches the age of 16.

NOTE: If you are approved for a hardship license and it is less than 6 months until your 16th birthday, you will be required to renew a Class PD upon expiration of your hardship license. You will need to hold the learner permit until you have attained a total of 180 days driving experience between the two license types and meet the Graduated Driver License Requirements as outlined in Section A-3 of this manual.

Identification Licenses ("ID Only")
There are two types of licenses for identification purposes available to United States Citizens and persons with lawful permanent resident status. No testing is done, but the applicant must meet the same standards for proof of identity and residency as for any driver license. The sole purpose of the ID is for identification and is not valid to operate any vehicle or

motorcycle. If an applicant is under the age of 18 years of age a responsible adult must complete a portion of the Minor/Teen-age Affidavit form (available at any driver license service center) at the time of application.

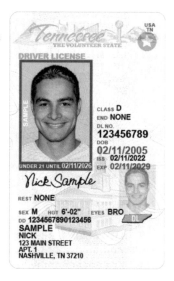

As a service to Tennessee residents, families with children, including infants, may obtain these identification-only licenses for their children. Children must meet all documentation requirements.

1. The first type of identification is an **"Expiring Identification License"** that may be issued to any person not currently holding a valid driver license. The person must present proof of identification and all other requirements detailed in the next chapter. NOTE: At age 65 or older, this ID does not expire.
   - Any applicant who does not have a social security number shall complete an affidavit, under penalty of perjury, affirming that the applicant has never been issued a SSN, and must provide a certified copy of one of the following:

     (a) Certified Birth Certificate issued by Tennessee or another state, possession, territory or commonwealth of the USA – or Valid United States Passport

     (b) Documentation proving lawful permanent resident status issued by the United States Citizenship and Immigration Services acceptable to the Department of Safety.

2. The second type is a "permanent identification license" that any person who is mentally challenged or physically disabled may obtain. In addition to presenting proof of identification, the applicant must submit a certified statement from a licensed medical doctor stating that the applicant is unable to operate a vehicle. Those who qualify for this ID may receive it free of charge. ID licenses issued in this manner do not expire.

Driving while revoked, canceled, or suspended is a class B misdemeanor. The penalty is a fine up to one-thousand dollars ($1,000) and/or six months in jail.

PENALTIES FOR DRIVING WITHOUT A LICENSE

While driving in Tennessee you must have your driver license or Temporary Driver License in your possession to show on request to any law enforcement officer. It is a Class D misdemeanor. If you do not have your license with you, you may be fined not less than two dollars ($2.00) and no more than fifty dollars ($50.00).

WHO IS NOT REQUIRED TO HAVE A TENNESSEE DRIVER LICENSE?

- Any member of the armed forces while operating a motor vehicle owned or leased by any branch of the Armed Services of the United States, including the National Guard.
- Operators of any road machinery, farm tractor, or other farm equipment which is temporarily operated or moved on a highway.
- Non-Tennessee residents who have in their immediate possession a valid driver license issued by their home state or country, equivalent to the appropriate class or type of Tennessee license.
- Non-U.S. citizens and who, in connection with their employment in managerial or technical positions in Tennessee, may operate vehicles with a valid driver license issued by another state, country, or international body for a period of 6 months. These individuals must apply for a Tennessee license at the end of 6 months.
- Students enrolled in a Tennessee Department of Safety and Homeland Security approved driver training course in a public or private secondary school, or in a licensed commercial driver training school for passenger vehicles, when accompanied by a certified instructor.

WHO IS NOT ELIGIBLE?

- Anyone whose license is currently suspended or revoked in this, or any other state.
- Anyone the Commissioner (or the Commissioner's designee) has determined would not be able to operate a motor vehicle safely because of mental or physical disabilities.
- Anyone required to show proof of car insurance/financial responsibility who has not done so.
- Anyone under the age of 18, who has dropped out of school before graduating, or who does not make "satisfactory progress" in school.
- Anyone who cannot provide the required proof of U.S. Citizenship, Lawful Permanent Residency (LPR) or Temporary Legal Presence, will not qualify for a driver license or identification license (ID Only).

TEMPORARY DRIVER LICENSE (TDL) OR TEMPORARY IDENTIFICATION LICENSE (TID)

Temporary Driver Licenses (TDL) are issued to Tennessee residents who are not U.S. Citizens or Lawful Permanent Residents but have temporary legal presence status and authorized stay in the United States. Their presence in the U.S. has

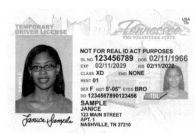

been authorized by the federal government for a specific purpose and for a specific time period. All other applicants for Tennessee Driver Licenses or Identification Only Licenses must provide proof of U.S. Citizenship (USC) or Lawful Permanent Residency (LPR). Proof of temporary legal presence is generally made with one or more of the following documents: (a) Conditional Resident Alien Card (I-551), (b) Temporary Resident Identification Card (I-688), (c) Employment Authorization Card (I-766), or (d) Valid Foreign Passport with a valid Visa and I-94 attached. Valid Foreign Passport with an I-94W. (Holders of F1 or F2 status should also present a valid SEVIS I-20. Holders of J1 or J2 status should also present a valid DS-2019)

This license type is issued as proof that the holder has successfully passed Tennessee's driver license examinations/ requirements for the operation of Class D and/or Class M vehicles. The Temporary Driver License (TDL) also serves as a valid identification document.

Other TDL features include:
- TDL class types will be preceded by the letter "X" (XD, XM, XPD)
- TDL may be issued as a Learner Permit (XPD, XMPD) or as a combo type (XDM, XMPD)
- The expiration date of the TDL will be tied to the corresponding dates of the legal presence documentation.

A Temporary Identification License (TID) is also now available for those non-driving applicants who are not U.S. Citizens or Lawful Permanent Residents but have proof of temporary legal presence status and authorized stay in the United States. The Temporary Identification card will be shown as Class XID.

- The expiration date of the TID will be tied to the corresponding dates of the legal presence documentation.
- Maximum length of time a TID can be issued is 5 years

Applicants for either the Temporary Driver License or Temporary Identification card must meet all other identification and residency requirements as mandated in Handbook Chapter A2 of this manual.

OTHER DRIVER RELATED TOPICS

Organ & Tissue Donation- Donate Life Tennessee

Sign Up to be an organ and tissue donor by circling "YES" on your license or state ID application or renewal.

With this simple step, your name will be added to the Donate Life Tennessee organ and tissue donor registry and serve as legal consent to donate your organs and tissues. Minors who are between the ages of 13 and 17 years old, and who have driver's license, permit or state ID can choose to register as a donor, according to the Tennessee Uniform Anatomical Gifts Act. A red heart will be printed on

your license or ID, to reflect your decision. Please share this decision with your family and loved ones.

Be the Gift! One organ donor can save as many as 8 lives and one tissue donor can improve the lives of 75 or more individuals.

Currently, there are more than 100,000 individuals waiting for a lifesaving organ transplant, including an average of 3,000 Tennesseans. Each year, organ transplants save the lives approximately 40,000 Americans, who move from the waiting list to their second chance at life. More than 2.5 million tissue transplants heal men, women, and children in the United States every year.

An average of 20 die each day waiting for an organ transplant, while every 10 minutes a name is added to the national organ transplant waiting list.

Lifesaving, transplantable organs include the heart, lungs, kidneys, liver, pancreas, and small intestine. Healing tissue grafts are made from skin, bones, ligaments, vertebral bodies, heart valves, pericardium, veins, blood vessels, nerves, and eyes/corneas.

Registered donors can specify, update or remove their registration on the DonateLifeTN.org website.

To remove the heart from your license or ID, you must visit a Tennessee Department of Safety Driver Service Center and complete an application to obtain a duplicate license.

For more information, call (877) 552-5050 or visit: DonateLifeTN.org

Veterans

If you are an Honorably Discharged Veteran you may now have "Veteran" displayed on your license. At the time of application you will need to certify on the driver license application that you are an honorably discharged veteran and want it displayed on your license. You must present a certified copy of your Department of Defense Form DD-214, the NAVPERS-660 honorable discharge certificate or your Department of Defense form DD Form 2 (Retired) identification card.

Voter Registration – Motor Voter

To make it easy for citizens to register to vote, you may apply to register to vote or update your voter record, when you apply for a driver license or ID. The Department does not process your voter registration application. The application is forwarded to your local election commission.

- REMEMBER: Only the Election Registrar can process and issue a voter registration card. The Driver Service Center sends your application to the appropriate County Election Commission to save you an additional trip. If you have not received your Voter Registration Card within 30 days of applying at the Driver License Service Center, you should contact your local County Election Commission immediately.

International Driving Permit (IDP)

Possession of an International Driving Permit does not mean that the holder is valid to operate an automobile in Tennessee or any other state. Do NOT be fooled by Internet sites that claim that you can drive on such a permit if your license is suspended or revoked in any state. The facts about International Driving Permits (IDP) are as follows:

- An International Driving Permit is an official translation of a driver's home state or country driver license into the official languages of the United Nations, including English. This translated document is to be used in conjunction with the valid driver license issued by the driver's home state or country.

- U.S. Citizens traveling abroad and/or foreign visitors to the United States are NOT required to have an International Driving Permit. However it can be useful in emergencies such as traffic violations or auto accidents when a foreign language is involved.

- The International Driving Permit MUST be obtained in the home country of the driver.

U.S. Citizens: In order to obtain an IDP a United States citizen must:

- Be at least eighteen (18) years of age

- Hold a VALID U.S. State, Territorial or U.S. Department of State Driver License, which is NOT under revocation or suspension at the time the IDP is issued.

- The IDP is valid for one (1) year only from the date of issuance and if the applicant's state license expires and is not renewed or is suspended during that year the IDP becomes invalid.

- **The IDP is NOT valid for driving in the United States or its territories and it is NOT valid by itself for driving.**

- The IDP **MUST** be carried with the driver's regular valid U.S. Driver License.

- NON-U.S. Citizens: must obtain their International Driving Permit in their native country prior to arrival in the U.S. if desired.

- An IDP can NOT be issued to a foreign visitor by any agency in the United States.

- The Tennessee Driver Service Centers do NOT issue International Driving Permits.

- Any Tennessee resident who is interested in obtaining an IDP before traveling abroad should contact a local American Automobile Association (AAA) office or visit their website at: www.aaasouth.com

Registered Sexual Offender and Violent Sexual Offender

If you are a registered sexual offender or violent sexual offender and making application for a new driver license, or renewing your current driver license, it is your responsibility to inform the Department of Safety Driver License Examiner that you are required to register as a sexual offender or violent sexual offender.

A Sex Offender Declaration and Supplemental Application must be completed along with documentation acceptable to the Department of Safety, evidencing identity, legal presence, and residency if the license requested requires such documentation. If you are ineligible to be issued a driver license, the Department of Safety will issue a photo identification license, or identification certificate. The applicant is required to pay any applicable fees related to the issuance of the driver license or photo identification card.

Sexual Offender and Violent Sexual Offenders shall always have their driver license, photo identification card or identification certificate in their possession.

STOP DO YOU HAVE THE RIGHT DOCUMENTS ?

IMPORTANT: All Documents Must be Originals or Certified. No Faxes or Photocopies. ✓ = REQUIRED FOR TYPE OF LICENSE:	Temporary Driver TDL	Temporary Photo-ID TID	Driver License DL or CDL	Photo ID ID
PROOF OF U.S. CITIZENSHIP OR LAWFUL PERMANENT RESIDENT EXAMPLE: U.S. Birth Certificate, U.S. Passport, I-551 / Permanent resident card, etc.			✓	✓
PROOF OF TEMPORARY LEGAL PRESENCE EXAMPLE: Conditional Resident Alien Card (I-551), Employment Authorization Card(I-766), Valid Foreign Passport with Visa & Valid I-94, etc.	✓	✓		
PRIMARY PROOF OF IDENTITY EXAMPLE: Certified Birth Certificate, Military ID Card, Passport, Valid Driver License Or ID Card Issued By Another State, etc.	✓	✓	✓	✓
SECONDARY PROOF OF IDENTITY EXAMPLE: SSN Card, Work ID, Voter Registration Card, School ID, etc.	✓	✓	✓	✓
PROOF OF ANY NAME CHANGES IF DIFFERENT THAN PRIMARY ID EXAMPLE: Certified Marriage Certificate, Divorce Decree, Certified Court Order, etc.	✓	✓	✓	✓
TWO PROOFS OF TENNESSEE RESIDENCY WITH YOUR NAME AND RESIDENT ADDRESS – NO P.O. BOXES (CURRENT=FROM LAST 4 MONTHS) EXAMPLE: Utility Bills, Vehicle Registration/Title, Bank Statement, LES Statement, etc.	✓	✓	✓	✓
SOCIAL SECURITY NUMBER* EXAMPLE: SSN Card, Paycheck stub with full SS# AND Name, IRS Forms, etc. *SSN Affidavit may be signed IF no SSN assigned by the U.S.	✓	✓	✓	✓
If under eighteen (18) years of age you will also need:				
TEENAGE AFFIDAVIT/FINANCIAL RESPONSIBILITY If guardian or step-parent is not named on school attendance; proof of relationship will be required such as custody or adoption papers or marriage certificate if step-parent is signing.	✓	✓	✓	✓
PROOF OF SCHOOL ATTENDANCE / PROGRESS – SIGNED AND DATED WITHIN PAST 30 DAYS – Form SF1010 completed and signed by School Principal/Guidance Teacher – OR – letterhead statement from out-of-state or private schools, clearly stating student is not truant.	✓		✓	
CERTIFICATION OF 50 HOURS BEHIND THE WHEEL DRIVING EXPERIENCE (SF-1256) – after holding learner permit for six months.	✓		✓	
If applying for or currently holding a Commercial Driver License (CDL) you may also need:				
VALID DOT MEDICAL CARD			✓	
PROOF OF TENNESSEE DOMICILE – STRICT LIMITS ON ACCEPTABLE DOCUMENTS – NO P.O. BOXES (CURRENT=FROM LAST 4 MONTHS) EXAMPLE: Utility bill, Vehicle Title/Registration, Lease/Mortgage papers, Tax return.			✓	
SOCIAL SECURITY NUMBER: *Federal regulations require CDL holders to have an SSN. The SSN Affidavit is NOT allowed when applying for a commercial license.*			✓	
FORM 2-C FOR PUBLIC SCHOOL BUS DRIVERS – OR – SCHOOL LETTER FOR PRIVATE SCHOOL BUS DRIVERS.			✓	

Please Note

A Detailed List of Acceptable Documents is available at www.tn.gov/safety

Practice knowledge tests are available on-line at www.tn.gov/dlpractice

The checklist and overview will provide you with a handy reference guide to the various documents and forms needed for obtaining a Tennessee issued driver license or identification document. Please be sure to review the entire chapter to become familiar with the requirements and items acceptable by the examiner. Tennessee has intensive identification requirements for all applicants including new and returning residents as well as Tennesseans needing to renew an existing license, certificate or identification.

If you have moved from out of state, your valid driver license from your former state can be used to prove your identity. The out-of-state driver license cannot be used to prove U.S. Citizenship or Lawful Permanent Resident status. Because identification and citizenship documentation requirements are very specific, it is very important that you read through these requirements carefully to avoid unnecessary trips to a Driver Service Center.

WHAT DO YOU NEED TO BRING?

To protect your identity and to reduce the potential for fraud, we must determine that you are "who you say you are." This is why you must bring proof of your full legal name and date of birth. The proof must be original or certified documents.
NO PHOTOCOPIES WILL BE ACCEPTED.

If your current name is different from the one shown on these documents, you must provide all the necessary information to document changes in your name currently on file and the name(s) you want to have shown. Each supporting piece of information to establish the change must be original or certified legal documents. We cannot accept name changes through the mail.

Proof of U.S. Citizenship, Lawful Permanent Residency

Proof of U.S. Citizenship or Lawful Permanent Residency is required to obtain a Tennessee driver license or Identification Only License. (See Table 2.1.) Documentation that they are either a U.S. Citizen or a Lawful Permanent Resident (LPR) must be provided by the following:

- First-time applicants

- New and returning Tennessee residents

- Applicants reinstating a driver license after being revoked, suspended or cancelled (regardless of when the license was issued) or

- Anyone issued a Tennessee driver license or photo identification license since January 1, 2001 who is renewing for the first time.

Table: 2.1

Acceptable documents proving an applicant is a U.S. citizen or a lawful permanent resident include, but are not limited to, the following:
• Certified Birth Certificate issued by a U.S. state, jurisdiction or territory (Puerto Rico, U.S. Virgin Islands, Northern Mariana Islands, American Samoa, Swain's Island, Guam);   • U.S. Government-issued Certified Birth Certificate;   • U.S. Certificate of Birth Abroad (DS-1350 or FS-545);   • Report of Birth Abroad of a Citizen of the U.S. (FS-240);   • Valid U.S. Passport;   • Certificate of Citizenship (N560 or N561);   • Certificate of Naturalization (N550, N570 or N578);   • U.S. Citizen Identification Card (I-197, I-179);   • I-551 Permanent Resident Alien Card;   • Foreign passport stamped by the U.S. Government indicating that the holder has been "Processed for I-551",   • Permanent resident Re-entry Permit (I-327);   • Temporary I-551 stamp on Form I-94 Arrival/Departure Record, with photograph of the applicant;   • U.S. Department of Receptions and Placement Program Assurance Form (Refugee) and I-94 stamped refugee;   • Form I-94 Record of Arrival and Departure stamped Asylee; Parolee, refugee, asylum, HP (humanitarian parolee or PIP (public interest parolee).

If an applicant is unable to provide the required proof or only has "temporary" legal presence status he/she will NOT be eligible for a driver license or identification only license. However, the applicant may be eligible for a Temporary Driver License (TDL) or Temporary Identification License (TID) if proof of temporary legal presence status and authorized stay can be provided. One or more of the following documents may provide the necessary proof:

- Conditional Resident Alien Card (I-551)

- Temporary Resident Identification Card (I-688)

- Employment Authorization Card (I-766)

- Valid Foreign Passport with Visa and I-94 Arrival/Departure Record

The above documents usually have an expiration date(s) for legal presence status. These dates are important in issuing TDL licenses.

REMEMBER: To receive a Temporary Driver License or Temporary Identification License in addition to establishing Temporary Legal Presence status, **all** Tennessee's driver license examinations/requirements for operation of Class XD and/or Class XM vehicle must be met.

Primary Identification Table: 2.2

Acceptable primary identification includes but is not limited to original or certified documents with full name and date of birth, such as the following items:

Document	Notes
• U.S. photo driver license or photo ID card or license from another country. Photo document must be issued by state or federal agency.	May also include photo learner permits - Licenses not issued in English, must be translated and accompanied by a Certificate of Accurate Translation —or— a valid International Driving Permit.
• Certified Birth Certificate	- Must be certified and have a seal and be issued by an authorized government agency such as the Bureau of Vital Statistics or State Board of Health. **- HOSPITAL ISSUED CERTIFICATES AND BAPTISMAL CERTIFICATES ARE-NOT ACCEPTABLE.** - Foreign birth certificates, not issued in English, must be translated and accompanied by a Certificate of Accurate Translation.
• Military Identification	Active Duty, Retiree or Reservist military ID card Discharge papers Military Dependent ID card
• Passport (Valid)	Passports, not issued in English, must be translated and accompanied by a Certificate of Accurate Translation. Passports are not acceptable if expired.
• U.S. Citizenship and Immigration Services	*Certificate of Naturalization* N-550, N-570, N-578 *Certificate of Citizenship* N-560, N-561, N-645 Northern Mariana Card, American Indian Card U.S. Citizen Identification Card (I-179, I-197) Temporary Resident Identification Card (I-688) *Travel Documents* - Record of Arrival and Departure (I-94) I-551 U.S. Re-entry Permit (I-327) Employment Authorization card (I-688A, I-688-B, I-766) *Refugee I-94* Record of Arrival and Departure stamped "Refugee", not likely to be in a foreign passport Refugee Travel Document (I-571)
• Marriage Certificate	Must include the applicant's full name and date of birth. The certificate must be the copy that is registered AFTER the marriage; NOT just the "license" authorizing the union.
• Federal Census Record	Must include the applicant's full name and date of birth (age)
• Applicant's Own Child's Birth Certificate	Must include the applicant's full name and date of birth (age)
• Adoptive Decree	Must include the applicant's full name and date of birth
• Legal Change of Name (Divorce, etc.)	As recorded in court decree with judge's original signature and/or official court seal
• Any confirmation of date of birth in court of law	As recorded in court document(s) with judge's original signature and/or official court seal

Any other documentary evidence which confirms to the satisfaction of the Department the true identity and date of birth of the applicant.

Secondary Identification

Document	Notes
• Computerized Check Stubs	Must include the applicant's full name pre-printed on the stub.
• Union Membership Cards	Must include the applicant's full name
• Work IDs	Preferably with photo
• Financial Institution Documents	Computer printouts of bank statements, savings account statements, loan documents, etc.
• Social Security Documents	SS Card (original only not metal or plastic replicas), printout, benefits statements, etc.
• Health Insurance card	TennCare, Medicaid, Medicare, etc.
• IRS / state tax form	W2 Forms, Property tax receipts, etc.
• Military Records	Assignment orders, selective service cards, Leave & Earnings Statement, etc.

Proof of Identity

The Driver License Examiner will require proof of identity and date of birth from any person of any person applying for a driver license or photo identification license. The Driver license examiner will require the same information for an applicant applying for a temporary driver license or temporary identification license.

The Examiner will ask for two (2) items of proof as follows:

• ORIGINAL applicants must have at least one item from the Primary Identification list. The second item may be from the Secondary Identification list or another item from the Primary Identification list. (See Table 2.2 above)

• Applicants for DUPLICATES or RENEWAL of an existing Tennessee DL/ID must provide 2 items from either list.

• NEW RESIDENTS must surrender their license from their former state. If a new resident's license from the other state has been lost, the new resident must provide the same two (2) items of proof, as required of an ORIGINAL applicant.

• CHANGE OF NAME: Applicants will need proof (such as an original certified court order, marriage certificate, divorce

Proof of Tennessee Residency   Table: 2.3

Documents must show the residence used for the application and the applicant's name (or name of the applicant's parent, guardian or spouse)

Two Documents From the List Below
Showing residence address used on application and your name, or name of your parent, guardian or spouse (Proof of relationship will be required)

- Current utility bill including telephone, electric, water, gas, cable, etc. (Must include postmarked envelope bill was mailed in) Initial Deposit Receipt is NOT acceptable.
- Current bank statement (not checks)
- Current rental or mortgage contract fully signed and executed or receipt including deed of sale for property
- Current employer verification of residence address or letter from employer as long as it is on company letterhead with original signature. If employer does not have letterhead then signature must be notarized.
- Current automobile, life or health insurance policy (not wallet cards)
- Current driver license or ID issued by the State of Tennessee to a parent, legal guardian or spouse of applicant (proof of relationship required)
- Current Tennessee motor vehicle registration
- Current Tennessee voter registration
- Current IRS tax reporting W-2 Form
- Receipt for personal property or real estate taxes paid within the last year
- In case of student enrolled in public or private school in this state, student may provide a photo student ID and acceptable documentation that student lives on campus.

REMEMBER — NO PHOTOCOPIES

decree, etc.) of **name** changes when any of the primary or secondary identification documents listed below have a name different than the applicant's current name.

Proof of Any Name Change

You will be required to provide proof of any name changes if the name differs on the documents presented from the application.

For a Marriage, a Marriage License/Certificate is acceptable if it includes the applicant's full name and date of birth. The certificate must be the original or certified copy that is registered AFTER the marriage; NOT just the "license" authorizing the union.

For a Divorce Decree, acceptable proof is the documentation as recorded in the court decree with judge's original signature and/or official court seal.

NOTE: Copy of court document with an original signature/seal that is affixed to copy is acceptable. Copy of court document with copied seal/ signature is not acceptable. All documents are subject to verification with the issuing

agency or source. Documents subject to verification may delay the issuance of your permit, driver license, identification only license, temporary driver license or temporary identification license.

Proof of Tennessee Residency

The Driver License Examiner will require proof of Tennessee residency for the following applicants:

- ORIGINAL applicants for a first time ID, TDL, permit or license of any class.
- NEW RESIDENT applicants for an ID, TDL, permit or license of any class.
- RETURNING RESIDENT applicants for an ID, TDL, permit or license of any class (even when the applicant may have previously held a Tennessee ID or license before moving out of state).

Proof of residency requires applicants to provide two (2) documents from the list shown in the Acceptable Proof of Residency Table 2.3. Documents listed are valid for residency proof as long as the documents contain the following information:

1. The applicant's name - OR -
2. The name of the applicant's spouse, if the applicant has a spouse (proof of relationship will be required if this type of proof is used) - OR -
3. If the applicant is a minor, the name of a parent or legal guardian (proof of relationship will be required if this type of proof is used)
4. The Tennessee residence address used on the application for ID, TDL, permit or license of any class. Most items in List B will NOT have the address but are still acceptable.
5. Documents must be originals; **no photocopies or facsimile (FAX) copies can be accepted**.

NOTE: Proof of relationship can be established with a certified marriage certificate or a birth certificate (the long-form).

Proof of Social Security Numbers

Tennessee law requires the Social Security number for all applications where the U.S. Government has issued the applicant a Social Security number. The department maintains this information on each applicant's record. Your social security number will not be printed on your license.

Tennessee has a computer link with the Social Security Administration. This link will return a message indicating that the number matches (or not). If the Social Security number provided fails to match with the computer records, the Examiner will ask for additional proof of the number from the applicant. If adequate proof is not available to resolve the conflict, the applicant may be required to contact the Social Security Administration for resolution prior to acceptance of their driver license application.

The documents listed below can by used by the Examiner to prove the Social Security number and to prove identity.

- An original Social Security card.

- The Internal Revenue Service W-2 Wage and Tax Statement form. (Full SS# required)
- An employer's computer generated payroll check (check stub) or an original bank statement with your Social Security Number on it.
- Health insurance card with both name and Social Security number

If You Have Never Been Issued a Social Security Number

Applicants who have never been issued a Social Security number must appear in person and sign a sworn affidavit to that effect. This affidavit is available at any Driver License Service Center and must be signed in the presence of a Driver License Examiner or Notary Public. By signing this affidavit, the applicant attests, under the penalty of perjury, that no Social Security number has ever been issued to him/her by the U.S. Government. This affidavit allows the Department of Safety to process the application without the requirement of the Social Security number. Each subsequent application will require a new affidavit to be signed in person unless a Social Security number can be provided.

LICENSE FEES AT A GLANCE

As of January 1, 2016, Tennessee licenses for persons over the age of 21 expire every eight years from the date of issuance. This means your license will normally no longer expire on your birthday. The fees shown on Page 12 (Table 2.4) as "standard fees" are calculated for an 8 year driver license and include an application fee.

Acceptable Methods of Payment

Accepted methods of payment for a Driver License or Identification License at our Driver Service Centers are Cash, Check, Money Order, MasterCard, Visa and Discover Credit Cards.

Temporary Driver License (TDL) & Temporary Identification License Fees at a Glance

A Temporary Driver License (TDL) or Temporary Identification License (TID) will be issued for the period of authorized stay in the U.S.

The fees for a Temporary Driver License (TDL) and Temporary Identification License (TID) are fixed rates that do not change with the length of time the TDL or TID is issued. The cost for a Temporary Driver License or Temporary Identification License will be $28.00 regardless of the type of license issued (XD, XPD, etc.) and whether it is issued for one day, one year or the maximum of five years.

Additional fees applied to the TDL cost the same as with a license. For example a minor applying for a GDL Temporary Driver License will pay the additional $5.00 GDL fee at the applicable levels for a total of $33.00.

If getting a TDL for a motorcycle the additional $1.00 motorcycle fee will apply for a total of $20.50 for XM. Also if the applicant is getting a TDL for two types there is a charge for each type plus any applicable additional fees (for example $38.00 for a Class-Type XDM).

Other Applicants

New Residents-Returning Residents

New residents or those returning to Tennessee and holding a driver license from another state, must obtain a Tennessee driver license no later than thirty (30) days after establishing residency. New residents holding a valid learner's permit from another state must meet separate requirements to obtain a Tennessee learner permit or driver license.

- All new or returning residents must take a Tennessee vision screening at the Driver Service Center. There are additional requirements for commercial driver license holders. Only foreign country licenses/IDs may be retained.
- New or returning residents whose out of state license has been expired for more than six months must take the Tennessee knowledge exam, road skills test, and vision screening.
- New residents from other countries are required to take the following tests: vision screening, knowledge exam, and road skills test. They will be allowed to keep the license issued by that country.

At time of application, new or returning residents must present:
- Your current license (or certified copy of driving record and another acceptable ID)
- Proof of U.S. Citizenship, Lawful Permanent Resident Status or Proof of authorized stay in the United States
- Primary Proof of Identity
- Secondary Proof of Identity
- Proof of any Name Changes if the name differs from the documents presented
- Two Proofs of Tennessee Residency with your name and resident address - NO P.O. BOXES (Documents must be current and dated within last 4 months.)
- A Social Security Number or sworn affidavit if no Social Security number has ever been issued.

PLEASE NOTE: All documents are subject to further verification with the issuing agency or source. Documents subject to verification may delay the issuance of your permit, driver license or identification only license.

Items must be original documents. No photocopies will be accepted!

If a person holds a valid Tennessee license and is in the United States Armed Forces, that license shall remain valid regardless of the displayed expiration date as long as: the person remains on active duty; and is based outside the State of Tennessee, and the license is not surrendered, canceled or suspended.

License Fees* Table: 2.4

License Class (standard 8-year cycle)	License Fees	Minimum Age	Temporary Driver License & Identification License Type*	Temporary License Fees
D-Operator	$28.00	16	XD-Class D Vehicle	$28.00
D w/For Hire	$30.50	18	XD w/For Hire	$30.50
Adding for Hire	$4.50	18	NA	$4.50
PD- Learner Permit (over age 18)	$5.50 (1yr)	18	XPD-Class D Permit (over age 18)	$28.00
PD- Learner Permit (under age 18)	$10.50(1yr)	15	XPD-Class D Permit (under age 18)	$33.00
H-Hardship	$5.50	14	XH-Hardship	$28.00
Photo ID (under age 18)	$4.50	Under 18	XID-Photo ID Only (under age 18)	$12.00
Photo ID (over age 18)	$12.00	Over 18	XID-Photo ID Only (over age 18)	$12.00
M-Motorcycle	$29.00	15	XM-Class M Vehicle	$29.00
DM-Operator & Motorcycle	$55.00	16	XDM-Class D & M Vehicles	$55.00
Class A	$70.00	21	NA	NA
Class B or C	$62.00	21	NA	NA
1st Duplicate- D or M	$8.00	-	1st Duplicate XD or XM	$28.00
2nd or subsequent Duplicate D or M	$12.00	-	2nd or subsequent Duplicate XD or XM	$28.00
1st Duplicate-CDL	$12.00	-	NA	NA
2nd or subsequent CDL	$16.00	-	NA	NA
Intermediate Restricted- D	$23.25	16	Intermediate Restricted -XD	$33.00
Intermediate Unrestricted- D	$2.00	17	Intermediate Unrestricted- XD	$28.00
Graduating to Class D	$8.00 or $12.00	18	Graduating to Class XD	$28.00

*Fees listed above include the applicable rebate and application fee.

MILITARY PERSONNEL

A Members of the National Guard and family members of military personnel are not eligible for this provision.
While on active duty and stationed outside of Tennessee, military personnel may have a "Code 30" placed on the license to indicate that the license does not expire. To add this code, bring a copy of your military orders to the driver license service center and pay the appropriate fees.

To add this code, military personnel must provide proper identification and required military documents to the Driver Service Center and pay the appropriate fees or submit by mail. Renewals and duplicates can also be handled through the mail with the proper documents and fees.

Once the person has been discharged or separated from such services or has been reassigned to a duty station within the state, he or she must renew his/her license within sixty (60) days following the date of separation on the DD214 form or reassignment to Tennessee.

NOTE: Assignment to Fort Campbell Army Base is considered reassignment back to Tennessee. Fort Campbell Army Base is located in both the states of Tennessee and Kentucky.

FREQUENTLY ASKED QUESTIONS

Q: How Do I Replace a Lost License?
If your driver license, learner permit or identification license is ever lost, stolen or destroyed, you may obtain a duplicate by applying at any driver license service center, or you can visit our website at tn.gov/safety to see if you are eligible to apply for a duplicate online. Temporary Driver Licenses and Temporary Identification Licenses cannot be replaced online.

If you must apply in person, you will need to present proper identification. You will have a new photo taken and pay the appropriate fee. The fee may vary depending upon the number of duplicates applied for during the current renewal cycle of your license.

Q: How Do I Renew My License?
Your Class D license issued before January 1, 2016 normally expires in 5 years on your birthdate. Permits normally expire one year from date of issuance.

Tennessee law requires anyone issued a Tennessee driver license or photo identification license after January 1, 2001 to provide documentation that you are a United States Citizen or a lawful permanent resident at the time of your first renewal. In these instances, you may not renew by mail or by the internet and you will be required to visit a Driver Service Center to renew your license.

The department mails every driver a courtesy renewal notice eight to ten weeks before his/her license expires. Read your renewal notice carefully. The notice explains several ways to renew a driver license.
- If you have a current valid photo license, you may be eligible to renew by mail, or online through our website (www.tn.gov/safety).

- If you renewed by mail or internet on your last renewal, or have certain types of licenses, your renewal notice will direct you to go to your nearest Driver Service Center to have a new photograph made.

- If your license is a temporary driver license, temporary identification license or commercial driver license, your renewal notice will direct you to go to your nearest Driver Service Center to have a new photograph made.
- If you are 60 years old or older and choose to have a nonphoto license, you may obtain this by mail or internet. You will be sent a new non-photo license to replace your old license. Please note: if you travel, you may wish to consider obtaining a photo license to assist with the necessary credentialing to board a commercial aircraft, passenger rail service such as Amtrak and cruise ships. This will require you to go to your nearest Driver License Service Center to have a new photograph made.

Don't Let Your License Expire.

No matter how you renew, the important thing is to renew your license before it expires. If your license has expired more than thirty (30) calendar days, there will be a five-dollar ($5.00) late fee. After six (6) months, the late fee doubles to $10.00. If you let five (5) years go by without renewing, not only will you have to pay the $10.00 late fee, you will also have to pass the vision screening, knowledge, and skills test.

These are no "grace periods." When your license expires, you are no longer entitled to drive a vehicle or motorcycle and will be subject to the same penalties as someone who has never been licensed. It is your responsibility to maintain the validity of your license.

If you do not receive a renewal notice, you may simply take your current license to any driver license service center. The renewal notice itself is not necessary for you to be able to renew your license.

Q: How Do I Change My Address?

It is important to notify the Department of Safety if your address changes. If your residence address changes (even though you may not have moved) you are required by state law to notify the Department of Safety within **ten (10) days** of this change. This includes when you move as well as address changes made by the United States Postal Service or your local 9-1-1 Emergency Communications District when you have not physically relocated. Notifying the post office of an address change will not provide the information to us. By failing to notify us, you could miss the renewal date of your license, or other important correspondence from the Department of Safety.

The law does not require the address to be changed on your actual license, just on our files. The easiest way to update your record is go online to: https://dl.safety.tn.gov/_/

You may also notify the Department of your change of address by writing to us and giving us your name (as it appears on your license), driver license number, date-of-birth, your address as it appears on your current license and a good daytime phone number in the event we need to contact you. If you wish to write to us, please mail to:

TN DEPT OF SAFETY AND HOMELAND SECURITY
DRIVER LICENSE RECORDS
PO BOX 945
NASHVILLE TN 37202

You can also pick up a change-of-address form at any driver license service center.

If you want a new license issued that reflects your new address, you may go to a driver license service center, pay the appropriate fees, and have a new license issued or you may visit our website at https://dl.safety.tn.gov/_/ to see if you are eligible to apply for a duplicate with the new address online.

When giving us your new address, remember that by law, your license must show your legal residential address: a house, and/or apartment number and the street, road or highway.

The city along with the correct zip code is also required. A post office box alone will not be accepted as a residential address.

Q: Can Personal Information From My Record be released?

The Federal Driver Privacy Protection Act (DPPA) prohibits the dissemination or disclosure of personal information from a motor vehicle record without the "express consent" of that driver. This means that the personal information contained in your driver license record is protected. Without your express consent, we will not release your personal information to people wanting a mailing list or individuals who ask for your record for an unspecified purpose. If you want us to release your information, visit the local Driver License Service Center to file your request or visit our website at: tn.gov/safety.

Q: For persons 18 years old and over OR if under 18 years old who have graduated high school or received their GED, must they participate in the Graduated Driver License (GDL) Program?

No. The GDL law does not apply to anyone age 18 or older or to those persons under 18 who have graduated high school or received a GED.

Section A-3 INTERMEDIATE LICENSES FOR DRIVER UNDER 18—GRADUATED LICENSE PROCEDURES

Drivers under 18 years old are required to go through graduated steps of driving experience to gain full, unrestricted Driver License status. Parents and teen drivers are encouraged to read Chapter C4 titled *"Helping Teens and New Drivers Learn to Drive"* in Section C of this manual.

The graduated Driver License steps are designed to incrementally teach young drivers how to drive by requiring minimum levels of driving experience and a safe driving history record before allowing teenage drivers to receive a "full-fledged" Class D driver license. Motor vehicle crashes are the major cause of death for young people between the ages of 15 and 20. By requiring more supervised practice, the State of Tennessee hopes to save lives and prevent tragic injuries.

There are four steps to becoming a full, unrestricted Driver License holder:

1. Learner Permit
2. Intermediate Restricted License
3. Intermediate Unrestricted License
4. Regular Driver License.

The above four steps are part of the Graduated Driver License Program. A license issued under the first three steps will have "GDL" printed in the bottom left corner. See page 15 for pictures of graduated licenses.

Learner Permit

- You must be 15 years old and pass the standard written exams and vision screening.
- You must hold a learner permit for 180 days in order to move to the Intermediate Restricted License step.
- You may drive a car only when accompanied by a licensed driver 21 years or older who is riding in the front seat of the vehicle.
- You may not drive between the hours of 10 P.M. and 6 A.M.
- Driver and passengers must wear a safety belt.

Intermediate License

There are two Intermediate License levels for drivers under 18 years of age. The first level is the Intermediate Restricted License and the second level is the Intermediate Unrestricted License.

First Level - Intermediate Restricted License

- You must be 16 years old and pass the driving skills test, also known as the road test.
- You must have held a learner permit for 180 days.

- You cannot have been convicted of moving violations or contributed to accidents that equal to 6 or more points within a 12 month period.
- You must have verification from a parent, legal guardian or licensed driving instructor stating you have completed fifty hours (ten hours at night) of driving experience. Certification of driving experience must be made on the official form (SF-1256) provided by the Department of Safety. This form is available at all Driver License Service Centers or may be downloaded from our web site at:http://www.tn.gov/safety/forms/index.shtml. This form must be signed by either a parent, legal guardian or licensed driving instructor.
- Driver and passengers must wear a safety belt.

Second Level - Intermediate Unrestricted License

To apply for the Intermediate Unrestricted from the Intermediate Restricted License, you must be 17 years old and meet the following conditions:

- You must have held an Intermediate Restricted License for 1 year.
- You cannot have accumulated more than 6 points on your driving record or you must hold the Intermediate Restricted License for an additional 90 days.
- You cannot have had a traffic accident that was your fault.
- You cannot have 2 safety belt violations.
- Driver and passengers must wear a safety belt.
- No additional tests are required.

Final Level - Regular Driver License

You may obtain a Class D regular driver license when you are 18 years of age, or when you graduate from high school or receive a GED, whichever is sooner. The word "Intermediate" will be removed from your license when you move to the Regular Driver License. However, the license will still include the "Under 21" indicators.

NEW RESIDENTS UNDER 18

If you are fifteen years old and have a valid permit from the state you previously lived in, you will only qualify for issuance of a Tennessee learner permit. You must hold a valid learner permit for a total of 180 days and turn sixteen (16) years old before being eligible for the Intermediate Restricted License Class D. The length of time that you held the permit in your previous state may be included in the 180-day period as long as you can provide a certified driving record from your previous state. The certified driving record must be issued within the thirty (30) days immediately preceding the date of the Tennessee application

Effective July 1, 2018 all licenses issued to persons under 21 years of age are in a vertical format. Examples are shown below.

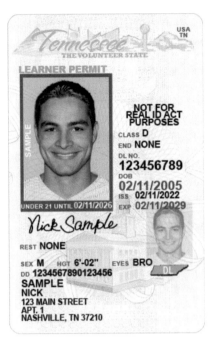

Learner Permit

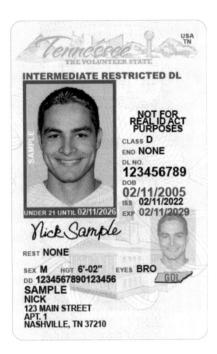

Intermediate Restricted

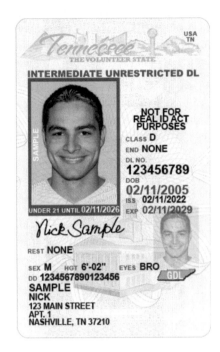

Intermediate Unrestricted

Front of PD Card

Learner Permit GDL Restrictions

- Must have licensed driver age 21 or older in front seat
- Cannot drive between 10:00 PM - 6:00 AM
- Seatbelt use is mandatory for all passengers age 4 through 17

Front of IR Card

Tennessee INTERMEDIATE GDL RESTRICTIONS

- **Only one passenger allowed, UNLESS:**
  - 1 passenger is 21 or older and has a valid driver license, or
  - All additional passengers are siblings from driver's house going to / from school (*WP**)
- **Cannot drive between 11:00 PM - 6:00 AM, UNLESS:**
  - Accompanied by a parent, guardian OR a licensed driver age 21 or older, who has been designated by the parent or guardian (*WP*)
  - Driving to or from work, or scheduled specifically-identified school sponsored activities (*WP*)
  - Hunting or fishing between 4:00 AM to 6:00 AM with a valid hunting or fishing license.
- **Seatbelt use is mandatory for all passengers age 4 through 17**
  NOTE: WP indicates that written permission from parent/guardian identifying the person(s) event or work place is needed.

Back of PD Card

For the next level of GDL the teen driver must:
- Hold the valid learner permit for at least 180 days.
- Maintain a safe driving record with less than six points.
- Acquire a minimum of 50 hours of behind the wheel driving experience, including 10 hours at night.
- Be 16 years old.

PENALTIES:	
IF YOU:	*YOU MUST:*
Get 6 or more points on your driving record during the 180 days prior to applying for the next level...	...continue to hold the learner permit until your record has been clear for 180 days.

Dept. of Safety 349232 - Rev. 8/11 - cost .02 ea.

Back of IR Card

In order to proceed to the next level of GDL you must:
- Hold the valid Intermediate Restricted license for at least 1 year.
- Maintain a safe driving record with less than six points.
- Not contribute to an accident.
- Not get a 2nd seatbelt or 2nd moving violation.
- Be 17 years old

PENALTIES:	
FOR:	*YOU MUST:*
6 or more pts., contributing to accident, or 2nd seatbelt ticket...	...hold Intermediate Restricted license for an *additional* 90 days
2nd moving violation...	...complete a Driver Ed. Class
Contributing to fatal accident, or a forged approval letter...	...drop back to a learner permit until you are 18 years old

Dept. of Safety 349233 - 1/07 - cost .019 ea.

This certified driving record must show no violations or accidents on the record. If there are any violations on the previous state record you will be required to retain the Tennessee Learner Permit until your driving record can be reviewed by the Department of Safety and Homeland Security's Driver Improvement Section to see if the record complies with Tennessee's "less than 6 points" requirement.

If the applicant is 16 years old and holds a valid license (regular, provisional, probationary, graduated, etc.) from a previous state (issued at least 90 days before applying for a Tennessee license), the application will be for an Intermediate Restricted license.

If the applicant had an out-of-state license for LESS than 90 days, an Intermediate Restricted License can only be issued if a clear driving record from the previous state is provided. The driving record must confirm:

1. That a valid learner permit and/or license class has been held for a combined period of at least 180 days. (e.g. - Georgia permit held for 120 days + Georgia license held for 60 days = 180 days total) and
2. That there are no violations or accidents on the driving record. If there are any violations on the record, a learner permit only may be issued until the previous state record can be reviewed and evaluated by the Department of Safety's Driver Improvement Section. It must comply with Tennessee's "less than 6 points" requirement.

Regardless of the length of time a license is held in the previous state, a Tennessee Intermediate Restricted license must be held for **one year** before qualifying for the Intermediate Unrestricted license.

Upon graduating from high school or after receiving a GED before age 18, a regular Class D operator's license may be issued as described on page A2 (Section A1 of this manual).

Restriction Cards for Learner Permit and Intermediate License Holders

A driver with a learner permit will be given a "Restriction Card" to carry along with the permit that explains the restrictions of driving with the permit. The Restriction Card also explains the requirements for advancing to the Intermediate Restricted level of the Class D license. An example of the PD Restriction Card is shown on page 15.

- Both levels of the Intermediate License (Restricted and Unrestricted) show the license class as Class D and have the words Intermediate Driver License displayed in the yellow header bar on the front of the license.
- A driver with the first level Intermediate Restricted (IR) Class D will be given a "restriction card" to carry along with the license that explains the restrictions of driving with the IR. The Restriction Card also explains the requirements for advancing to the Intermediate Unrestricted level of the Class D license. An example of the IR Restriction Card is shown on page 15.

Unsafe driving incidents or violations that could result in the suspension or automatic downgrade of license level under the GDL Program are outlined in the following table:

GDL Penalties Table: 3.1			
Incident	**After PD Issued**	**After Intermediate Restricted Issued**	**After Intermediate Unrestricted Issued**
(a) Six or more points on driving record	Requires the applicant to continue to hold the learner permit for an additional time period until they are able to maintain a record with less than 6 points for 180 consecutive days	Adds 90 days to the minimum 1 year teen required to hold Intermediate Restricted (Total = 1 year & 3 months)	If any of the violations listed in (a), (b), (c) or (d) occurred during the time the teen had an Intermediate Restricted license, but the DOS did not receive notice from the court until *after* we had already issued the teen an Intermediate Unrestricted license, **the penalties in the preceding column will still apply.** The teen will be "dropped back" to an Intermediate Restricted license for 90 days.
(b) Contributing to the occurrence of an accident	N/A	Adds 90 days to the minimum 1 year teen required to hold Intermediate Restricted (Total = 1 year & 3 months)	
(c) Conviction of a 2nd Seatbelt violation	N/A	N/A Adds 90 days to the minimum 1 year teen required to hold Intermediate Restricted (Total = 1 year & 3 months)	
(d) Conviction of a 2nd Moving violation	N/A	Requires completion of a certified driver education course	
(e) Forged letter of parental approval	N/A	Revocation of Intermediate Restricted and Re-issuance of a Learner Permit only until teen reaches the age of 18	If DOS notified *after* Intermediate Unrestricted issued, **teen's Intermediate privileges will still be revoked and a Learner Permit re-issued until the 18th birthday.**
(f) Contributing to the occurrence of a fatal accident	Must maintain a Learner Permit only until teen reaches the age of 18	Revocation of Intermediate Restricted and Re-issuance of a Learner Permit only until teen reaches the age of 18	Revocation of Intermediate Unrestricted and Re-issuance of a Learner Permit only until teen reaches the age of 18

- A driver with the second level Intermediate Unrestricted (IU) Class D does not have any restrictions on driving. Therefore there is no restriction card for this license level.

ADDITIONAL DOCUMENTATION REQUIREMENTS FOR MINORS

In addition to the documentation requirements described in Chapter 2 (Proof of Identity, TN Residency, Social Security Number and U.S Citizenship / Lawful Permanent Resident) all applicants under the age of eighteen (18) must also meet the requirements described in this section.

Minor/Teenage Affidavits

Applicants under eighteen years old must have an adult sign a Minor/Teenage Affidavit and Cancellation form, available at all driver license service centers. This form confirms that the adult signing the form joins in the application for the license and will be responsible for the actions of the minor driver. This includes assuming financial responsibility for the minor driver. It must be signed by a parent, foster parent, or step-parent living at the same address as the applicant, legal guardian, or a grandparent authorized by the parent, step-parent or guardian.

If adults cannot accompany the minor to the driver license service center to sign the form, it may be completed ahead of time and signed before a notary public.

If a grandparent is assuming financial responsibility for the youth, the grandparent must bring a notarized statement authorizing this, signed by the parent, a step-parent, custodian or guardian, as appropriate.

- If a minor applies for an additional class of license (such as motorcycle), the parents or legal guardian will be required to sign a second teenage affidavit for that license type.

The statement is not required to be on a Department of Safety form, but should be in the following general format:

"I do hereby authorize _____
to sign for a driver license for_____."
Signed: _____
(Notary certificate)

Proof of School Attendance/Progress

Applicants under the age of eighteen (18) must prove they are either enrolled in or have already graduated from high school. Acceptable proof of this status must be provided to the examiner in one of the following methods:

1. If the applicant has graduated, the applicant must **bring the original high school diploma or G.E.D. certificate** when applying (no photo copies).
2. If still enrolled in a Tennessee school, the applicant must **ask the school to complete a Certificate of Compulsory School Attendance (Form SF1010). The applicant must take the original, completed form to the Driver Service Center.** This form is only valid for **thirty (30) days** from the date of signing by the school official.

NOTE: During the traditional summer vacation months, a properly completed SF1010 form signed within the last 30 days of the school year will be accepted throughout the summer until 30 days after the start of the following school year (e.g. a form signed in May is accepted through Aug/Sept, approximately).

3. If the applicant is enrolled in school outside of Tennessee (or in an approved private or church school in Tennessee without access to the SF1010 forms), the applicant must provide a statement from the school principal or headmaster on official school letterhead specifically confirming that the applicant is not truant. (Copies and Faxes cannot be accepted.)

IMPORTANT: Grade cards or school transcripts are not acceptable as proof of compliance with this law. Due to the various grading scales, evaluation of excused / unexcused absences and other factors that differ from school system to school system, the Driver License personnel are not authorized to interpret the information in these documents. It is the responsibility of the school system or Department of Education to confirm the applicant's eligibility. It is the responsibility of the applicant to provide satisfactory documentation of this requirement.

4. **Home Schooled Applicants must provide the following documentation:**
   - **A letter from the local director of schools** in the district of the applicant's legal residence confirming the district received the proper annual notice of intent to home school.
   - **Verification of Home School Enrollment (Department of Safety Form SF-1193)** signed and completed by the parent or legal guardian, at time of application at the Driver License Center, affirming the student's satisfactory attendance.

If a student fifteen years old or older drops out of school, the school is required to notify the Department of Safety which suspends the student's driving privileges. The first time a student drops out, he or she may regain the privilege to drive by returning to school. However, **there is no second chance**. The second time a student drops out, he or she must wait to turn eighteen (18) years old before being eligible to apply for a license again.

If a person who dropped out returns to school, the appropriate school official can certify the student has returned by completing a different section of the Certificate of Compulsory School Attendance. The official will give the student a copy of the form to take with them to a driver license service center. The student will be required to pay a $20 reinstatement fee, in addition to the appropriate application and license fees. Other fees may be added as well, depending on the individual's history.

Novice Teen Drivers at Higher Risk

In 2019 there were 1,603 young drivers (15 to 20 years old) killed and an estimated 205,000 injured in motor vehicle crashes (NCSA, 2021). Distracted driving, inexperience, risk-taking, as well as speeding are some of the major reasons why.

Loud music, changing discs as well as tuning the radio are also potentially deadly distractions when behind the wheel. And when a teen driver has friends in the car, the risk is even higher - the more passengers, the greater the chance of a serious crash.Here are common teen driver distractions that can be deadly:

- Friends in other vehicles: Don't let saying "hi" or other fun and games take your attention off the road.
- Loud music or headphones: Hearing what's going on around you is just as important as seeing. It is extremely dangerous to wear headphones or earbuds and have the volume of your radio so high that it interferes with your "hearing" of traffic conditions, such as other vehicle's warning horns or emergency sirens. In most states it is illegal to wear headphones and earbuds while driving.
- The "show-off" factor: It may be tempting to go faster, turn sharper or beat another car through an intersection. Many teens fail to realize that they are no longer just "competing for fun" and are now using a 5,000 pound "weapon" in this competition.

Keep focused on DRIVING in order to stay safe and stay alive.

Cell Phone Usage Prohibited

IMPORTANT FOR TEENAGE DRIVERS

NO CELL PHONES WHILE DRIVING

Tennessee law prohibits any driver possessing a learner permit or intermediate driver license from using a cell phone while driving on any Tennessee roadway. A cell phone is defined as:
(a) handheld cellular telephone
(b)cellular car telephone or
(c) other mobile phone

CONSEQUENCES OF CONVICTION

- **Class C misdemeanor**
- **$50.00 fine**
- **6 points on to a minor's driving record**
- **90 day delay in eligibility for intermediate Restricted Driver License**

Channeling Devices used to direct traffic flow

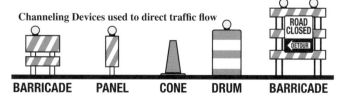

BARRICADE   PANEL   CONE   DRUM   BARRICADE

Texting while Driving is Prohibited

As of July 1, 2009, texting while driving is also prohibited for teenage drivers as well as adult drivers. This includes a hand-held telephone or hand-held personal digital assistant to transmit or read a written message while the driver's motor vehicle is in motion. Violations can result in a fine not to exceed Fifty Dollars and court costs not to exceed Ten Dollars.

Teen Driving in Work Zones

Every three days a teen is killed and seven are injured in a work zone crash in this country according to NETS, The Network of Employers for Traffic Safety. This could be you and your driver, if you drive carelessly through a roadway work zone. They are considered the most hazardous place for workers in the U.S., but they can be even more dangerous for drivers – particularly young, inexperienced ones. Statistics show that drivers comprise four out of five deaths in highway work zones.

Teen drivers have higher rates of fatal crash involvement than any other age group. Studies show young drivers are more likely to become involved in work zone accidents than others, as they are more likely to engage in risk-taking behavior, exercise negative driving habits, are easily distracted while driving, and lack the basic driving skills needed to respond quickly to work zone demands. When it comes to driving, there is no such thing as beginner's luck!

Some work zone safety tips:

- Slow down! Drive within the posted speed limits, which are usually reduced in work zones. If you don't, you'll pay the price. The Tennessee Highway Patrol's program Project CAR (Construction Accident Reduction) places Highway Patrol State Troopers in work zones across the state targeting motorists who violate traffic laws while traveling through roadway work zones when workers are present.
- Don't tailgate! Most work zone accidents are caused by rear-end collisions.
- Eliminate distractions! Put down the cell phone; leave the radio dial alone. This is not the time to look for a new CD!
- Keep your ears open! Do not wear earphones or earbuds while driving.
- Merge early! You can be ticketed and be the cause of an accident for being a last chance merger.
- Watch for flaggers! Follow their signals, and don't change lanes within the work zone unless instructed to do so.
- Expect the unexpected! Work zones change constantly.
- Turn your lights on before you enter the zone! Turn on your vehicle's headlights to become more visible to workers and other motorists.
- Stay calm! Remember the work zone crew members are working to improve your future ride.

1. **What is the Graduated Driver License law?**
   The graduated driver licensing system places certain restrictions on teens under the age of 18 who have a learner permit and driver license.

2. **What are the restrictions for those with learner permits?**
   Anyone under the age of 18 who has a learner permit is prohibited from driving between the hours of 10 p.m. and 6 a.m. When driving, permit holders must have a licensed driver age 21 or older in the vehicle with them in the front seat. Everyone inside the vehicle must wear a seat belt. The driver may not use a handheld device while operating the vehicle.

3. **How long must I have a learner permit before applying for an Intermediate Restricted license?**
   - Anyone under the age of 18 must have their learner permit for a minimum of six months before applying for an intermediate restricted license.

   - The minimum age for applying for an intermediate restricted license is 16.

   - If someone with a learner permit has driving offenses adding up to 6 or more points on their driving record during the 180 days before applying for the Intermediate Restricted license, the applicant has to continue to hold the learner permit until his/her record has less than 6 points for a full 180 consecutive days.

   - After the record is clear for 180 consecutive days (i.e., less than 6 points), the driver may apply for the next level, an Intermediate Restricted License.

4. **What are the restrictions for an Intermediate Restricted License?**
   Those with an intermediate license can only have 1 other passenger in the vehicle. UNLESS:

   - One or more of the passengers is age 21 or older and has a valid, unrestricted license; OR

   - The passengers are brothers and sisters, step-brothers or step-sisters, adopted or fostered children residing in the same house as the driver and AND the Intermediate License holder has in their possession a letter from the driver's parent authorizing passengers to be in the motor vehicle for the sole purpose of going to and from school.

   Those with an Intermediate Restricted License are prohibited from driving between the hours of 11 p.m. and 6 a.m. UNLESS the meet one of the following circumstances:

   - They are accompanied by a parent or guardian;

   - They are accompanied by a licensed driver 21 or older who has been designated by the parent or guardian. This designation must be in writing and be in the possession of the teen driver;

   - They are driving to or from a specifically identified school sponsored activity or event and have in their possession written permission from a parent or guardian to do this;

   - They are driving to or from work and have in their possession written permission from a parent or guardian identifying the place of employment and authorizing the driver to go to and from work; OR

   - They are driving to or from hunting or fishing between 4 a.m. and 6 a.m. and have in their possession a valid hunting or fishing license.

5. **What would happen to an Intermediate Restricted License holder caught with a forged or fake letter regarding permission to drive outside of the allowed hours?**
   A driver with an Intermediate Restricted License who is convicted of having a forged or fraudulent letter or statement will have his/her Intermediate Restricted License revoked and will only be reissued a learner permit until he/she reaches the age of 18.

6. **What will an Intermediate license look like?**
   You may view examples of these licenses on page 15.

7. **How long must an Intermediate Restricted License be held?**
   Teens must hold their Intermediate Restricted License for a **minimum of one year**. After one year, an unrestricted Intermediate license may be applied for. There is a $2 application fee. The word "Intermediate" will still be on the license, but the restrictions will be lifted.

IMPORTANT: A teen driver will be ineligible for an Unrestricted Intermediate License for additional ninety (90) days beyond the minimum one year if:

1. The driver has received six (6) or more points (the equivalent of two (2) minor traffic citations) on their Intermediate Restricted License, or

2. The driver has contributed to a traffic crash, or

3. The driver has been convicted of a second seatbelt violation,

ALSO: If the teen driver gets a second moving violation while holding the Intermediate Restricted Driver License, an approved Driver Education class MUST BE COMPLETED before receiving an Intermediate Unrestricted Driver License.

NOTE: At age 18, a driver can apply for a regular unrestricted license without the word "Intermediate" printed on it. There is an $8 duplicate fee unless the driver chooses to keep the license with the word "Intermediate" on it until that license is at the end of its five-year renewal cycle.

Table: 3.2

PD	At least 6 months →	Level 1	At least 12 months →	Level 2	Until age 18 →	Level 3

	LEARNER PERMIT CLASS PD	INTERMEDIATE RESTRICTED	INTERMEDIATE UNRESTRICTED	REGULAR CLASS D
Requirements:	▪ Must be 15 years old ▪ Vision Exam ▪ Knowledge Test ▪ SF 1010 Form *(Proof of Compulsory School Attendance and Satisfactory Progress)* ▪ Parent or Legal guardian must sign Teenage Affidavit of Financial Responsibility ▪ Birth Certificate* ▪ Social Security Number ** ▪ Proof of citizenship or lawful	▪ Must be 16 years old ▪ Held a valid PD for 6 months ▪ Certification of 50 hours behind-the-wheel experience including 10 hours at night ▪ **Cannot have:** ☒ six or more points on driving record during the 180 days immediately preceding application ▪ Driving Test	▪ At least 17 years old ▪ Held a valid Restricted Intermediate for 1 year ▪ **Cannot have:** □ six or more points on driving record □ have been at fault in a traffic crash □ have been convicted of a 2nd seatbelt violation *[these would add a 90 day waiting period to the 1 yr*	▪ Must be at least 18 years of age ▪ Optional: can apply for a duplicate of license without 'the word "Intermediate" on' the face
Fees:	$10.50, any age under 18 years old.	Age 16 = $24.50 Age 17 = $21.00 Age 18 = Eligible for regular driver license	Age 17 = $2.00 Age 18 = Eligible for regular driver license ($8 duplicate fee if had Intermediate license)	$8.00 or $12.00, regular duplicate fee depending upon if 1st or subsequent duplicate
Issued for:	12 months	until age 21	Same expiration date @ age 21	Same expiration date @ age 21
Restrictions:	▪ Must have licensed driver age 21 or older in front seat ▪ Cannot drive between 10:00 PM - 6:00 AM ▪ Seatbelts mandatory for all passengers age 4 thru 17 (or child restraint device if under age 4)	▪ Only one passenger ▪ Cannot drive between 11:00 PM - 6:00 AM ▪ Seatbelts mandatory of all passengers age 4 thru 17 (or child restraint device if under age 4)	▪ Seatbelts mandatory for all passengers age 4 thru 17 (or child restraint device if under age 4) ▪ No additional restrictions, however, license still states "Intermediate" prominently on the face of the license	▪ No restrictions and license looks like regular "Under 21 license"

* See page 9 for information on acceptable forms of identification.
** See page 10 for more information on SSN requirements.

8. Are there any teens not required to complete the steps in the Graduated Driver License program?

The Graduated Driver License requirements do not apply to anyone age 18 and older OR anyone under the age of 18 who has graduated high school or received their GED. If you are 16 years of age you may also obtain a Class D regular driver license if you are emancipated by active duty military service, marriage or court order.

Effective July 1, 2018 all licenses issued to persons under 21 years of age are in a vertical format. Example of a Class D Under 21 license is shown to the right side of this page.

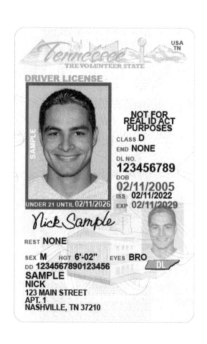

General Information:

- Your driver license examination will consist of a vision screening, a knowledge test, and a road test.

- Driver license tests are given at all Driver Service Centers except for the express service centers. The knowledge tests are administered on a first-come, first-served basis.

- Due to the length of time to administer, road tests are taken **by appointment**.

- Road tests are not given in extreme weather (heavy rain/ snow, dense fog, hail, high winds, icy roads, etc.)

- During winter months road tests are not given in the dark.

- **No test may be repeated on the same day.**

- **Mandatory 1-day waiting period is required after failing the knowledge test.**

- **Mandatory waiting periods are required when an applicant fails the road test for the original issuance of a Class D license.** For details on these waiting periods, see Table 4.2.

- When you return to take a test over, you must bring back all of the original documents you are required to provide.

- You will be required to pay the $2 application fee each time you take a test and fail. This fee applies to PD, D and H tests.

Determining Which Tests Are Required:

Table: 4.1

Original License	Class D or Class H Full Tests: Knowledge, Road Skills, Vision Screening Class PD Vision Screening and Knowledge tests Exchanging PD to D Vision Screening and Road Skills
Duplicate, Renewal	No Test
Adding For-Hire Endorsement	Vision Screening and Knowledge tests
New residents, with current and valid out-of-state license	Vision Screening only, if out-of-state license is valid and not expired; otherwise, knowledge and road skills test, Vision Screening
New residents, from other countries or no prior license	Vision Screening, Knowledge and Road Skills test

Note: See Motorcycle Manual for Class M tests, and CDL Manual for Classes A, B, and C

VISION SCREENING

To determine if a driver can see well enough to drive, a vision screening is required before any license or permit is issued. An applicant is required to have at least 20/40 vision in each eye individually and both eyes together. This may be with or without your glasses or contact lenses. If you are unable to successfully complete the vision screening, you must have an eye specialist of your choice fill out an eye statement for the Department to evaluate.

KNOWLEDGE TEST

You will be given an exam covering knowledge needed to drive safely. The test will consist of multiple choice questions based on information contained in sections B and C of this manual. You can expect the test to approximately consist of the following four areas:
Traffic signs and signals—25%
Safe driving principles—25%
Rules of the road—25%
Drugs and alcohol—25%

1. Test Formats
The knowledge tests are administered in our Driver License Service Centers using computerized testing machines. In very limited circumstances, tests are administered in written formats.

Our Driver Service Centers that have the computerized testing are also currently able to offer the test in 3 alternate language formats of Spanish, Korean or Japanese. Applicants for whom English is not their first language may also use a translation dictionary as long as there are no notes or other handwriting visible within the pages of the book. The use of Personal Digital Assistants (PDAs), Smart Phones, Electronic Dictionaries and other similar electronic devices are NOT allowed during testing. Interpreters are NOT allowed to assist with any of the driver license testing.

Oral tests are available by appointment at selected Driver License Service Centers for applicants who have a learning disability or cannot read. If the applicant requesting an oral test is under age eighteen (18), a written statement from a physician or educational specialist stating that the applicant has a medical condition or learning disability will be required before the test can be administered in the oral format. In the event the applicant requesting an oral test is deaf, the Department of Safety will furnish a certified sign language interpreter to assist with the administration of the exam.

Any form of cheating by an applicant on a required examination will result in an automatic failure and the applicant will not be allowed to re-attempt the test for 30 days. Forms of cheating include, but are not limited to the following:

- Use of any form of written notes (including notes on paper, clothing, body, digital pagers, etc.)

- Talking during the examination (includes cell phone use)

- Attempting to allow another person to take the examination

- All cell phones, pagers or text messaging devices must be turned off during both written and road test administration.

2. When You Don't Pass the Knowledge Test

In order to encourage the applicant to thoroughly study Section B of this manual and cut down on repeat visits by applicants who are not yet prepared for the examination, a mandatory 1-day waiting period is required after failing any driver license knowledge test.

All applicants will be required to wait a minimum of one day before returning to any Driver License Service Center to attempt the knowledge examination again. The date and information on failures is keyed into the Driver License computer system to ensure that all locations are aware of prior test dates and scores.

The waiting period outlined above will also be applied to wait times between additional re-testing if the applicant does not pass the examination on the second or subsequent attempts.

ROAD TEST

1. Make an Appointment to Schedule Your Road Test

All applicants that require a road test should make a pre-scheduled appointment at the Driver License Service Center of their choice. These appointments may be made using the Driver License Appointments system found on our Internet website at: tn.gov/safety/ or by calling toll-free 1-866-849-3548. **For the Hearing Impaired, TTY USERS SHOULD HAVE THE TENNESSEE RELAY SERVICE CALL (615) 532-2281.**

NOTE: Because road tests are not given in the dark, these times will be adjusted during winter hours to compensate for the shortened daylight hours.

All applicants will need to be aware of the following guidelines for road test appointments:

- You must have successfully passed the required knowledge test(s) prior to your road test appointment. If you arrive for your road test appointment and have not passed the knowledge test your appointment will be canceled.
- Applicants who do not successfully pass the Knowledge test on the first attempt or subsequent attempts, are not permitted to retake the examination for a second time on the same day.
- You will be able to make your appointment up to 45 days in advance of your desired test date. When scheduling, keep the following mandatory requirements in mind:
- If you do not already have a valid Tennessee learner permit you will be required to bring proof of U.S. citizenship or lawful permanent residency with you to your appointment. (When getting a TDL you will need current proof of Temporary Legal Presence (TLP).)
- You should plan to arrive at the Driver License Service Center at least 15 minutes prior to your scheduled appointment time to allow for paperwork processing and review of your required documentation mentioned above.

- You must speak and understand enough of the English language to communicate with the Examiner during the road test.
- You must provide your own vehicle for use during the road test with all the operational equipment and safety features as outlined in the next section on vehicle inspection.
- If you are more than 5 minutes late for your appointment time, your road skills test will be canceled and you will need to reschedule for a later date.
- The Department of Safety reserves the right to cancel road test appointments for emergency situations or dangerous weather conditions. Road tests will be given in light to moderate rain, fog or snow. However, they will NOT be given in heavy rain, thunderstorms, thick fog cover, when roads are flooded, covered/packed with snow and ice, during severe weather warnings (i.e. tornado) or other similarly dangerous driving situations.

2. Pre-Trip Vehicle Inspection

The motor vehicle you bring for the road test must meet all Tennessee motor vehicle registration (valid tags) and safety law requirements and have equipment in proper working order. In addition, applicants will be asked to demonstrate their ability to use each of the following eight items.

Safety Belts. Any passenger motor vehicle manufactured or assembled in 1969 or later must be equipped with safety belts and must be in good usable condition for both the applicant and the examiner.

Brakes. (Emergency and regular). By law all automobiles must have two separate methods of applying brakes. They must have a regular foot brake and a parking brake.

Headlights. (High and low beam). Motor vehicles must be equipped with at least two headlights but no more than four white headlights.

Tail and Brake Lights. Passenger vehicles must be equipped with a rear license light, two red tail lights, and two red brake lights.

Windshield Wipers. Every vehicle equipped with a windshield should have 2 windshield wipers for cleaning rain or any other moisture in order to permit clear vision for the driver, unless 1 wiper cleans to within 1 inch of the inside of the windshield.

Windshield Defroster and Fan Control. Applicants need to be able to demonstrate how to 'defog' the windshield.

Rearview Mirrors. The vehicle must have at least one rearview mirror not interfering with the driver's view of the rear. For applicants with certain vision or hearing impairments, two outside rearview mirrors are also required.

Horns. A horn is required on all motor vehicles.

Also required:

Windows and windshields. Clear vision for the driver is required to the front, rear and both sides. It is unlawful to drive a motor vehicle with a windshield that is so cracked, or covered with steam or frost that clear vision is prevented.

No tinting material may be affixed to the windshield of any motor vehicle. Standards for the other windows depend on the vehicle as follows:

Passenger Car. No material which transmits less than 35% of visible light may be attached to any window.

Multi-Purpose Vehicles: All windows behind the front seat are exempt. Windows immediately to the left and right of the driver must comply the same as for passenger vehicles.

Mufflers. Every vehicle must be equipped with a muffler to prevent excessive or unusual noises and polluting smoke.

Doors. Both the driver door and the passenger door must open from the inside and the outside.

Bumpers. Passenger cars must have bumpers which are within a range of 14 to 22 inches from the ground; 4x4 recreational vehicles must have bumpers with a range of 14 to 31 inches.

Speedometer. Every vehicle must have a working speedometer in order to gauge vehicle speed.

3. The Driving Test

The examiner will give you directions and evaluate whether or not you can drive safely. You will not be asked to do anything illegal. The only people allowed in the vehicle are you and the examiner (or other authorized personnel). No animal may be in the vehicle.

During the test, the examiner will be observing the following:

1. **How you prepare to drive.** Have you checked your mirrors, fastened your safety belt, turned on any necessary lights or wipers?
2. **How you start your vehicle.** Do you look for other cars? Do you signal and wait until it is safe before entering traffic?
3. **How you control your vehicle.** Do you accelerate smoothly? Do you use your gas pedal, brake, steering wheel, and other controls correctly? Handle curves properly?
4. **How you handle intersections and make left and right turns.** Are you in the proper lane? Do you look both left and right for approaching vehicles? Do you make sure your path is clear before proceeding? Do you simply rely on the traffic signals? Do you signal and change lanes carefully?
5. **How you obey the traffic signals and posted signs.**
6. **How you drive in traffic.** Do you pay full attention to driving? Do you scan carefully for signs, signals, pedestrians and other vehicles? Do you yield and take the right-of-way correctly?
7. **How you stop.** Do you stop smoothly and at the right spot? Can you stop quickly and safely in an emergency?

8. **How you back up.** Do you look over your shoulder? Can you back in a straight line? Can you turn safely while backing? Can you back into/out of a parking space?
9. **How you judge distance.** Do you maintain a safe distance from other cars?
10. **How you communicate to other drivers.** Do you make sudden changes, or signal too late or too early? Do you slow down as early as it is safe to do so, or do you catch other drivers by surprise?
11. **How you share the road with others.** Are you courteous and watchful?
12. **How you change your speed to suit the situation.** Do you take into account the speed limit, other cars, light, weather and road conditions?

4. Causes for Immediate Failure

The applicant will be failed immediately for any of the following:
- Violation of any traffic law
- Lack of cooperation or refusal to follow directions
- Any dangerous action
- Contributing to an accident

5. When You Don't Pass the Road Test

Upon completion of the driving test, the examiner will advise you of your errors, how to correct them, and what maneuvers you should practice to improve your driving skill. You should review the related material and/or practice the driving skills before returning. Applicants who do not successfully pass the skills test on the first attempt or subsequent attempts are not permitted to take the examination again on the same day.

Applicants may be allowed to re-test after mandatory practice times as determined by their total score (number of errors) under the guidelines in Table 4.2. These guidelines are designed to encourage the applicant to thoroughly practice their driving skills and cut down on repeat visits by applicants who are not yet prepared for the examination.

Guidelines for Retesting Table: 4.2

Number of errors committed during the skills test:	Allow retest after the following mandatory practice time period:
1 to 6 errors / points	PASS no re-test needed
7 to 9 errors / points	Next (1) Day
10 to 12 errors / points	Seven (7) Days
13 to 15 errors / points	Fourteen (14) Days
16 or more errors / points -OR- Automatic Failure	Thirty (30) Days

NOTE: The guidelines established above will also be applied to wait times between additional re-testing opportunities if applicant does not pass the examination on the second or subsequent attempts.

☑ **Study and Practice Driving Ahead of Time**

Both the knowledge test and the road test will go more smoothly if you spend time reviewing this manual, and spend time on the road with an experienced driver before you come to apply.

☑ **Bring A Proper Vehicle**

All safety equipment must work (horns, lights, safety belts, brakes, signals and windshield wipers). The vehicle registration must also be current. Bring a vehicle that you are familiar with driving.

☑ **Arrive at least 15 minutes before your scheduled Road Test appointment.** This will allow time for application paperwork before your appointment time.

☑ **Don't Be Late - for Road Test Appointments.** Road tests average 20-25 minutes. To insure we can provide timely service to you and your fellow applicants, if you are five (5) or more minutes late for the start of your road test appointment, it will have to be rescheduled.

PARENTS Be sure to review Section C-4 starting at page 116 of this manual. It provides helpful information to assist you and your teen in learning to drive as well as a useful driving experience log that has been recommended by many parents and safety advocate groups.

IMPORTANT INFORMATION FOR PARENTS AND KNOWLEDGE TEST APPLICANTS AGE 15-17

Teenagers between the ages of 15 to 17 seeking to obtain their driver's license who are required to take a written test, can now take that test on-line under a proctor's supervision (parent/legal guardian) via Tennessee Proctor Identification (PID) App.

Please Note you must comply with the testing rules and follow the instructions listed on the web test portal.

What is the Tennessee Proctor Identification (PID) App?

The Tennessee Proctor Identification (PID) App allows eligible Tennesseans to securely proctor online knowledge tests by obtaining a highly secure personal identification via the Proctor Identification (PID) App. Personal identification information must be registered by verifying the proctor against their Tennessee Department of Safety & Homeland Security (TDOSHS) record.

For more information please visit our webpage at:

https://www.tn.gov/safety/driver-services/driver-license-knowledge-test-online.html

SECTION B

INTRODUCTION

This section is designed for all new drivers. Reading and studying Sections B and C of this manual will help prepare for the driver license and learner permit tests. The section explains Tennessee's licensing requirements, driving responsibilities and basic "rules of the road." All drivers need to know the information in this section to pass the driver license test and become safe, courteous drivers. Alone, the guide will not teach you how to drive. Mastering driving skills is done with a good instructor and plenty of practice.

In order to help users study, there are a few sample questions at the end of each chapter. These are actual questions from the driver license test. There are many possible questions that can be included on the driver license test. These questions are included to help you review the material and get a sense of what the test may cover. Study the chapters and test your understanding of the information by using these questions.

Website Resources: Additional study questions and practice tests are available as part of the online services at: www.tn.gov/safety/ There are different practice tests that focus on specific areas of study. Practice test topics and the related chapters in this publication include:

Alcohol, Other Drugs and Driving (Chapter B-7)
Guidelines for Driving (Chapters B-1 and B-2)
Rules of the Road (Chapters B-4, B-5, B-6 & B-8)
Traffic Signs and Signals (Chapter B-3)

Be Prepared for the Driving Task

To help you safely prepare for the actual operation of the vehicle, follow the tips below. There is much more to driving than just "grabbing the keys and getting in the car." Give your complete attention to knowing the proper operation of the vehicle's equipment.

GETTING READY TO DRIVE

Vehicle Condition

1. Check around the outside of the vehicle. Look for small children, pets and any other sort of obstruction.

2. Check the condition of the vehicle (windows, lights, body damage, condition of the tires and potential fluid leaks).

3. Enter the vehicle, place the key in the ignition and lock the doors.

4. Identify the location and purpose of all switches, gauges and pedals.

5. Know the location of the following controls even if there is no need to use them at the moment:
   • Horn
   • Turn Signals
   • Emergency/Four-Way Flashers
   • Headlights (on/off and dimmer switch)
   • Windshield Wipers and Washer Controls
   • Parking Brake and Release Lever
   • Air Conditioner/Heater/Defroster Controls
   • Gearshift Location (and clutch if manual transmission)

Seat Adjustments

Adjust the seat and, if equipped, the steering column, for the "Proper Driving Posture"

Align your body to your seat.
   • Adjust the seat to a comfortable upright position.
   • ***DO NOT DRIVE WITH THE SEAT IN A RECLINED OR SEMI-RECLINED POSITION.*** This is dangerous and reduces both your vision and your ability to react to emergency situations.

Be sure you are the proper distance from the steering wheel and foot pedals.
   • The pedals must be easily reached.
   • Have good clear vision through the windshield, each side window and all mirrors.
   • Your foot should move smoothly from the accelerator to the brake while the heel is kept on the floor.
   • Your body should be about 10 to 12 inches back from the steering wheel with or without an air bag. At this distance, an air bag would hit the driver in the chest if there were a collision. Sitting closer could result in serious head or neck injuries from an air bag hitting the chin or face.
   • Do not move the seat so far forward or extend the steering column to a point where you cannot easily steer.

   • The top of the steering wheel should be no higher than the top of the shoulders.

Properly adjust seat head restraints to a level even with the back of the head. Head restraints are designed to prevent whiplash if hit from behind.

Mirror Adjustments

1. Adjust mirrors properly. Remember that all three of the rear view mirrors must be adjusted so that the widest possible view is given. Also, keep blind spots to a minimum.
   • Adjust mirrors after the seat is adjusted correctly. (Always adjust before driving.)

2. Outside mirrors should be adjusted to reduce blind spots and provide maximum visibility.
   • INSIDE Rearview Mirror: Adjust the inside rearview mirror to frame the rear window. To get the smallest blind spot at the right side of the car, turn the inside mirror so that only the edge of the right rear window post is seen.
   • LEFT Side Mirror: To adjust the driver's side-view mirror, seated in an upright position place your head against the left side window and adjust the left side mirror. Set the mirror so you can just barely see the side of your car in the right side of the mirror which is the part that is closest to the window.
   • RIGHT Side Mirror: Seated in an upright position, to adjust the passenger's side-view mirror, position your head so that it is just above the center console. Set the mirror so you can just barely see the side of your car in the left side of the mirror which is the part of the mirror that is closest to the window. If the vehicle is not equipped with remote mirror-adjustment controls, you may need assistance when properly positioning this mirror.

3. After mirror adjustments, if you lean slightly backward and see more than a glimpse of the rear corners of the vehicle in your outside mirrors, adjust them outward.

4. To make sure mirrors are in the correct position, let a car pass you on the left. As it passes out of view in the inside mirror you should see its front bumper in the outside left (driver side) mirror.

5. Before driving with these updated mirror settings, see how they work while your vehicle is parked. For example, you can parallel park along a street, then see how passing vehicles move through your mirrors and peripheral vision. This can help you become oriented to the new settings before heading out into traffic.

6. Remember, even properly positioned mirrors cannot eliminate all blind spots. To reduce risk, make a final check to the sides before attempting any lateral moves. Even with properly adjusted mirrors, always turn your head and check blind spots when you want to turn or change lanes.

Safety Belts Fastened

1. Fasten and adjust safety belts (both lap and shoulder if separate belts). Lap belts should be positioned firmly across the hips while the shoulder belt is firmly across the shoulder.

2. Make sure all passengers are using safety belts or child restraints before driving.
   - If you or your passengers are not wearing a safety belt or are not secured in a car seat or booster seat, you may have to pay a fine.
   - Full details on safety belts and child restraints are found in the *Protecting Passengers/Drivers* chapter.

STARTING THE VEHICLE ENGINE

Check the vehicle owner's manual to determine the proper way to start the specific vehicle. The following are basic tips that apply to most vehicles:

1. Place foot on brake pedal and ensure gearshift selector is in the PARK position for automatic transmissions or in NEUTRAL for manual/standard transmissions.
   - Make sure the parking brake is "on" before starting any manual transmission vehicle. In vehicles with manual transmissions, the clutch must be depressed before the vehicle will start.

2. Place the car key into the ignition switch and turn the key forward to "on." Check dash lights and instruments (antilock brake systems [ABS], air bags, fuel level, etc.) for any warnings or alerts.

3. Turn on low-beam headlights, particularly at night or in bad weather. NOTE: In normal daylight, vehicles are visible at twice the distance when headlights are on.

4. Using an automatic transmission: With automatic transmissions, the driver usually does not need to change gears. The vehicle is put in "R" for reverse when to back-up and in "D" for drive to drive forward. (Some newer cars have an "O" gear selection for overdrive, which is for use when driving on interstates or other expressways where there is very little stop and go traffic.)
   - Most automatic transmissions also have lower gears that will be indicated by an "L", "2", or "1" on the gearshift indicator. These gears are generally not used except for special or emergency situations, such as:
     - Driving down steep mountain grades.
     - Slow speed driving on icy or other slippery roads.
     - Emergency deceleration if there is a brake failure.

5. Using a standard transmission: With a standard or manual transmission, the driver can control the gear-speed ratio and use gears, rather than brakes, to help slow down the vehicle. The following techniques for smooth shifting will help you handle driving vehicles with standard transmissions.
   - Hold the clutch pedal all the way down when starting, shifting gears and when speed drops below 10 MPH as you are coming to a stop.
   - Don't "ride the clutch", meaning don't drive with your foot resting on the clutch pedal if it is not needed to change gears.
   - Practice to get smooth coordination in using the clutch and accelerator pedals.
   - Don't coast with the gears in neutral (it's illegal) or with the clutch pedal pushed down except when shifting gears.
   - When going down steep hills, place the vehicle in a lower gear.

SPECIAL WARNING: FOR DRIVERS WITH STEERING WHEEL INTERLOCK SYSTEM

The basic rule a driver must follow when operating a vehicle with a steering wheel interlock system is: *never turn the ignition to the lock position when the vehicle is in motion The steering wheel will lock when trying to turn and the control of the vehicle will be lost.*

STEERING THE VEHICLE

To begin driving the vehicle, use a relaxed grip on the steering wheel and always drive with BOTH hands on the wheel. A firm (but not tight) grip allows you to "feel" the road (vibrations, etc.) better. Don't develop the habit of driving with your elbow or arm propped on the door or out the window. You won't have full control of the steering wheel and a sideswipe could take off your arm.

You not only steer with your hands, but also with your eyes! Always look where you want to go. This tells your brain what to do with your hands. Your peripheral vision (i.e., your vision to each side) helps you to keep your road position.

The following information outlines the steering methods for safe vehicle operation:

1. Looking at the steering wheel as a clock face, drivers should place the left hand at the 9 o'clock position and the right hand at 3 o'clock position on the steering wheel. This position helps avoid injury from air bag deployment during an accident.

   When using the turn signal indicators, headlight dimmer and windshield wiper controls, hand placement will change. You should have a slight bend in the elbow when the palm of your hand reaches the top of the steering wheel. Never sit in a position where your elbows are locked in a "stiff arm" type position.

2. Do not let the steering wheel slip through your fingers when turning/steering. Reverse the hand and arm movements made during the turn when coming out of a turn. This "counter-steering" makes for smooth turns and will also help in skids and when driving on snow and ice.

3. Do not cross your arms when steering or turning. It is OK to cross wrists while turning. But crossing arms may cause clothing and jewelry to interfere with safe turning. Also, you would suffer more serious injuries should the air bag deploy.

4. There are two generally accepted steering methods: **Push-Pull and Hand-over-Hand.**

- The Push-Pull method is recommended because it slows down turning movements making for a smoother, safer turn. It also keeps both hands on the steering wheel through the entire maneuver. Both hands move in an up and down motion on the sides of the steering wheel—the right hand on the right-hand side and the other on the left-hand side.

  - **Left Turn:** Start with your hands at the proper placement of 9 and 3 o'clock positions. Pull down with your left hand to approximately 7 o'clock, and then push up with your right hand until it reaches approximately 1 o'clock. As your left hand pulls the wheel down, during the same movement you will move the right hand down to the three o'clock position so it is ready to take over. The right hand then pushes the wheel up as you reposition the left hand up to repeat this pattern until you complete your turn. Counter-steer to straighten out the vehicle.

  - **Right Turn:** Start with hands at the proper placement of the 9 and 3 o'clock positions. Pull down with your right immediately 5 o'clock. Then, push up with your left hand until it reaches approximately 11 o'clock. Repeat this pattern until the turn is completed. Counter steer to straighten out the vehicle.

- The **Hand-over-Hand:** When turning the vehicle with this method, be careful to keep speed down. Steering this way crosses the hands at the top of the wheel. This method allows for quicker wheel movement, but there will be times when only one hand is on the wheel. Also, loose clothing or jewelry can get in the way, and the body can become unbalanced. For these reasons, the Push-Pull method is recommended for normal everyday driving.

  - For a right turn, start with hands at the proper 9 and 3 o'clock positions. Lean forward and grasp the outside of the rim at the 1 o'clock position with the right hand palm down. Lean back and pull with the right hand to the 5 o'clock position. Lean forward and grasp the outside of the rim with the left hand, palm down at the 1 o'clock position. Lean back and pull to the 5 o'clock position with the left hand. Repeat the process until the front wheels of the vehicle are at the desired angle. Before you straighten out, return hands to the original 9 and 3 o'clock positions. Counter-steer to straighten out the vehicle.

  - For a left turn, simply follow the steps above, reversing the hand references and steering wheel references to the opposite of what is indicated above in each step

BACKING, MOVING FORWARD AND STOPPING

The following instructions are for vehicles with automatic transmissions:

1. **Backing** - Common mistakes committed by new drivers when backing are (a) moving too fast, (b) providing too much steering input and (c) turning the steering wheel in the wrong direction.
   - With foot on the brake, move gear selector lever to "R" for reverse.
   - Grasp steering wheel at 12 o'clock position with left hand.
   - Turn to the right and place right arm over the back of the seat.
   - Look over your shoulder through the rear window for a safe, clear path.
   - Use idle speed or accelerate gently and smoothly, keeping a slow speed.
   - Turn the wheel to the right to back to the right; turn to the left to back to the left.
   - Continue looking to the rear until coming to a complete stop.

2. **Moving Forward** -Learning to avoid sudden or quick jolts forward will take some practice as follows:
   - With foot on brake, move gear selector lever to "D" for drive.
   - Check forward for safe, clear path.
   - Check for traffic to the sides and behind.
   - Signal if pulling away from a curb.
   - If safe, pivot foot to accelerator and press down gently.
   - Look at least one block ahead and steer toward a reference point.

3. **Stopping** - Planning ahead for smooth stops will help you avoid brake wear and potential rear-end collisions. Like most states, Tennessee reports that rear-end collisions are the most common type of accident recorded annually.
   - Check mirrors to the side and rear for traffic.
   - If moving to the curb or other lane, check over the right (or left) shoulder and signal intention.
   - Release accelerator and pivot foot to brake pedal slowly.
   - Press down on the brake pedal with a steady pressure for a smooth stop. Do not "stomp" on the brake pedal.
   - If stopping at stop sign or traffic signal light, stop before the crosswalk, a marked stop line, and if there is no stop line, at the point of the nearest intersecting roadway, where you can view the approaching traffic on the intersecting roadway, before entering the intersection.
   - If stopping at a curb, move to within 18 inches of the curb for proper parking.

As you may have noticed, driving is a complex and detailed activity that requires your complete attention. The "safest" thing you can do is to make sure you don't let your attention to driving safely decline after you have become competent.

SPECIAL WARNING: CARBON MONOXIDE POISONING

Avoid Carbon Monoxide Poisoning: Carbon monoxide gas from a car engine can kill (it has not taste, no smell or visibility). It generally leaks when the car heater is running, when the exhaust system is not working properly or in heavy traffic when breathing fumes from other vehicles.

How to avoid carbon monoxide poisoning:

- Have the exhaust system checked regularly.
- Be alert for unusual roars from under the car.
- Never let the engine run in a closed garage
- Do not use a heater/air conditioner in a parked car with the windows closed.
- Close the fresh-air vent in congested traffic

The information in this chapter covered how to become "prepared for the driving task." It will take some practice for new drivers to translate these written details into common habits for safe driving. Therefore, review this information frequently. Once you are comfortable with the operation of the vehicle, you will be ready to drive in various traffic situations, such as interstate driving.

TEXTING WHILE DRIVING

Effective July 1, 2009 drivers are prohibited from using a hand-held telephone or hand-held personal digital assistant to transmit or read a written message while the driver's motor vehicle is in motion. Violations can result in a fine not to exceed Fifty Dollars, and court costs not to exceed Ten Dollars. Law enforcement officers, firefighters, emergency medical persons and emergency management agency officers when in the actual discharge of their official duties, are exempt from the provisions of the law.

OPERATING A HAND-HELD PHONE IN A SCHOOL ZONE

Effective January 1, 2018, it is an offense for persons 18 years or older to use a hand-held mobile phone while a motor vehicle is in motion in any marked school zone in this state, when a warning flasher or flashers are in operation. There is an exception if the phone is being used in hands free mode. This exception also does not apply to persons under eighteen (18) years of age and creates a delinquent act for these individuals.

VIDEO DEVICES IN VEHICLES

Careful planning and consideration should be given for the placement of video devices in vehicles. State law prohibits the installation of a video monitor or video screen capable of displaying a television broadcast or video signal that is intended to display an image visible to the driver of a vehicle while in motion. A navigation or global positioning device, a vehicle information system display, visual displays for the driver's view forward, behind and the sides of the vehicle are not prohibited. Careful consideration should be given to the placement of this equipment to insure no visual obstructions.

HANDS FREE TENNESSEE

Public Chapter No. 412, was implemented in 2019. It is now illegal for a driver to:

(a) hold a cellphone or mobile device with any part of their body,
(b) write, send, or read any text-based communication,
(c) reach for a cellphone or mobile device in a manner that requires the driver to no longer be in a seated driving position or properly restrained by a seat belt,
(d) watch a video or movie on a cellphone or mobile device, and
(e) record or broadcast video on a cellphone or mobile device.
for more information, please visit www.handsfreetn.com.

Chapter 1– Chapter Sample Test Questions

Here are some sample test questions. Because these are just study questions to help you review, you may receive a test with completely different questions, in whole or in part. The page number is shown for where the correct answer can be located for each question. Also, answers to all study questions can be found in the back of the book.

1. Properly adjusted seat head restraints:
   A. Are designed to prevent whiplash if hit from behind.
   B. Both A and C
   C. Should always be at a level even with the back of head. Page 27

2. The driver should drive with both hands on the steering wheel approximately in the:
   A. 9 o'clock and 3 o'clock positions
   B. 11 o'clock and 6 o'clock positions
   C. 7 o'clock and 5 o'clock positions
   Page 28

3. When adjusting the driver's seat for best driving posture, set the seat in an upright position where your body is about how far from the steering wheel?
   A. 6 to 8 inches
   B. 10 to 12 inches
   C. 18 to 24 inches
   Page 27

"It's the Law"

The use of safety belts, child restraint safety seats and child booster seats are required by Tennessee law. These can help save you and your passengers' lives in the event of a traffic crash. Tennessee law enforcement officers can stop drivers and issue citations for failure to observe the safety belt or child restraint laws. Officers can stop and ticket drivers solely for disobeying Safety belt and Child Restraint Device (CRD) laws.

A. Safety belts are required for ALL drivers and all passengers in the FRONT seat, any time the vehicle is in motion.

B. Safety belts are also required for BACKSEAT passengers in the following situations:
- If the passengers are under 17 years old.
- This provision no longer applies when back seat passengers are 18 years or older.
- If the driver has either a learner permit or an intermediate license, and when the passengers are between four and 17 years old.
- If the passenger is four through eight years old and is shorter than four feet, nine inches in height. These passengers must be in a child booster seat at all times. Children in booster seats must be in the back seat of a vehicle, if the vehicle has a back seat. (This booster seat must meet federal motor vehicle safety standards as indicated on its label.)

Child Safety Restraint Rules

Tennessee was the first state in the country to pass a Child Passenger Protection Law requiring children to be restrained in child safety seats (car seats and booster seats).

A. A child under one year old, or any child weighing less than 20 pounds, must be in a child passenger restraint system (car seat) that is facing the rear of the car.

B. Children who are one through three years old, and who weigh more than 20 pounds, must be in a child passenger restraint system that is facing forward.

C. Children who are four through eight years old and whose height is under four feet, nine inches, must be in a belt positioning booster seat system (child booster car seat) and wearing a seatbelt.

NOTE: These "Child Safety Restraining"seats should be in the rear seat of the car, if possible.

All child passenger restraint systems (car seats and booster seats) referenced above must meet federal motor vehicle safety standards and be used consistently with the manufacturer's and the vehicle's instructions.

D. Children are further protected by the law, which makes the driver responsible for their protection up to the age of sixteen (16). If children under age 16 are not properly restrained, the driver may be charged and fined $50.00 for violation of the law.

If the child's parent or legal guardian is present in the car but not driving, then the parent or legal guardian is responsible for making sure that the child is properly transported and may be fined for non-compliance.

If the violation is one relating to not using a car seat or booster seat for children under nine years old or whose height is less than four feet, nine inches, the punishment is greater. The driver can be charged with a Class C misdemeanor, required to attend a class on safely transporting children and required to pay possible fees and fines.

E. Provisions are made for the transportation of children in medically prescribed modified child restraints. A copy of a doctor's prescription should be carried in the vehicle utilizing the modified child restraint device (CRD) at all times.

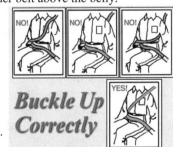

SAFETY BELT FACTS

Safety belts and child safety seats help prevent injury five different ways, by:

1. **Preventing ejection:** Ejection greatly increases the chance of death or serious injury. The chance of being killed in a crash by being ejected from a vehicle is one in eight. Safety belts virtually eliminate ejection. The belted driver stays inside the car and is better protected from injury.

2. **Shifting crash forces to the strongest parts of the body's structure. To get the most benefit from a seat belt, be aware of the following points:**
   - The lap belt should be worn low over the pelvis with the bottom edge touching the tops of the thighs snugly.
   - The shoulder belt should be worn over the shoulder and across the chest, not under the arm and over the abdomen. Make certain that the shoulder belt is not worn so loosely that it slides off the shoulder.
   - Pregnant women should wear the lap belt below the abdomen and the shoulder belt above the belly.

3. **Spreading crash forces over a wide area of the body.** Safety belts reduce the possibility of injury from "hostile" surfaces inside the car (steering wheel, dashboard, windshield, controls, etc.). Even if the belted driver

collides with some of these surfaces, it happens with much less force and often results in less serious injury.

4. **Keeping the body more closely in the "proper driving posture."** The belt keeps the driver "in the driver's seat." The belted driver is better able to deal with emergencies and often avoids more serious trouble.

5. **Protecting the head and spinal cord.** The belted driver is less likely to be stunned or made unconscious by the crash and is better able to cope with the situation. Research has found that proper use of lap/shoulder belts reduces the risk of fatal injury to front seat passenger car occupants by 45 percent and the risk of moderate-to-critical injury by 50 percent (for occupants of light trucks, 60 percent and 65 percent respectively).

VITAL STATS

- In 2019, almost 2,400 teens in the United States aged 13–19 were killed and about 258,000 were treated in emergency rooms for injuries suffered in motor vehicle crashes.

- Vehicle occupants were 32 times more likely to die in a crash if they were unbelted. They were 3 times more likely to sustain serious injuries if they were unbelted

- Failure to use a safety belt contributes to more fatalities than any other single traffic safety-related behavior.

- According to the CDC in 2020, motor vehicle crashes are the leading cause of fatal injuries for children ages 3 to 14. In 2020 an average of 6 children are killed and 423 were injured EVERY DAY in the United States.

COMMON FEARS AND MISCONCEPTIONS ABOUT SAFETY BELTS:

Many people still have "bad information" about using safety belts. For example:

"Safety belts can trap you inside a car." It takes less than a second to undo a safety belt. Crashes seldom happen where a vehicle catches fire or sinks in deep water and you are "trapped." Only one-half of one percent of all crashes ends in fire or submersion. Even if they do, a safety belt may keep you from being "knocked out." Your chance to escape will be better if you are conscious.

"Some people are thrown clear in a crash and walk away with hardly a scratch." Most crash fatalities result from the force of impact or from being thrown from the vehicle. Your chances of not being killed in an accident are much better if you stay inside the vehicle. Safety belts can keep you from being thrown out of a vehicle and into the path of another one. Ejected occupants are four times more likely to be killed as those who remain inside the vehicle.

"If I get hit from the side, I am better off being thrown across the car, away form the crash point." When a vehicle is struck from the side, it will move sideways. Everything in the vehicle that is not fastened down, including the passengers, will slide toward the point of the crash, not away from it.

BUCKLE UP
IT'S WORTH
THE EFFORT

In 2016, traffic crashes on Tennessee's roadways killed 1039 people. Sadly, many of these deaths could have been prevented if the victims had taken the time to buckle up.

TENNESSEE'S CHILD PASSENGER PROTECTION LAWS

By promoting child passenger safety, Tennessee attempts to protect children from needless death or injury. Many of these needless injuries result in permanent disabilities, such as paralysis, brain damage, epilepsy, etc. Why needless? Consider the following:

- Motor vehicle injuries are a leading cause of death among children in the United States. But many of these deaths can be prevented.

- Infants (under one year old) who are properly secured in safety seats survive almost 75 percent of the crashes that would otherwise be fatal. Toddlers (one-to-four years old) who are properly secured in safety seats survive more than half of the crashes that would otherwise be fatal.

- The proper use of child restraint devices could prevent 9 out of 10 deaths and 8 out of 10 serious injuries to child passengers under the age of four. If child safety restraint seats were used properly 100 percent of the time, the percentage of children who survive crashes would go up by 23 percent.

Set a Good Example – Always Buckle Up
Think about what your child sees you do in the car. Do you wear your safety belt? Children follow their parents' examples. Studies show that children's behavior in the car improves when they learn how to ride in a child restraint device. Make it a habit for you and your child.

Tips For Using Safety Belts With Children
When your child "graduates" from the child restraint system to safety belts, it is very important for the belts to lie across the correct area of the child's body.

Basically, a child is big enough to use the vehicle lap and shoulder belt when (1) they can sit with their back against the vehicle seat back and (2) their knees bend over the edge of the vehicle seat. The lap belt should lie securely on the child's upper thigh, low and snug around the hips. The shoulder belt should fit snugly across the chest and rest between the neck and shoulder. NEVER put the shoulder belt behind the child's back or under their arms.

"Belts to Bones"

The pelvic bone and the collarbone should bear the pressure of the safety belts. If the safety belt system rides too high on the child's stomach, or if the shoulder harness lies across the face or neck area of the child, go back to using a booster seat or a high back booster model that uses the vehicle's existing safety belt system.

AIR BAG SAFETY

Air bags can HELP save your life. Air bags combined with safety belts are the best protection currently available in a car, SUV, or truck. The National Highway Traffic Safety Administration (NHSTA) estimates that between 1987 and 2012, air bags have been credited with saving more than 39,976 lives from information provided by the NHTSA.

Remember: Most tragedies involving air bags can be prevented if air bags are used in combination with safety belts.

Air bags were developed to prevent occupants from striking the steering wheel or dashboard. The air bag deploys and immediately deflates—faster than the blink of an eye.

If you drive, own or ride in a vehicle equipped with either a driver-side and/or passenger side air bag, you should follow the following safety points:

Air Bags and Children

CHILDREN ages 12 and under are safer in the back seat of a vehicle.

- "The Back Is Where It's At" for children 12 and under. While air bags have a good overall record of providing supplemental protection for adults in the event of a crash, they pose a severe risk for children ages 12 and under. Research shows that children and air bags simply do not mix.

- Children are safer when they are properly restrained in a child restraint device or safety belt in the rear seat of a vehicle, regardless of whether the vehicle is equipped with a passenger side air bag.

- It is not advisable to place a child safety seat in the front seat of a vehicle, when a passenger side air bag is present. Instead, the child safety seat should be placed in a rear seat, if available.

- Infants in rear-facing seats should be placed in the rear seat,

if available, of a vehicle with a passenger-side air bag. If a child must ride in the front seat of a vehicle such as a pick-up truck, with a passenger side air bag, the seat should be moved back as far as possible, and the child should be properly buckled up.

Air Bags and Adults:

- Always wear the lap AND shoulder safety belts.

- If you have an adjustable steering wheel, always try to keep it tilted down in a level or parallel position.

- Sit as far as possible from the steering wheel (or dashboard on passenger side) to give the air bag room to deploy and spread its energy. Ten (10) to twelve (12) inches between the chest and the air bag module is recommended by the National Highway Traffic Safety Administration (NHTSA).

Other Child Passenger Protection Laws

It is illegal in Tennessee to allow any child under the age of 6 to ride in the bed of a pickup truck. It is also against the law to allow any child between the ages of 6 and 12 to ride in the bed of a pickup truck on any state or interstate highway. Cities and counties may prohibit by ordinance, children between the ages of 6 and 12 from riding in the bed of a pickup truck on any city or county roads or highways.

There are two exceptions. One exception to this law is when a child is being transported in the bed of the vehicle when it is part of an organized parade, procession or other ceremonial event and the vehicle must not exceed the speed of twenty (20) miles per hour. The other exception is when the child being transported in the bed of the vehicle is involved in agricultural activities.

DO NOT LEAVE CHILDREN UNATTENDED IN A MOTOR VEHICLE

TCA Code 55-10-803 is a provision in the law for the offense of leaving child unattended in motor vehicle.

It is an offense for a person responsible for a child younger than 7 years of age to knowingly leave that child in a motor vehicle located on public property or while on the premises of any shopping center, trailer park, or any apartment house complex, or any other premises that is generally frequented by the public at large without being supervised in the motor vehicle by a person who is at least 13 years of age, if:

(1)   The conditions present a risk to the child's health or safety;

(2)   The engine of the motor vehicle is running; or

(3)   The keys to the motor vehicle are located anywhere inside the passenger compartment of the vehicle.

    (b)   A violation of this section is a Class B misdemeanor punishable only by a fine of two hundred dollars ($200) for the first offense.

    (c)   A second or subsequent violation of this section is a Class B misdemeanor punishable only by a fine of five hundred dollars ($500).

SPECIAL WARNING: DURING HOT WEATHER, DO NOT LEAVE CHILDREN OR PETS UNATTENDED IN A VEHICLE

On a typical sunny, summer day, the temperature inside a car can reach potentially deadly levels within minutes. Experts say the damage can happen in as little as ten minutes. Even on a mild day at 73 degrees outside, an SUV can heat up to 100 degrees in 10 minutes and to 120 degrees in just 30 minutes. At 90 degrees outside, the interior of a vehicle can heat up to 160 degrees within several minutes.

Heat exhaustion can occur at temperatures above 90 degrees and heat stroke can occur when temperatures rise above 105 degrees. If not treated immediately, heat exhaustion can lead to heat stroke. With respiratory systems that are still developing, children are particularly vulnerable to heat exhaustion.

Depending on the seriousness of the offense, a person can be charged with penalties ranging from a Class A Misdemeanor to a Class A Felony for leaving a child unattended in a vehicle. TCA Code 39-15-401 provides that "any person who knowingly, other than by accidental means, treats a child under eighteen years of age in such a manner as to inflict injury commits a Class A misdemeanor. If the abused child is six years of age or less, the penalty is a Class D felony. TCA Code 39-15-402 carries a possible Class B or Class A felony for aggravated child abuse and aggravated child neglect or endangerment. Class A Misdemeanors carry a penalty of not greater than 11 months, 29 days or a fine up to $2,500, or both. Class A Felonies can carry a penalty of not less than 15 and no more than 60 years. In addition, the jury may assess a fine not to exceed $50,000.

Remember :
- Children should never be left alone in a vehicle, not even to run a quick errand.
- Be sure that all occupants leave the vehicle when unloading. Don't overlook sleeping babies.
- Children can set a vehicle in motion. Always lock your car and ensure children do not have access to keys or remote entry devices.
- If a child gets locked inside, call 911 and get him/her out as soon as possible.
- If you see a child or animal unattended in a car, be proactive and call 911.

Chapter 2 – Chapter Sample Test Questions

Here are some sample test questions. Because these are just study questions to help you review, you may receive a test with completely different questions, in whole or in part. The page number is shown for where the correct answer can be located for each question. Also, answers to all the study questions can be found in the back of the book.

4. A child in a child passenger restraint system (car seat) should:

    A. be facing the rear of the car if weighing less than 20 pounds and under 1 year old.

    B. be facing forward if the child is one through three years old, and weighs more than 20 pounds,

    C. A & B

    Page 31

5. The lap belt should be worn:

    A. at the abdomen for extra comfort .

    B. above the pelvis so it doesn't touch the top of the thighs.

    C. by pregnant women below the abdomen and the shoulder belt above the belly.

    Page 31

6. The safest place for children 12 and under to ride in a vehicle equipped with air bags is:

    A. The front seat

    B. The back seat

    C. The bed of a pick-up truck

    Page 33

TRAFFIC SIGNS

Traffic control devices include traffic signals, signs and pavement markings. Traffic control can also be provided by law enforcement, highway construction personnel or school crossing guards. Drivers must obey directions from these individuals, even if the directions are different than what the traffic lights and signs indicate.

Traffic signs give you information about the road, the highway system, traffic flow and the local regulations and laws. They warn you about hazards, identify your route and direct the speed and movement of traffic. These signs also provide directions and let you know about places of interest, from the huge overhead green interstate signs to the little blue rectangles that direct you to a library or hospital.

Every traffic sign has a definite shape and colors that announce its purpose and specific meanings. You should be able to recognize them immediately. Even if a stop sign is damaged or blocked by dirt, limbs or snow, you should know by the octagonal shape and red color that you must stop.

Sign Colors and Shapes

Learn the standard colors and shapes (shown below) so you know what a sign means, even at a distance. For example, a regulatory sign is always a rectangle, telling you about laws and regulations or giving you instructions such as speed limits or lane uses.

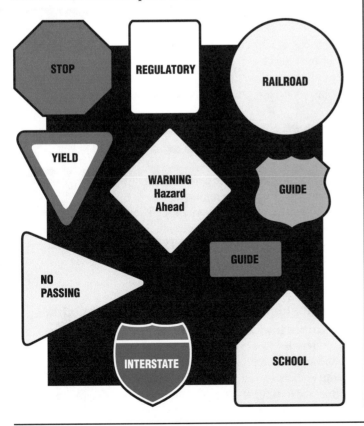

Color Codes on Highway Traffic Signs

The meanings of the nine basic background colors of sighs should be memorized. The colors used on standard signs are as follows:

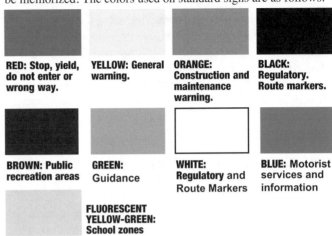

RED: Stop, yield, do not enter or wrong way.

YELLOW: General warning.

ORANGE: Construction and maintenance warning.

BLACK: Regulatory. Route markers.

BROWN: Public recreation areas

GREEN: Guidance

WHITE: Regulatory and Route Markers

BLUE: Motorist services and information

FLUORESCENT YELLOW-GREEN: School zones

RED is used only as a background color for STOP signs, multiple supplemental plates (FOUR-WAY or ALL WAY), DO-NOT-ENTER messages, WRONG WAY signs and on Interstate route markers. Red is also used as a legend color for YIELD signs, parking prohibition signs, the circular outline and diagonal bar prohibitory symbol.

BLACK-WHITE is used for **regulatory signs**. Regulatory signs are used to inform road users of selected traffic laws or regulations. Black is used for a message on white, yellow and orange signs. Whenever white is specified as a sign color, it includes silver-colored reflecting coating or elements that reflect white light.

WHITE is used as the background for route makers, guide signs, regulatory signs, except STOP signs and for the legend on brown, green, blue, black and red signs. Whenever white is specified as a sign color, this is referencing the silver-colored reflective coating and other materials that reflect white light.

ORANGE is used as a background color for construction and maintenance signs and shall not be used for any other purpose.

YELLOW is used as a background color for warning signs, except where orange is specified, and for school signs.

BROWN is used as a background color for guide information signs related to points of recreational cultural interest.

GREEN is used as a background color for guide signs (other than those using brown or white), mileposts and as a legend color with a white background for permissive parking regulations.

BLUE is used as a background color for information signs related to motorist services (including police services and rest areas) and the Emergency Route Marker.

FLUORESCENT YELLOW-GREEN IS THE COLOR FOR SCHOOL ZONES!

FLUORESCENT YELLOW-GREEN is now in use for signage in school zones and other pedestrian traffic areas such as crosswalks. These signs are much easier to see in low light and foggy/rainy weather. Where these signs are posted, motorists are encouraged to carefully watch for all forms of school traffic, including pedestrians, school children, bicyclists, as well as motor vehicles.

FLUORESCENT PINK (sometimes called "coral") is used for incident management traffic control signage when needed for incidents such as traffic accidents, wildland fires, floods, and hazardous material spills, that take place on or adjacent to a road, interrupting the normal flow of traffic.

Temporary Traffic Control Zones

Temporary traffic control zones allow traffic to flow safely through incidents while reasonably protecting motorists, incident responders, vehicles, and equipment. Zones also are established when necessary to restrict use of road systems to incident management personnel. Availability of message signs, warning lights, flags, barricades, and cones may be used to enhance the visibility of traffic control zones.

IMPORTANT: Whenever white is specified as a sign color, it includes silver-colored reflecting coating or elements that reflect white light.

Traffic signs are placed to help you and to instruct you in the best and safest use of the highway. All signs must be obeyed at all times, unless a policeman or other traffic officer directs you to do otherwise. Study and learn the following signs and notice the shape of each sign has a general or specific meaning.

Octagon Shape — Stop

This sign is the only eight-sided sign on the roadway. It always means that there is danger. It will always be red with white lettering. It tells you that you are

approaching an important street or highway and that you must bring your car to a complete stop, not going beyond the crosswalk. IF you cannot see, then proceed cautiously to a point where you can see, and then go only if you can do so safely.

ALL WAY: Red Rectangle –Added below a stop sign. It means all traffic approaching this intersection must stop.

Triangular Shape — Yield

This three-sided sign means that you are approaching an intersection and must stop and wait when other vehicles are approaching from the right or left on the other roadway. If you are sure no other

cars are coming you need not come to a complete stop but you must slow down and enter the intersection with caution. Always stop when traffic is heavy.

Round Shape — Railroad Ahead

This circular sign always means that you are approaching a railroad grade crossing. You must slow down and be ready to stop. This sign tells you that it is up to you to stop if you see a train coming. NEVER TRY TO "BEAT" THE TRAIN. YOU WILL USUALLY MISJUDGE ITS SPEED. More than 200 traffic crashes occur each year at railroad crossings. Do not play with your life trying to "beat the train."

Broad "X" Shape — Railroad Here

This is known as a crossbuck sign. It is placed at all railroad grade crossings and shows exactly where the tracks are located. Notice the smaller signs placed on the post directly below the crossbuck. They show the number of tracks at a particular crossing. This is very important because, when there are two or more tracks, one train passing might hide the approach of a train from the other direction.

Some crossbucks are equipped with two lights underneath the "X." Flashing lights on a crossbuck mean that a train is coming. Always stop when the lights are flashing. Remain stopped until the train has passed. If there is more than one track, be sure all tracks are clear before crossing.

Some crossbucks are equipped with both flashing lights and a gate. Stop when the lights begin flashing and before the gate comes down. Remain stopped until the gates are raised and the lights stop flashing.

Diamond Shape — Hazardous Or Unexpected Condition Ahead

These signs call for caution and usually for a slower speed. Some carry written information. Others are miniature symbolic road maps that warn of highway conditions ahead. This sign tells you that you are approaching an intersection. The black lines show just what kind of intersection this is. This sign tells you it is a crossroad.

Rectangular Shape - Special Laws, Regulations or Important Information, Some Guide Signs

The signs below are examples of lane control signs. Some indicate that certain vehicles (trucks) must use specific lanes. While others indicate that traffic in the respective lanes must either move straight through or turn left. These signs are

LEFT LANE MUST TURN LEFT

TRUCK LANE 500 FEET

TRUCKS USE RIGHT LANE

sometimes mounted overhead. This sign (High Occupancy Vehicle) indicates lanes reserved for buses and vehicles with the minimum number of occupants specified on the sign.

Speed Control: These signs show the maximum speed allowed, the minimum speed required or a change in speed limit. The sign on the far right is used whenever children are within walking distance of school. It tells you that children may be crossing the street on their way to and from school. This type of sign is controlled by a time clock and flashes yellow lights while illuminating the speed limit. Failure to obey the posted school zone limit could result in serious injury or loss of life.

SPEED LIMIT 70

SPEED LIMIT 55

SCHOOL SPEED LIMIT 15 WHEN FLASHING

Regulatory Signs

STOP FOR SCHOOL BUS LOADING OR UNLOADING

PEDESTRIANS BICYCLES MOTOR-DRIVEN CYCLES PROHIBITED

COMMERCIAL VEHICLES EXCLUDED

WEIGHT LIMIT *T *T

END SCHOOL SPEED LIMIT

PEDESTRIANS AND BICYCLES PROHIBITED

NO PARKING 8:00 AM TO 4:00 PM

ONE WAY

SLOWER TRAFFIC KEEP RIGHT

This sign is used on a highway that has more than one lane going each direction. It means that you must drive in the extreme right lane unless you want to pass a slower moving car or make a left turn. Never straddle lanes or drive in the center lane when moving more slowly than other traffic around you.

No Passing Signs: These signs tell you where passing is not permitted. Passing areas are based on how far you can see ahead. They consider unseen hazards such as hills and curves, intersections, driveways and other places a vehicle may enter the roadway.

DO NOT PASS

NO PASSING ZONE

A triangular No Passing Zone sign can also be used. These signs are yellow or orange and placed on the left side of the roadway.

Signs having a white background and a red circle and a line diagonally through them mean "NO" according to what is shown behind the red symbol. For example:

NO TRUCKS   NO BICYCLES

NO LEFT TURN   NO U TURN

This sign tells you that, in the area where this sign is placed, parking is forbidden.

This sign tells you that you are approaching a one-way street and that you must not enter from the direction you are traveling.

DO NOT ENTER

In Tennessee, it is illegal to stand on a roadway to solicit a ride. Hitchhiking is not only dangerous for the pedestrian, but also to the driver of the vehicle who stops to pick up a stranger.

Warning Signs - Diamond Shape *(Yellow)*

Warning signs alert road users to conditions that might call for a reduction of speed or an action in the interest of safety and efficient traffic operations. Become familiar with these signs so that each message can be quickly understood and followed.

 This sign tells you to be prepared for a rather sharp turn to the left. The turn sign is used to mark turns with a recommended speed of 30 m.p.h. or less.

Curve Sign: This sign tells you that you must be prepared for a curve to the right. The curve sign is used to mark curves with recommended speeds in the range between 30 and 55 m.p.h.

 **Reverse Turn Sign:** This sign tells you that you must turn right, then left. The reverse turn sign is used to mark two turns in opposite directions that are less than 600 feet apart.

Advisory Speed Plate: The smaller sign on the post beneath this sign is used to supplement warning signs. It gives you the recommended maximum safe speed.

You will see this sign in some hilly areas. This sign warns of rocks that may be in the road, not of rocks which may strike you from overhead. Watch the roadway, not the hill.

 This sign indicates that there is a STOP sign just ahead that you cannot yet see. At this point, start to slow down. A similar sign using a symbol shaped like a traffic light and the black arrow indicates there is a "traffic signal ahead."

This sign indicates that there is a YIELD sign just ahead that you cannot yet see. At this point, start to slow down.

This sign indicates that children are likely to be in the area with a school bus loading and unloading during the school season.

 This sign is warning of the lane ending and that drivers should merge left. Be sure to signal your intentions.

This sign alerts you to the possibility of traffic blending into the main stream of travel. After checking to your rear, you should move into the other lane, if possible, to allow the merging motorist a clear path.

 This sign tells you that the bridge is narrow and may require passing cars to reduce speeds.

You will see the following sign near school grounds or buildings. It warns you to slow down, drive with caution and watch for children. This sign is placed as you approach a school.

SLIPPERY WHEN WET

TWO-WAY TRAFFIC

CATTLE CROSSING

LEFT LANE ENDS

BIKE CROSSING

WINDING ROAD

LOW CLEARANCE
Shows the distance from road
surface to the bottom of a bridge
or overpass

T-INTERSECTION AHEAD

These Chevron signs displayed below are used to provide additional
emphasis and guidance for a change in horizontal alignment.

T-INTERSECTION
You must turn right or left.
Be prepared to yield.

CHEVRON
A sharp change in
direction ahead

Work Area Signs

These construction, maintenance or
emergency operations signs are generally
diamond or rectangular shaped, orange
with black letters or symbols and warn
you that people are working on or near the
roadway. These warnings include reduced
speed, detours, slow moving construction
equipment and lane closures. In work areas, a person with a sign
or flag may control traffic. You must obey the directions of these
persons.

Construction Signs

Construction signs are generally **diamond** or **rectangular**
shaped and **orange with black letters symbols**. Their purpose is
to warn drivers to be prepared to stop and that workers are
preswent near the roadway. The warnings include reduced
speed, detours, slow moving construction equipment and lane
closures.

Channeling Devices

Barricades, vertical panels, concrete barriers, drums and cones
are the most common devices used to guide drivers safely
through work zones. When driving near these devices, keep your
vehicle in the middle of the lane and obey the posted speed limit.
As you leave the work zone, stay in your lane and maintain your
speed. Don't change lanes until you are completely clear of the
work zone.

Channeling Devices
Used to direct traffic flow.

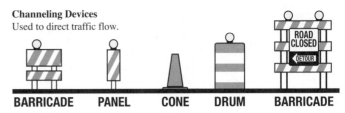

BARRICADE   PANEL   CONE   DRUM   BARRICADE

Electronic Message or Arrow Signs: These are mobile devices
that are often used on some roads to give advance warning of
construction zones, special traffic directions, road closures or
in some cases weather hazards. Flashing arrow panels alert
approaching drivers of lane closures. You must begin to merge
into the remaining open lane(s) well in advance of this sign.

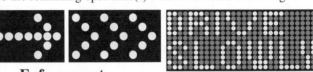

Law Enforcement

You will see Law Enforcement
Officers in the Fluorescent
Yellow-Green Vests and rain
coats during traffic related
emergencies to make sure they
can be seen under normal
conditions and under low light
and poor weather conditions.

Highway Flaggers

Flaggers, at most worksites, will
be using paddles with the word stop on one side and slow on
the other. However red flags are used in emergency situations
as shown below.

The basic hand movements for stop and proceed remain the
same, whether a flag or paddle is used. Please learn these
three simple signals displayed below, since they are the most
commonly used by construction flaggers.

Flaggers along with utility workers, construction worker and
other emergency personnel directing traffic, can also be seen
wearing FLUORESCENT YELLOW-GREEN clothing, vests
and hard helmets in these construction work zones. This is in
addition to fluorescent orange to make sure they can be seen by
drivers under normal conditions and improve being seen under
low light and poor weather conditions.

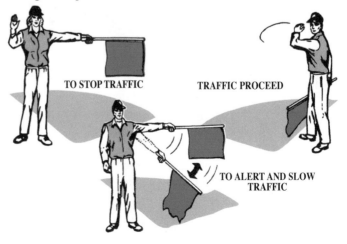

TO STOP TRAFFIC   TRAFFIC PROCEED

TO ALERT AND SLOW
TRAFFIC

  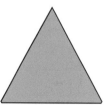

RED REFLECTIVE BORDERS — **SLOW-MOVING VEHICLE EMBLEM KIT** — **ORANGE FLUORESCENT CENTER**

Slow-Moving Vehicle (SMV) Emblem
Recognize this sign. Some day (or night) it may save your life. Look at it!

During daylight, the bright fluorescent orange solid triangle in the center of the SMV emblem is highly visible. At night, the SMV emblem glows brilliantly in the path of approaching headlights.

You may see this emblem on slow-moving vehicles, such as farm tractors, machinery, construction equipment or horse-drawn vehicles.

Object Marker
These markers warn you of objects, not actually in the roadway, but so close to the edge of the road that need marking.

Typical applications include bridge ends, underpass abutments and other obstructions closely adjacent to the edges of roadways.

Hazard to left — Hazard to right

Guide Signs for Highways
A sign, such as the one to the right, (shown as State 44 and US 41) will indicate two highways are coming together or separating. The sign (marked as 44) is a state secondary route. The sign to the right (marked as Highway 41) indicates a U.S. highway route that will reach into another state. **U.S. Route signs consists of black numerals on a white shield surrounded by a black background without a border.**

PRIMARY ROUTE
(Primarily Connects Cities)

The sign in lower left is a state primary route. Drivers should become thoroughly familiar with route numbers and signs they must follow when beginning a trip from one area to another.

Interstate Route Marker

Blue and red signs, like the one on the right, indicate that the route is part of the national system of interstate and defense highways. These highways join centers of population and defense establishments. They also join with the major international highways at the Mexican and Canadian borders. They are part of a nationwide network of the most important highways.

Guide Signs On Highways

These are signs to help you while driving on Tennessee's Interstate Highways. The signs are above or to the right of the highway with the arrows pointing to the lane you should be in if you intend to enter or leave the road.

This sign is seen on Interstates and Expressways. The background is green with white letters and/or numbers visible at some distance. Such signs give information vital to selection of lane, proper exits, etc.

If an interstate guide sign is marked with the above sign, all traffic in the lane(s) directly below the arrows MUST exit.

Service Signs

The blue color of these signs directs motorists to service facilities. Word message signs will also be used to direct motorists to areas where service stations, restaurants and motels are available.

Handicap Symbol

Parking spaces displaying this blue sign are reserved for vehicles bearing disabled veteran or handicapped license plates, or a special handicapped decal. The convenience and availability of these spaces is important for disabled citizens. The use of reserved handicapped spaces by others is prohibited by law.

Directional Signs

The green background signs indicate that the message is providing directional information. Directional signs point to bike and hiking trails.

Emergency Reference Markers

In order to help motorists better identify their location on urban interstates, the state has installed interstate reference markers every 1,000 feet along heavily traveled sections. These have been installed in Nashville, Knoxville, Memphis, Jackson and Chattanooga. The signs display information about the route number, direction of travel and the "log mile" in tenths of a mile. Most are mounted on median dividers. Motorists with mobile phones who notify emergency operators about incidents can give an accurate description of the exact location where assistance is needed. This will help emergency personnel respond more rapidly, and possibly make the difference between life and death. It will also help clear the highways more quickly. In the sample (at right), this sign indicates the location as: West Bound on Interstate 40 at mile marker 205 and 2 tenths. So the driver would be between mile markers 204 and 206.

MAIN LINE SIGN

TRAFFIC SIGNALS

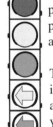

Traffic Signals are used to control vehicle drivers and pedestrians at some intersections and crosswalks. Signals promote better movement of traffic on busy roads by assigning right of way.

Traffic Signals are usually placed at heavily traveled intersections. These lights tell you when or where to stop and go. A green light means you can go if it is safe. A yellow light means caution—prepare to stop for the red light. The red light always means stop. Standard traffic lights are red, yellow and green, from top to bottom respectively.

RED: Stop behind crosswalk or stop line. Unless otherwise posted, you may turn right on red after coming to a complete stop and when no pedestrians or cross traffic are present.

YELLOW: Caution—prepare to stop. The red stop signal will be exhibited immediately after the yellow light appears. Adjust speed immediately to come to a smooth stop. You must stop if it is safe to do so. Do not speed up to beat the light. If you are already IN the intersection when the yellow light

---

comes on, do not stop, but continue cautiously through the intersection. Tennessee law only requires the yellow light to be exhibited for a minimum of **three seconds before the red light**.

Collisions often happen at intersections on yellow lights. Not only is it dangerous to ignore the yellow light, you may hold up oncoming traffic that receives the green light. Please be aware that some drivers often "jump the green" and start through an intersection, because they have seen the yellow light come on from the crossing directions. *If you try to "beat the yellow" and another driver decides to "jump the green" the results could be deadly!*

GREEN: Go **IF** the intersection is clear. You must yield to pedestrians and vehicles still in the intersection at light change. The green signal gives permission to proceed, BUT you must still observe the laws of the right-of-way. Yield to oncoming vehicles if you are turning left. Never attempt to "jump the gun" by starting through the intersection early or by making a quick left turn in front of oncoming traffic. This is extremely dangerous!

PROTECTED ARROWS: At many intersections, you may see what is called a "protected turn arrow." When the arrow is green, you have the right-of-way and may drive the vehicle only in the direction of the arrow, after yielding to vehicles and pedestrians already in the intersection. When the arrow changes to yellow, prepare to yield to oncoming traffic. When the arrow is red or your lane has the red light, all turns are prohibited. This is true even if other lanes of traffic have a green signal and your path through the intersection appears to be clear.

FLASHING YELLOW

Slow down and proceed with caution at the intersection.

FLASHING RED

Complete stop. Same as stop sign. Look both ways, yield to traffic and pedestrians and proceed when it is safe to do so.

PERMISSIVE ARROWS: If you see a flashing yellow arrow, you are allowed to turn left after yielding to all oncoming traffic and to any bicyclists and pedestrians in the crosswalk. You must wait for a safe gap in oncoming traffic before turning in the direction of the arrow.

Busy intersections can sometime leave vehicles stranded inside the intersection. Don't let this happen to you, do not pull into an intersection to make a turn until your path is clear.

Malfunctioning Traffic Light:
What to do when the light is out!

Tennessee state law requires that if a signal is not working, the intersection is to be treated as if it were a ll-way stop intersection. Stop as you would if there were stop signs in all directions (This is covered in the Rules of the Road chapter). Do not proceed until it is safe.

The right-of-way law says that if there are two or more vehicles at the intersection stopping at the same time, the driver on the left would yield to the driver on the right. The driver on the right who arrives first gets to go first. However, stay cautious and be sure it is safe to proceed even when you are in the first car to reach the intersection.

Pedestrian Signals: Allow pedestrians to know when it is legally permitted and safe to cross a street or intersection. Tennessee law defines a pedestrian as any person afoot or using a motorized or non-motorized wheelchair. Pedestrians can protect themselves by observing the following rules:

A. **"Walk" Sign:** Many streets with significant pedestrian traffic will have a pedestrian signal. The displays the word "WALK" or a symbol of a person walking when it is safe to cross the street or intersection. Pedestrians, who have started to cross the street or intersection when the "WALK" signal or walking person sign appears, should continue as quickly possible to the other side of the street before the signal shifts to "DON'T WALK."

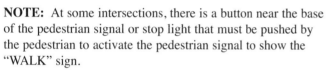

NOTE: At some intersections, there is a button near the base of the pedestrian signal or stop light that must be pushed by the pedestrian to activate the pedestrian signal to show the "WALK" sign.

B. **"Don't Walk" Sign:** Pedestrian signals indicate when it is not permissible or safe to cross a street or intersection. When the pedestrian signal shows the words "DON'T WALK," or a symbol of a raised hand appears, it is not safe to begin crossing a street or intersection. As a driver, pay attention to the traffic signals and pedestrian signals in order to anticipate when a pedestrian may begin to cross the street.

2. **Lane Control Signals:** The signals below may appear as single or multiple units over each lane of the road. They are most often used when the direction of the flow of traffic changes during different hours of the day. Also, these signals indicate whether toll plaza lanes are open or closed.

| Driving in this lane is permitted | If flashing lane is for turning only; if solid direction of lane is changing | Driving is NOT permitted in this lane |

Uniform Highway Markings

The information in this chapter is based on the United States Department of Transportation's Federal Highway Administration's (FHWA) Manual on Uniform Traffic Control Devices, which all states' highway agencies must use in marking and signing roadways. Because states continue to update signage to conform with the federal requirements, drivers may encounter both old and new markings and signs. BE ALERT and follow directions.

(See the section on *Traffic Lanes and Lane Usage* starting at page 59 in the *Rules of the Road* chapter).

Lines and symbols on the roadway (1) divide the road into lanes, (2) tell you when you may pass other vehicles or change lanes, (3) indicate which lanes to use for turns, (4) define pedestrian walkways and (5) show where you must stop for signs or traffic signals. Line colors tell you if you are on a one-way or two-way roadway.

l. **Edge and Lane Lines:** Lines along the side of the road show you where the edge of the road is located. A solid white line indicates the right edge of the traffic lane on a road. A solid or broken yellow line indicates the left edge of traffic lanes going in your direction.

- If you ever find yourself with yellow to your right and white to your left, you are going the wrong way.

- Remember, on a divided highway, the side of the roadway to the left of the driver and nearest the median always has a yellow line.

- The right side of the roadway will always have a white line.

It is a good way to confirm you are traveling the right direction when entering an unfamiliar roadway.

A. **Yellow Lane Markings:** Lines separating traffic moving in opposite directions are yellow. Yellow lines are also used to mark a boundary or barrier of the travel path at the location of a particular hazard, such as bridge supports, etc.

- Broken yellow lines mean that you MAY cross the line to pass if there is no oncoming traffic and it is safe to do so.

- Two solid yellow lines between lanes of traffic mean you MAY NOT cross the lines from either direction, even if no oncoming traffic is in view. You may cross a solid yellow line to turn into a driveway or side road if it is safe to do so.

- One solid yellow line and one broken yellow: Where

there is both a solid and a broken yellow line between opposing lanes of traffic, you may not pass if the solid yellow line is on your side. If the broken yellow line is on your side, you are in the "passing zone" and may pass if it is safe to do so. You must safely return to your side of the roadway before the passing zone ends.

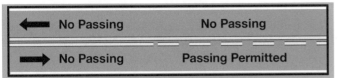

B. White Lane Markings - Multiple lanes of traffic that flow in the same direction are separated by white lane markings. You will find white lane markings on freeways, limited access highways, bypasses and one-way streets.

- Broken white lines between lanes of traffic mean you may cross the lines to pass or change lanes if it is safe to do so.

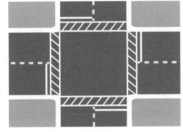

One solid white line between lanes of traffic means that you should stay in your lane and should not cross the line to pass (unless an emergency situation requires you to change lanes). Also, you should not cross a double solid white line.

2. Crosswalks - White crosswalk lines are painted across a road to indicate pedestrian crossing areas. Crosswalks define the area where pedestrians may cross the roadway and may be located at intersections or in the middle of a block. However, not all crosswalks are marked. You must yield the right-of-way to pedestrians who are in or are about to enter the crosswalk or street.

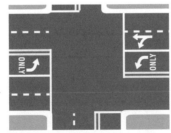

3. Stop Lines - White stop lines are painted on the pavement across traffic lanes, usually at intersections, to indicate the vehicle stopping position, before traffic signs or signals. (A) If the motorist is required to stop at the

intersection, the vehicle must be stopped behind this stop line. If no stop line is painted on the pavement, all vehicles required to stop must: (B) Stop the vehicle before crossing the first line of the crosswalk (if the crosswalk is marked), and (C) Stop the vehicle before the front bumper crosses the white edge line of the cross street, in order to keep the vehicle from protruding out into the cross street traffic.

4. High Occupancy Vehicle (HOV) Lanes are designated on highways by a diamond-shaped marking in the center of the lane. HOV lanes may also be special lanes separated by a barrier. During heavy traffic periods, HOV lanes are reserved for buses, vanpools, motorcycles, carpools and other high occupancy vehicles. Road signs indicate the minimum number of passengers a vehicle must carry to use the HOV lanes and the times that HOV restrictions are in effect.

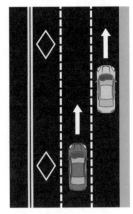

5. Turn Lane Arrow: If you are traveling in a lane marked with a curved arrow and the word ONLY, you must turn in the direction of the arrow. If your lane is marked with both a curved and a straight arrow, you may turn in the direction of the arrow or you may go straight.

- Double or triple arrows indicate more than one movement is permitt

- Single arrows indicate only one ma allowed.

6. White Crossbuck with RR: A white crossbuck and the letters RR are painted on the pavement as a warning marker for many railroad/highway grade crossings.

Stop Line (A)	Crosswalk (B)	Neither (C)

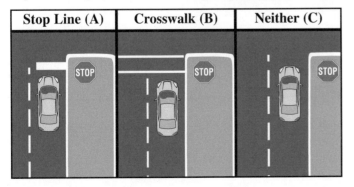

Chapter 3 – Chapter Sample Test Questions

The page number shown with each question tells where correct answers can be located. Remember, these are just samples of possible questions that may be included in your actual test. You may receive a test with completely different questions in whole or in part. Here are some sample test questions. Also, answers to all the study questions can be found in the back of the book.

7. The sign at the right means:
   A. Slow down and yield to traffic on main road when merging.
   B. Always come to a complete stop.
   C. Give your turn signal and proceed into traffic at regular speed.

   Page 36

8. What does a traffic signal with a yellow left arrow indicate to the driver?
   A. Prepare to yield to oncoming traffic.
   B. Protected left turn is about to end.
   C. Both of the above.

   Page 41

9. The center of the roadway is marked with one solid yellow line and one broken yellow line. If the broken yellow line is on the right of the solid yellow line (your side) it means:
   A. You are not allowed to pass in this area.
   B. You are in a "passing zone" and it is safe to pass other vehicles if no oncoming traffic is present.
   C. You are only allowed to make right turns in this area.

   Page 43

This chapter highlights key traffic laws and safe driving principles related to those laws. A more complete discussion of driving techniques is found in Section C of this manual, Safety Tips for Safe Driving and Sharing the Road.

Even on a short trip, you may be faced with many dangerous driving conditions. Statistics show that half of all vehicle crashes occur within 25 miles of home. The rules of the road are those laws, regulations and practices that provide safe vehicle movement on the roadways: **signaling, turning, passing and stopping.**

- Learn the traffic rules and follow them.
- Be willing to yield to other drivers to avoid a crash.
- Always watch carefully for advance warning and information signs.
- Be a courteous driver.
- Always obey instructions of traffic officers.

SOME BASIC RULES ARE:

Driving on the Right Side of the Road

In the United States, Canada and most other countries, right hand traffic is the rule. This means we drive on the right side of the road, and turn right when going around traffic circles, roundabouts or town squares.

Obeying Officers

You must obey traffic officers at all times. There will be times when an officer will instruct you to do something that ordinarily would be a violation of traffic regulations. The officer will do this only in case of an emergency when it is the only way to keep traffic flowing smoothly and safely. A common example: A police officer holding up traffic at a green light and permitting a funeral procession to continue through a red light.

Coasting Prohibited

While traveling on a downgrade, NEVER coast with the transmission of the vehicle in neutral. Also, drivers of manual transmission vehicles must not coast with the clutch depressed. Driving in neutral and/or with the clutch depressed reduces the driver's control of the car.

Use of Headlights

- **Required Night Use:** Your car headlights must be turned on 30 minutes after sunset until 30 minutes before sunrise.
- **Required Daylight / Inclement Weather Use:** Also, your car headlights must be turned on:
  1. At any time when daylight is not good enough for

you to see persons or vehicles clearly at a distance of 200 feet ahead; and

2. When rain, mist, snow, or other precipitation requires constant use of windshield wipers.

Headlights turned on during daylight hours will make your vehicle easier to see to oncoming vehicles and pedestrians. Use headlights when driving at dusk. Even if you can see clearly, headlights help other drivers see you as much as they help you see them. Get into the habit of turning headlights on when using windshield wipers. **Remember, using headlights when wipers are in use is not just a good safety precaution — it's Tennessee law!**

- **Dimming of Headlights Required:** When your vehicle's high beam headlights are on, you must dim or lower the beam when an oncoming vehicle is within **500** feet (approximately the distance of one city block) or when you are following another vehicle within **500** feet.

  Dimming headlights when following other vehicles is an important safety step. The glare from your headlights in a rear view mirror can blind another driver including a motorcyclist.

- **Limited Use of Parking Lights or Auxiliary Fog Lights:** The following procedures should be followed when using these types of lights:

  1. The law requires a vehicle stopped or parked on a road or shoulder to have parking lights on when limited visibility conditions exist.

  2. Do not drive a vehicle with only the parking lights on when driving at night or in inclement weather. The small size of parking lights may cause other drivers to think your vehicle is farther away than it actually is. When there is limited visibility, the use of parking lights alone is not only unsafe, it is against the law.

  3. It is also illegal to have auxiliary lights or fog lights on by themselves or on at times when you are required to dim high beam headlights. These very bright lights make it difficult for oncoming drivers to see, and the glare may reflect blindingly in the rear view mirror of vehicles you are following.

- **Daytime Running Lights:** Some newer vehicles have headlights that are on anytime the vehicle is running. These lights make it easier for others to see the vehicle, even in daylight. This reduces the likelihood of collisions.

Effective January 1, 2018, no vehicle operated in Tennessee shall be equipped with any steady-burning lights that display to the front of the vehicle in any color other than white or amber or in any combination of colors other than white and amber. There are exceptions for certain vehicles.

Also effective January 1, 2018, no vehicle operated in Tennessee shall be equipped with any flashing lights in any color or combination of colors that display to the front of the vehicle, other than factory installed emergency flashers. There are exceptions for certain vehicles.

Littering

Litter is an unsightly problem across the State of Tennessee creating an eyesore for our scenic roads and highways.

Throwing cigarette butts, food sacks, tobacco products, papers, cans, bottles or disposing of other material from vehicles are all forms of littering. Littering not only harms the environment we enjoy here in Tennessee but also poses a potential traffic hazard and risk to you and your family.

Tennessee law requires any motor vehicle transporting litter or any material, likely to fall or be blown off onto the highway, to be in an enclosed space or fully covered by a tarpaulin.

Prevention of littering is a major savings of your tax dollar. Costly cleanup of litter is required before our roadways can receive certain maintenance services such as roadside grass mowing.

Littering is against state law. Fines start at $50 and can be up to $3,000 based upon the amount of litter. A person convicted of littering is required to spend up to 40 hours of public service removing litter and at the discretion of the court, spend up to 8 additional hours of working in a waste recycling center. Littering can be very costly. Let's keep Tennessee clean – don't litter!

Slow-Moving Vehicles

It is against the law to drive slower than the posted minimum speed under normal driving conditions. You may drive more slowly than the minimum speed if you are driving in bad weather, heavy traffic or on a bad road. If there is no posted minimum speed, it is still against the law to drive so slowly that you block traffic.

NOTE: You are considered to be driving a slow-moving vehicle if you are traveling at a rate of speed that is 10 miles per hour or more below the lawful maximum speed. If five or more vehicles are lined up behind you, turn or pull off the roadway as soon as you can do so safely. Slow drivers, who block other traffic, cause many accidents.

Remember, slower is not always safer.

Funeral Procession

In Tennessee, it is a common and accepted practice for oncoming traffic to pull to the side of the roadway as a sign of respect when meeting a funeral precession. **Tennessee law instructs the following:**

- Vehicles following a funeral procession on a two-lane roadway may not attempt to pass such procession; and

- No operator of a vehicle shall drive between vehicles in a properly identified funeral procession except when directed to do so by a traffic officer.

The Basic Speed Rule

The speed at which you drive determines how much time you have to act or react and how long it takes to stop. The higher the speed, the less time drivers have to spot hazards. Judge the speed of other traffic, and react to avoid the mistakes of other drivers.

The Basic Speed Rule (BSR) is not a Tennessee law, but it is a general safety principle. The BSR does not set an exact speed limit; instead, it teaches that the speed you may drive is limited by current conditions. For example, if the posted speed limit is 65 m.p.h., and you are driving at night on a two-lane state highway and it's raining or foggy, 65 m.p.h. is too fast for those conditions.

To obey the BSR, think about your speed in relation to other traffic (including pedestrians, bicycles and motorcycles), the surface and width of the road, hazards at intersections, weather, visibility and any other conditions that could affect safety.

Principles of the Basic Speed Rule:

1. Your speed must be careful and prudent. Use skill and good judgment.

2. Your speed must be reasonable and proper, not too fast and not too slow, for any conditions including:

- Amount of Traffic - How many cars on the road

- Speed of Traffic - How fast or slow it's moving

- Whether Pedestrians are Present - Especially children in school zones or neighborhoods

- Surface of the Road - Rough or smooth, paved, gravel, etc.

- Width of the Road - One-lane, two-lane, four-lane

- Structure of the Road - Straight, curving, bridges, narrow shoulders, etc.

- Visibility - How far ahead you can see clearly

- Weather Conditions - Rain, snow, ice, fog, etc.

- Your Own Driving Ability

3. Do not drive so slowly that you block, hinder, or interfere with other vehicles moving at normal speeds.

4. Your speed must be adjusted to conditions so you can stop within a clear distance ahead.

If you drive at a speed that is unsafe for existing conditions in any area, you are violating the basic rule. This applies even if you are driving slower than the posted speed or maximum limit.

Example: You are driving in a line of downtown traffic and the car ahead of you stops suddenly. If you cannot stop in time to avoid hitting that car from behind, you are either breaking the BSR - even if you were driving within the posted speed limit - or you are following too closely.

TENNESSEE SPEED LAWS

Speed is a major contributing factor that causes fatal accidents in Tennessee. Unless otherwise posted, the speed limit on primary and secondary state and federal highways is 55 m.p.h.

When driving, adjust your speed to flow along with the speed at which other traffic is moving - provided the other traffic is traveling within the posted speed limit. Slow drivers are as likely to become involved in accidents as speeders. If most vehicles are traveling between 50 and 55 m.p.h., you are least likely to have an accident if you stay within that speed range.

Interstate Speed Limits

The maximum speed set by Tennessee law for interstate highways is 70 m.p.h. This speed does not apply to ALL sections of the interstate highway system as they have variable speed limits. It may be set as low as 55 m.p.h. in some larger urban areas where there is more traffic congestion. The maximum limit should be driven only in ideal driving conditions. You must adjust your speed to the conditions.

Example: Reduce speed for (1) curves, (2) when the roadway is slippery (during rain, snow, icy conditions), or (3) when it is foggy and difficult to see clearly.

Rural Interstate Limits

70 m.p.h. is the speed posted on most of the rural sections of Tennessee interstate highways.

Urban Interstate Limits

In the more congested urban or metropolitan areas of Tennessee interstates, the limit is typically 55 m.p.h.

NOTE: It is unlawful for any person to drive a vehicle less than 55 m.p.h. in the left most lane of any Interstate highway, unless traffic congestion and flow prevent safe driving at such speed. On the interstates, the minimum speed limit in the right lane(s) is 45 m.p.h., and under normal driving conditions, all vehicles must travel at least this fast so they are not a hazard to other drivers. If the minimum posted speed limit is too fast for you, use another road.

Watch for speed limit changes! The state, counties and municipalities each have the authority to set speed limits for the roadways/highways under their control. You could see some sections of interstate vary in speed set by TDOT. On the secondary streets and highways, these limits will change according to certain zones. Some

residential roads or city streets may have limits as low as 25 or 35 m.p.h. at all times. Watch carefully and obey speed limit signs in business, residential and school zones.

Speeding in School Zones: Speed limits in all school zones are regulated when children are going to or from the school or during a school recess hour. **Exceeding the school zone speed limit is by law considered to be reckless driving.** The penalty includes an automatic six points added to your driving record, which automatically results in an advisory letter being sent to you.

Speeding in Highway Work Zones: Highway work zones are those portions of a street or highway where construction, maintenance or utility work is being done to the road, its shoulders or any other items related to the roadway. This includes work, such as underground and overhead utility work, tree trimming and survey activities. Highway work zones are easily recognized by the presence of orange (or yellow-green) signs and other orange traffic control devices, flashing lights on equipment and workers dressed in highly visible clothing (orange or yellow-green).

Highway workers are trained on how to set up safe zones with directional traffic signs and devices. Motorists and pedestrians are responsible for knowing how to read and react to these directions. Paying attention and driving cautiously and courteously are the most important steps to preventing crashes while driving through highway work zones.

TENNESSEE LAW MANDATES A MINIMUM FINE OF $250 DOLLARS AND UP TO A MAXIMUM FINE OF $500 DOLLARS FOR VIOLATIONS OF THE SPEED LIMIT POSTED IN ACTIVE WORK ZONES.

Work zone crashes are preventable. Drivers must obey the reduced speed limit, as well as pay close attention to the ever changing traffic lanes and detours in the construction work zone. Law enforcement provides increased patrols in work zone areas. State figures for 2021 show 26 persons died, 1,105 were injured and there were 3,010 cases of property damage in work zones crashes in Tennessee.

BRAKING, FOLLOWING AND STOPPING DISTANCES

Drivers must know and understand the safe and proper braking procedures for vehicles. This includes the principles of allowing adequate following distances or "safety cushion" around your vehicle and the laws of required stops (signs, signals, railroad crossings, school buses, etc.). It is important to read the owner's manual of your vehicle to learn the safe and proper operation of your brake system.

By law, all automobiles must have two separate methods of applying brakes. Commonly, these are the vehicle's regular brakes (foot brake) and a parking or emergency brake (sometimes referred to as a "hand brake"). In this section, we will focus on use of the regular vehicle brakes. For information on use of the parking brake, see the section on backing and parking that begins on page 64.

1. Braking: You will encounter numerous driving situations, such as speed zone changes and merging traffic, that will require proper braking techniques. (1) You should apply your brakes slowly and evenly by applying gradual pressure. (2) Start braking early as a signal to the cars behind you. (3) If you brake too strong or quickly, you could skid and lose control of your vehicle. (4) A sudden stop makes it harder for drivers behind you to stop without hitting your vehicle.

IMPORTANT: As a general rule for vehicles without anti-lock brakes, if the car starts to skid, take your foot off the brake and turn the steering wheel in the direction of the skid; This is recommended, if you can do so without running off the road, hitting something, or steering into oncoming traffic.

- With a standard transmission, you can use the gearshift to slow down when approaching a stop sign or signal. First, flash the brake lights to signal any cars behind you. Then, shift down to a lower gear.

- Many of today's cars are equipped with 4 wheel anti-lock braking systems (ABS). Read the instructions in your vehicle's owner manual to learn the safe and proper operation of ABS.

A general overview of ABS braking procedures includes:
- When slowing or stopping, apply firm, steady pressure to the brake pedal. Never pump the pedal with ABS.

- **Always brake and steer when using anti-lock brakes --** With ABS, you "brake and steer." Push the brake pedal while steering around hazards and keep your foot firmly on the brake pedal until the car comes to a stop. Do not take your foot off the pedal or pump the brakes because that will disengage the anti-lock system.

- If you are braking to avoid an emergency or crash, gradually steer the car around any obstacles. ABS was designed to prevent vehicles from locking wheels and to allow drivers to steer when skidding.

- **Expect noise and vibration in the brake pedal when your ABS is in use** -- These sensations tell you ABS is working.

Additional information on ABS begins on Page 96 of this manual.

Regardless of the type of brake system you have, always be prepared to brake unexpectedly. There are some instances when drivers should be especially alert, including:
- When driving next to parked cars

- When approaching any type of intersection
- When approaching traffic signals and crosswalks
- When driving in a school zone or residential area
- When seeing brake lights of other cars
- When driving in heavy, slow moving traffic.

Drivers should know the difference between "covering the brake" and "riding the brake." In situations listed above, "covering the brake" means the driver's foot needs to hover over the brake or between the brake and gas pedals for quicker response time. "Riding the brake" is keeping your foot resting or slightly pressed down on the brake. This adds much wear and tear on the vehicle's brake system, and also gives other drivers the false impression that a stop is imminent. **Covering the brake** is often smart and a safe driving practice; **Riding the brake** is **NOT** a safe practice.

2. Following Distances: Obey speed limit laws and know the proper braking procedures that must be used for maintaining safe following distance between your car and other vehicles.

Tennessee law states: "The driver of a motor vehicle shall not follow another vehicle more closely than is reasonable and prudent, having due regard for the speed of such vehicles and the traffic upon and the condition of the highway."

When another driver makes a mistake, you need time to react. Give yourself this time by keeping a "space cushion" around your vehicle. This space cushion will give you room to brake and avoid hazards when needed. Good drivers keep this safe following distance or space cushion to have a better view of the road. The more space you allow between your car and the car ahead, the more time you will have to see and react to traffic hazards or crashes down the road.

Many drivers don't see as well as they should because they follow too closely (tailgating). The vehicle ahead of them blocks their view of traffic and road conditions. Rear-end crashes are very common and most of these crashes are caused by drivers who are "tailgating."

The Two-Second Rule

To share the road safely, stay a safe distance from the vehicle in front of you. Nationally, safety agencies and driver education programs have tried to define a safe following distance for drivers to maintain. This has ranged from a two to four second following distance. Use the following tips to determine if you are following too closely:

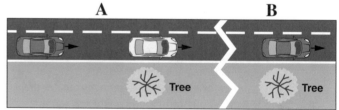

A. As the car ahead of you passes a stationary point on the road (a sign post, driveway, utility pole, etc.), count the seconds it takes you to reach the same spot. (In the illustration below, you are driving the red vehicle.)

B. Count to yourself "one-thousand and one, one-thousand and two," etc. You should NOT reach the same point on the road before you finish counting to at least "one-thousand-two." If you do, you are following too closely.

C. Slow down slightly to increase the space between you and the other vehicle. Find another spot to check your new following distance. Repeat this exercise until you are following no closer than two seconds.

This principle will hold true at any speed on state and U.S. highways with moderate speed limits. However, during inclement weather, interstate highway driving at higher speeds and night driving, the two-second rule should be increased to allow for improved visibility. A minimum of four seconds should allow for better reaction time and a safer space cushion under these conditions including following a motorcycle.

3. Stopping Distances: Be alert and know when you will have to stop well ahead of time. Stopping suddenly is dangerous and usually indicates that a driver was not paying attention, was speeding or was not allowing a safe following distance. Try to avoid panic stops by seeing events well in advance. By slowing down or changing lanes, you may not have to stop at all, and if you do, it can be a more gradual and safer stop. As a rule, it is best to never stop on the road, unless necessary for safety or to obey a law (stop sign, etc.). There are three steps in stopping a vehicle:

* **Perception time:** The length of time it takes a driver to see and recognize a dangerous situation.

* **Reaction time:** The time from perception of danger to the start of braking. The average is 2/3 of a second, as noted in blue section of charts on the next page.

* **Braking time:** This depends on the type and condition of vehicle brakes, as well as vehicle speed.

PERCEPTION, REACTION AND BRAKING TIME		
Step	**Time**	**Explanation**
Perception	**About .50 second**	See/hear danger
Reaction	**About .66 second**	Brain tells foot to brake
Braking/ Stopping	**Varies by speed**	Foot presses brake pedal until car stops

Stopping distance can vary widely due to many factors:
* Type and condition of the road/pavement;
* Type and condition of vehicle tires and brakes;
* Vehicle design and condition of the shock absorbers;
* Vehicle weight when loaded or towing.

It takes longer to stop than most people realize. Suppose you're driving on the interstate at night at the maximum limit of 70 m.p.h. A deer suddenly appears in your headlights. Will you be able to stop in time?

It will take 1.16 seconds for you to see the deer and move your foot to the brake. Before you even start to brake, you will have traveled 128 feet. If you're on a good road in good weather, the braking distance at 70 m.p.h. will be 290 feet.

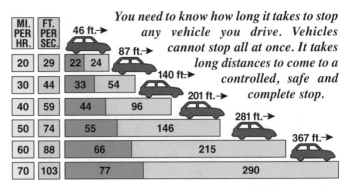

MI. PER HR.	FT. PER SEC.		
20	29	22	24
30	44	33	54
40	59	44	96
50	74	55	146
60	88	66	215
70	103	77	290

46 ft.➤
87 ft.➤
140 ft.➤
201 ft.➤
281 ft.➤
367 ft.➤

You need to know how long it takes to stop any vehicle you drive. Vehicles cannot stop all at once. It takes long distances to come to a controlled, safe and complete stop.

Your total stopping distance has now reached 418 feet, nearly 150 yards, the length of one-and-a-half football fields!

The chart (top right) shows "average" stopping distances (based on tests made by the Federal Highway Administration) for vehicles under ideal conditions. **Note:** This chart does not include the distance you will travel in the 1/2 second of time required for perception of the hazard. According to the National Safety Council, a lightweight passenger car traveling at 50 m.p.h. can stop in about 200 feet. The distance required to stop your vehicle is important in helping you choose a safe driving speed. These charts can be used as a rough guide, but your actual stopping distance will depend upon many factors specific to the situation you encounter.

STOPS REQUIRED BY LAW

Tennessee law states: Every driver approaching a stop sign shall stop before entering the nearest side of a crosswalk, or stop at a clearly marked stop line. If neither is present, then (1) stop at a point nearest the intersecting roadway where the driver has a view of approaching traffic on the intersecting roadway, and (2) stop before entering the actual intersection.

Tennessee Code defines "stop" as "complete cessation of movement."

You are responsible for knowing the proper stopping procedures required by this law. At stop signs and right-turn-on-red intersections, come to a **COMPLETE** stop (not a rolling stop) and go only when traffic is clear. Approaching traffic should not have to slow down or change lanes for your vehicle.

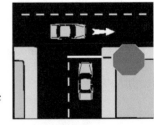

You should:

* Come to a full and complete stop at the stop sign or traffic signal. Often, a wide white stop line will be painted on the pavement in line with the sign. You must stop your vehicle behind this line.

* If no pavement markings are present, stop when the front of your vehicle is even with the stop sign's placement on the roadside.

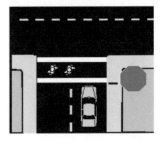

- If you cannot see whether the intersection is clear of crossing traffic, edge up slowly until traffic is clearly visible from both directions.
- If the intersection where the stop sign/traffic signal is placed has a crosswalk for pedestrians marked on the pavement, you must stop before the front of your vehicle reaches the nearest white line marking the border of the crosswalk.
- If there are pedestrians in the crosswalk or about to enter the crosswalk, you must wait for them to cross before proceeding.
- Once the crosswalk is clear, you may slowly edge forward to check traffic before crossing the intersection or entering the roadway.
- When stopping behind another vehicle already stopped at the intersection, make sure you allow adequate "gap" space between the vehicles so you are not "tailgating."

A basic rule of thumb is that you should be able to see the license plate and/or the other vehicle's back tire where it meets the pavement. This "gap" provides a safety zone in the event that the other vehicle rolls back slightly or stalls. If the vehicle stalls, you would still be able to maneuver around it safely. The gap provides a way out in the event of an emergency, such as another vehicle approaching from behind so fast that you may need to move to avoid a rear-end collision.

- Once the vehicle in front of you has moved on through the intersection, you may move forward to the stop line. Remember, you still must bring your vehicle to a FULL STOP at the stop line.
- A complete stop is required at a flashing red traffic light, just as with a stop sign.
- After you have stopped, if there is no traffic from the right or left, you may proceed. When there is traffic on the crossroad (right to left) and/or oncoming traffic (heading toward you) from the other side of the intersection, you must follow the right-of-way procedures. (Right-of-Way rules are discussed in depth later in this chapter.)
- You must stop completely when directed to stop by a flag person at a road construction site or by a police officer directing you to stop in any situation.

Rolling Stops:
Rolling stops are dangerous and illegal. A rolling stop occurs when the driver only slows down for a stop sign or traffic signal and proceeds through the intersection or turn without bringing the vehicle to a full and complete stop. **A complete stop is required by law.** Most law enforcement officers and driver education instructors agree that a vehicle has not come to a complete stop until the driver feels the car lurch forward after all motion has ceased. **Rolling stops are grounds for receiving a traffic ticket AND for failing the driver examination road test.**

The following are reasons to avoid rolling stops:
- A driver may not see a child or other pedestrian who may think the car will follow the law and come to a complete stop.
- There is a better chance of seeing possible hazards, because the driver who comes to a full stop has a longer observation period at the intersection.
- If two drivers are traveling at right angles to one another, and both fail to stop, a collision is almost a certainty.
- Police and insurance companies will hold the driver who fails to stop completely liable in the event of a crash, possibly resulting in fines, loss of license, increased insurance rates or loss of insurance coverage.

Stopping for Railroad Crossings

Railroad crossings have pavement markings that include a large crossbuck ("X"), the letters "RR", a no-passing zone stripe and a stop line. Railroad crossing collisions should not happen. When they do, it usually means drivers are not paying attention to signs, pavement markings and other warnings that tell when a train is coming.

Stop—Look—Listen—Look Again!

Every motor vehicle should be driven at a rate of speed that will permit the vehicle to be stopped before reaching the nearest rail of a railroad crossing. The vehicle should not be driven over the crossing until all railroad tracks are completely clear of train traffic. Violations of railroad signals or signs carry the same penalties as violations of other traffic control devices.

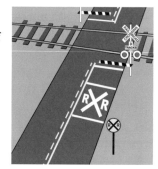

When you approach a railroad crossing and a train is coming, you must stop between 15 and 50 feet from the railroad tracks. Never stop on the railroad crossing tracks. Wait until the train has passed and it is safe to cross before proceeding across the tracks. The following are indications that a train is approaching an intersection:

- The crossing has a crossbuck sign with flashing lights to warn drivers when a train is approaching.
- The crossing has a crossing gate that is lowered, blocking access to the railroad tracks when a train is approaching.
- A human flagger signals drivers that a train is approaching.
- Trains are required to signal a horn when they are approximately 1,500 feet from passing through a railroad crossing.

- An approaching train is visible to the driver.

Never drive across a railroad crossing when any of the above indications of an approaching train are present. Trains move very quickly. Trying to "beat" a train is extremely dangerous for the vehicle driver, as well as people on the train.

Tennessee law requires certain vehicles to stop at all railroad grade/highway crossings, whether or not any signs or signals are activated when the vehicle approaches the crossing. As a driver, you must be aware of this requirement so you will be prepared to meet or follow these vehicles when they have stopped at the crossing.

The vehicles listed below are required by law to stop before crossing ANY railroad grade crossing:

- Church or school buses, regardless of whether such buses are carrying any passengers at the time of crossing;
- Common carriers, such as taxis or other vehicles transporting passengers for hire;
- Vehicles transporting flammables, explosives or other dangerous articles as cargo or part of a cargo.

Buses at a railroad crossing will pull to the right. The side movement of the vehicle, along with its stoplights, is a very clear signal, day or night, that the vehicle is preparing to stop. You must be alert to this type of movement by buses. Tanker trucks and other vehicles, required to stop at all railroad tracks, will usually signal such a stop by displaying emergency flashers of the vehicle to alert other drivers to the impending stop.

The School Bus Stop Law

Meeting A School Bus:
Any driver meeting a school bus or church bus on which the red stop warning signal lights are flashing should reduce his speed and bring the vehicle to a complete stop while the bus stop signal arm is extended. The vehicle must remain stopped until the stop arm is pulled back and the bus resumes motion.

Overtaking A School Bus:
Any driver approaching a school bus or church bus from the rear shall not pass the bus when red stop warning signal lights are flashing. The vehicle must come to a complete stop when the bus is stopped. The vehicle must remain stopped until the stop arm is pulled back and the bus resumes motion.

School Bus Warning Lights:
It is illegal to pass a school bus that has stopped to load or unload students. Never pass on the right side of the bus, as

this is where the children enter or exit. This is illegal and can have tragic results. You must stop and remain stopped until:

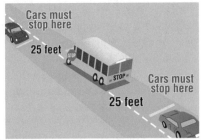

- The bus has started moving, OR
- The driver motions for you to proceed, OR
- The visual signals are no longer activated such as the red flashing lights go off and/or the stop arm is pulled back.

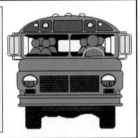

YELLOW FLASHING:
When the yellow lights on the front and back of the bus are flashing the bus is preparing to stop to load or unload children. Motorists should slow down and prepare to stop their vehicles.

A RED FLASHING:
When the red lights are flashing and the stop arm is extended this indicates that the bus HAS stopped and that children are now getting on or off the bus. Motorists must stop their cars and wait until the red flashing lights are turned off, the stop arm is withdrawn, and the bus begins moving before they start driving again.

When a school bus is stopped at an intersection to load and unload children, drivers from ALL directions are required to stop until the bus resumes motion (as shown by the red vehicles in the diagram at right). It is a Class A misdemeanor and the driver can be fined between $250 and $1,000 for not stopping for a stopped school bus.

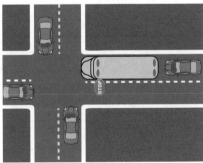

When driving on a highway with separate roadways for traffic in opposite directions, divided by median space or a barrier not suitable for vehicular traffic, the driver need not stop, but should proceed with caution. A turn lane in the middle of a four-lane highway is NOT considered a barrier, but a fifth lane that is suitable for vehicular traffic. Drivers meeting a stopped school bus on this type of road would be required to stop in both directions.

Stopping For Police Vehicles

Police vehicles attempting to stop drivers will do so by means of a visual, flashing blue or flashing blue and red lights, and/or an audible signal. Remember, a police officer never knows what to expect when stopping a driver. Do not let your emotions or sudden unexplained movements (or those of your passengers) raise tensions or anxiety in the situation.

A police officer may be more likely to listen to what you have to say and less likely to feel threatened by you (or your passengers) if you follow these guidelines:

- Drive as closely as is safely practical to the right-hand edge or curb of the road, clear of any intersection, stop and park.

- Limit the movements of the driver and/or passengers while stopping your vehicle.

- Drivers should keep their hands on the steering wheel and passengers should keep their hands in plain view. **Drivers should advise officers if they have a handgun permit and if they are armed.**

- Provide your driver license and/or vehicle registration when requested.

- Keep all vehicle doors closed and remain in the vehicle unless asked to get out.

- If the stop is made after dark, turn on the vehicle's interior light before the officer approaches.

- If enforcement action is taken against you that you disagree with, do not argue with the officer at the scene. Traffic violations and traffic crimes charged against you are decided in court.

- If you find yourself being directed to pull over and stop by someone in an UNMARKED police car, you may drive slowly a short distance to the nearest area where there are other people, such as the next business parking lot or the next exit, if on the interstate. This may be important if traveling at night and/or alone.

INTERSECTIONS

Now that you have studied the effects of speed, following distances, stopping distances and legally required stops, it is time to look at the complex issue of intersections. This includes rules for the right-of-way, pedestrians, right turns, left turns and turn signals. Intersections are places where traffic merges or crosses. They include:

- Cross streets,
- Side streets,
- Driveways,
- Shopping center or parking lot entrances.

More crashes happen at intersections than at any other place. Intersections constitute a very small part of the rural and urban street/highway systems, yet they are implicated in 33 percent of all motor vehicle crashes and 21 percent of all fatal crashes. There were 308 fatalities in Tennessee in 2021 for intersection related crashes. Be careful when approaching any intersection or driveway. Never assume the other driver will yield the right-of-way to you. **Always be prepared to stop.**

Approaching Intersections Safely

"Traffic checks" is the process of looking frequently and carefully for vehicle traffic approaching from each direction. "Traffic checks" is especially important when merging or changing lanes **AND** when approaching and crossing intersections. Below are five things to remember to navigate an intersection safely:

Look: Look both ways as you near an intersection. Before you enter an intersection, continue checking traffic from both the left and right for approaching vehicles and/or crossing pedestrians. Bicycles and motorcycles are smaller and more difficult to see.

1. **The Left-Right-Left Rule:** Look first to the left to make sure cross traffic is yielding the right-of-way. Then look for traffic from the right. If stopped, look both left and right just before you start moving. Look across the intersection before you start to move to make sure the path is clear through the intersection.

   A. As you enter an intersection, check again for unusual or unexpected actions to the left and right.

   B. It is also important to watch for vehicle traffic from the front (oncoming traffic) and rear (approaching/overtaking traffic) of your vehicle at intersections. Be especially aware of vehicles behind you. If the light changes and/or you encounter a vehicle violating the right-of-way that causes you to stop suddenly, will the vehicle behind be able to stop? It is not uncommon for drivers to run red lights or stop signs resulting in a head-on or rear-end collision.

   C. Look twice for motorcycles, bicycles and pedestrians.

2. **Control Speed:** Be prepared to brake or stop unexpectedly at intersections if the above traffic checks alert you to a possible hazard. You should slow down **before** reaching the intersection, drive at your slowest speed just before entering the intersection and gradually increase your speed as you cross the intersection.

3. **Use Proper Lane:** You should be in the proper lane for the direction you intend to travel before you reach the intersection. Do **NOT** make last minute lane changes as you start through an intersection. Do **NOT** pass a vehicle in an intersection.

4. **Know and obey:**

   - The proper right-of-way procedures for vehicles and pedestrians at intersections;

   - The purpose and meaning of pavement markings;

- The purpose and meaning of traffic signals, including stop or yield signs posted at intersections;
- The proper lane usage and speed at intersections;
- The proper use of your vehicle's turn signals.

5. Do Not Block: Do not move into an intersection and block it after the traffic lights have changed. This is not only common sense, but it's also illegal to block an intersection after the light has changed. Some intersections have signs posted nearby (often hanging next to the traffic light) advising "Do Not Block Intersection." It is always illegal to block an intersection, whether it is marked or not.

Right-of-Way Procedures

Vehicles or pedestrians are likely to meet one another where there are no signs or lights to control traffic. There are rules on who must yield the right-of-way. These rules tell who goes first and who must wait in different traffic situations.

However, if another driver does not follow these rules, give him the right-of-way. In all driving situations, think of the right-of-way as something to be given, not taken. All drivers should know and understand the rules which determine the right-of-way.

You Must Not Insist On the Right-of-Way: The law does not really give anyone the right-of-way. It only says who must yield the right-of-way. A driver must do everything possible to avoid a traffic crash. Rules for the most common situations drivers encounter include:

1. **Yield to pedestrians crossing the road or your path of travel:**
   - **Pedestrian means any person afoot or using a motorized or non-motorized wheelchair.**
   - When pedestrians are in a crosswalk (marked or unmarked) or when the pedestrian is upon the half of the roadway upon which your vehicle is traveling or when the pedestrian is approaching so closely from the opposite half of the roadway as to be in danger;
   - When in a marked school zone when a warning flasher or flashers are in operation, the driver of a vehicle shall stop to yield the right-of-way to a pedestrian crossing the roadway within a marked or unmarked crosswalk. The driver shall remain stopped until the pedestrian has crossed the roadway on which the vehicle is stopped.
   - When your car is turning a corner and pedestrians are crossing with the light;
   - When your vehicle crosses a sidewalk while entering or exiting a driveway, alley or parking lot. It is illegal to drive on a sidewalk except to cross it;
   - When a blind or visually impaired pedestrian using a guide dog or carrying a cane, which is white in  color or white with red tip, or a hearing impaired person with a dog on a blaze orange leash, is crossing any portion of the roadway, even if not at an intersection or crosswalk. Take special precautions as may be necessary to avoid accident or injury to the pedestrian. Stop at least 10 feet away until the person is off the roadway. Do not use your horn, as it could startle the blind pedestrian;
   - You must yield to children playing in the streets. In crowded downtown areas and in suburban residential neighborhoods, children play in the streets because there may not be parks or playgrounds nearby. Even though they have been told not to run into the street, children won't always put safety ahead of a runaway puppy or a bouncing ball. Children on bicycles can easily forget to slow down before entering an intersection or to signal and look behind before they turn. You are responsible for driving with extreme caution when children are present. Slow down near schools, playgrounds, and residential areas.

2. **Yield to Oncoming Traffic:** When meeting other traffic at intersections, or when entering the roadway, make sure the other driver sees you. Make eye contact whenever possible. Drive cautiously and defensively. Be a friendly driver. Remember, the right-of-way is something to be given, not taken.
   - When starting from a parked position, wait for all moving traffic to pass.
   - When turning left, you must wait for oncoming traffic going straight ahead or turning right.
   - When entering a main road from a driveway, alley, parking lot or roadside, you must yield to all vehicles already on the main road. *(The blue car in the graphic below must yield the right-of-way.)*
   - When entering a roundabout, traffic circle or rotary (also known as "town squares"), you must yield to traffic already in the roundabout.
   - When approaching a MERGE onto a busy highway or interstate, you must increase or decrease speed as needed to avoid an accident and yield the right-of-way, if necessary, to the oncoming traffic.
   - When approaching a fire station, you should yield to any emergency vehicle that is about to back into, or is already in the process of backing into, the driveway entrance to the station.

3. **Yielding at Intersections:** The right-of-way should be determined by each driver before entering an intersection. If you have the right-of-way and another driver yields it to you, proceed immediately. However, YOU must yield the right-of-way:
   - When oncoming vehicles (including bicycles) are proceeding straight or making a right turn;

- At intersections where YIELD signs are posted, the driver must slow down or stop to avoid a crash with oncoming traffic;

- To any vehicles already in the intersection, even if you have the green traffic light; (The red vehicle in the diagram at right must yield to the green vehicle.)

- At "T" intersections where one road dead-ends into another main crossing roadway, the vehicles on the road ending must yield to oncoming traffic from both directions on the main road;

- When turning left at intersections, you must yield to any oncoming vehicle proceeding straight or turning right, unless you have a traffic light where your left turn is on a protected green arrow; (The red vehicle in the diagram to the right must yield.)

- At intersections marked as ALL-WAY stops, the vehicle reaching the intersection first gets to go first (of course, ALL vehicles must stop). If more than one vehicle arrives at the same time, yield the right of way to the vehicle on the right;

- Where roads cross and there are no stop signs or signals, yield to any vehicle coming at the same time on your right;

- Do not enter an intersection unless you can get through it without having to stop. You should wait until traffic in front of you clears so that you are not blocking the intersection. If your vehicle is left blocking an intersection (with or without a traffic signal), it prevents other traffic from proceeding and you could be ticketed.

4. Yield to Emergency Vehicles and Transit Buses

- You must yield the right-of-way to a police vehicle, fire engine, ambulance or other emergency vehicle using a siren, air horn or a red or blue flashing light.

- It is against the law for an unauthorized private vehicle to have a blue flashing emergency light or combination of blue and red flashing emergency lights installed, maintained or visibly shown on the vehicle in any manner.

Following Fire or Other Emergency Vehicles:

It is against the law to follow a fire truck or other emergency vehicle responding to a fire alarm or other emergency.

It is also illegal to take your vehicle within the block of where the emergency vehicle has stopped to take care of the emergency. If your car passes an emergency site, do not drive over any unprotected fire department hose unless the fire department official in command says it is okay.

Tennessee law requires that when an emergency vehicle is approaching, all traffic meeting or being overtaken must yield the right-of-way and immediately drive to a position parallel to, and as close as possible to the right hand edge or curb of the roadway stop. You must remain in that stopped position until the emergency vehicle has passed or until you are directed to move by a police officer. You must still proceed with caution; there may be other emergency vehicles coming.

There are a few other important details about sharing the road with emergency vehicles:

- If you are in an intersection, drive on through the intersection before pulling over, or you may block the emergency vehicle's path through the intersection.

- Do not pull over to the right if it will block a side road or driveway. The emergency vehicle may need to turn into that road or driveway to get to the incident scene.

- If the traffic light is red, stay where you are. If the light turns green before the emergency vehicle has passed, do NOT proceed on green. Wait until the emergency vehicle has passed or turned onto a different street.

- When yielding to emergency vehicles, get in the habit of turning down the volume on the radio (if on) so you can hear any instructions or directions given out over the emergency vehicle's loudspeaker. Your immediate reaction to such directions may be critically needed.

You must yield the right-of-way to any transit vehicle (metro bus) that has signaled and is pulling back onto the roadway from a bus stop. Generally, this occurs on urban roadways in areas marked by "bus stop" signs or benches. Occasionally, you may encounter cross-country commercial buses signaling to re-enter traffic after allowing passengers to disembark on rural roadways in smaller communities and towns.

A. You are not required to stop for, nor forbidden to pass, transit buses when they are stopped for passenger pick-up or drop-off as you would be for a school bus in the same situation. (See "The School Bus Stop Law" section of this manual for complete details.)

B. Be extremely cautious near stopped buses and be watchful for passengers (including elderly individuals and children) attempting to cross the road in these areas.

5. Slowing and Yielding to Stationary Vehicles on the Roadside:

Tennessee's Move Over Law requires that when approaching any stationary emergency vehicle with lights flashing, you must make a lane change into a lane not adjacent to that of the vehicle, or proceed with caution by reducing the speed of the vehicle and maintaining a safe speed for the current road conditions. This requirement applies only on multi-lane roadways where there are two or more lanes of traffic moving in the same direction and the stationary vehicles are along the roadside in the direction of the driver's travel.

You are likely to see the following stationary vehicles using their flashing lights:

- Utility vehicles that provide your electric, phone, natural gas and water services
- Authorized emergency vehicles (police, fire, ambulance or rescue);
- Highway maintenance vehicles (state, county, city or vendor vehicles used for road repair, maintenance or construction);
- Recovery vehicles (tow truck or wrecker).

TURNING

The most common faults when making turns are (A) failing to signal, (B) not signaling long enough, (C) failing to search for hazards, (D) turning from the wrong lane and (E) failing to turn properly. Rules for turning apply at all locations, even driveways and alleys, not just at intersections.

The first rule of turning is to turn from the closest lane in the direction you are traveling to the closest legal lane in the direction you want to go. The law says which lanes and positions you must use when turning, and the required signaling distances for such turns. This section expands on those rules and helps you learn proper procedures for signaling and making safe turns.

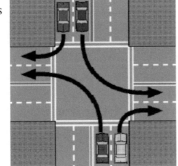

1. Signaling a Turn: Before making any turn, whether the turn is into another roadway, a parking lot, another traffic lane, or leaving a parked position, it is extremely important that you signal. Unless you signal, other drivers expect you to keep traveling the path of the roadway, using the lane in which your vehicle is positioned. Your signal lets other drivers, motorcyclists,

cyclists and pedestrians know your intentions to make a change in your vehicle's path of travel and gives them time to react. However, signaling does NOT give you the right-of-way.

You should always use turn signals before:

- Changing lanes or making any movement of your vehicle to the right or left;
- Turning at an intersection or into a driveway, alley or parking lot;
- Entering or exiting the interstate or other controlled access roadway;
- Pulling away from a parked position along the curb;
- Pulling over to the curb or roadside;
- Slowing down or stop your vehicle suddenly.

You may use either your vehicle turn signal lights or hand and arm signals. Make sure your signals can be easily seen by others.

A. Hand Signal Tips:

- When you use hand signals, bring your arm in during the actual turn to keep control of the steering wheel.
- During non-daylight hours, hand and arm signals are usually not visible except in well lit areas.
- Hand signals should be used when the sun is shining brightly. This makes your turn signal light harder for other drivers to see easily.
- In heavy traffic, a hand signal may be seen by drivers who are several cars back with an obscured view of your turn signal light.

The illustration below shows the standard positions for hand and arm signals. Extend your hand and arm well out of the car window and signal in plenty of time.

B. Electrical Turn Signal Tips:

- Check your vehicle's turn signals often to be sure they are working properly.
- Be sure that your turn signal lights (front and rear) are clean and free from dust, dirt, ice or snow.
- When signaling a stop, lightly pump your brakes a few times to attract attention with your brake lights.

LEFT TURN   RIGHT TURN   STOP OR SLOW

- Be sure to turn off your turn signal light after using it. An unintended signal still means "turn" to the other drivers. By leaving it on, you might tempt other drivers to pull out in front of you.

Your signal helps other drivers plan ahead. You should not assume that all drivers will respond to your signaled intentions. Also, be aware that some drivers will not signal their intentions. Therefore, maintain control of your vehicle at all times and "drive defensively." A surprise move often results in accidents. As a good driver, you should be alert and emphasize your intentions to turn by giving the proper signal or signals.

- At least 50 feet before the turn, you must turn on your turn signal lights.

- Use your turn signals ONLY to indicate when YOU plan to turn or change lanes.

- If you are parked at a curb or roadside and about to re-enter traffic, use a signal long enough to alert oncoming traffic that you are moving from the parked position back into the traffic lane.

- If you plan to turn beyond an intersection, do not signal until you are in the intersection. If you signal earlier, another driver may think you intend to turn at the intersection and might pull into your path.

- Get in the habit of signaling every time you change direction. Signal even if you do not see anyone else around. It is the car you do not see that is the most dangerous.

- When you slow down, your brake lights flash as a signal. Slowing down, itself, acts as a signal.

C. You should NOT use your signals:

- To signal a driver behind you to come around to pass your vehicle.

- To relay the turn intentions of vehicles ahead of you to those drivers behind your vehicle.

This is misleading to other drivers. Your brake lights will be sufficient to warn those behind you to slow down. If you see someone ahead signaling they are about to turn, do NOT turn on your turn signals unless you also plan to turn.

> **Proper signaling is a key to safe driving. Failure to signal is dangerous and inconsiderate. Communication while driving is a must. Safe drivers are always aware of surrounding conditions and readily communicate their intentions of other drivers by using signals whenever appropriate.**

D. Making Turns: Before making a turn, be sure you can do so safely. Check traffic ahead, behind and to the side. Become familiar with the following Do's and Don'ts:

DO:

- Use your turn signal at least 50 feet before the turn or lane change.

- Make thorough traffic checks, looking behind and on both sides to see where other vehicles are so you can change lanes and make the turn safely.

- Move into the correct turn lane as soon as possible. The faster the traffic is moving, the sooner you should move into the proper lane. Go from one lane to the other as

directly as possible without crossing lane lines or interfering with the traffic.

- Select the proper gear before entering the intersection, and accelerate slightly through the turn.

- As you turn, make sure to check for pedestrians, cyclists and other traffic. Make the turn correctly, staying in the proper lane and maintaining a safe speed.

- Finish the turn in the proper lane. Once you have completed the turn, change to another lane if you need to, and if traffic is clear.

DON'T:

- Don't turn unless the turn is permitted and can be made safely. Be aware of signs prohibiting right or left turns at certain locations.

- Don't try to turn from the wrong lane. If you aren't in the proper lane, drive to the next intersection and make the turn from the proper lane there. Circle back if necessary. This may take some extra time and miles, but it is the safe thing to do.

- Don't "swing wide" or "cut the corner" when making turns. Don't turn too short so as to cut corners on left turns or run over the curb on right turns. Turning too wide or too late, straddling lanes, or turning into the wrong side of the street will leave you in the wrong lane. Always follow the white lines in intersections using multiple turn lanes.

- Don't turn your wheels in the direction of the turn while waiting for oncoming traffic to pass. If you are hit from the rear while your wheels are turned, the impact can push you into oncoming traffic. Keep your vehicles wheels straight until you begin the turn. Wait until you are sure you can complete the turn before turning the wheels.

- Don't enter the intersection if traffic ahead may keep you from completing the turn before the traffic light changes. Stay behind the stop line or crosswalk until you can fully complete the turn without the risk of blocking the traffic flow.

- Don't brake or depress the clutch while actually turning.

- Don't shift gears in the intersection (If you stall you could cause an accident and/or block the intersection to other traffic).

2. Left Turns: When you meet another driver at an intersection and both of you want to turn left, each will turn to the left of the other. Leave from the left lane or as close to the yellow center line as possible and enter in the left lane or as close to the yellow center line as shown in diagram on page 57. Study the diagram that shows the five basic steps in making routine left turns from a two-way street onto another two-way street.

A. From a Two-Way Street on to a Two-Way Street Remember these tips:

HOW TO MAKE A LEFT TURN
These are five steps in making a left turn. Take care to keep close to the centerline, but don't cut it.

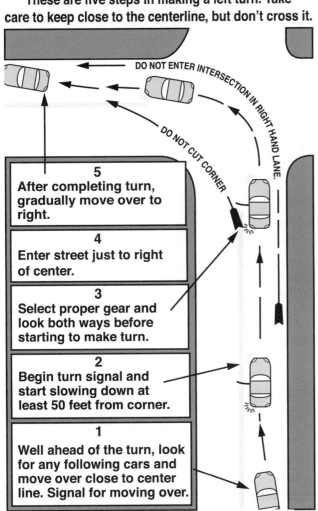

5 After completing turn, gradually move over to right.

4 Enter street just to right of center.

3 Select proper gear and look both ways before starting to make turn.

2 Begin turn signal and start slowing down at least 50 feet from corner.

1 Well ahead of the turn, look for any following cars and move over close to center line. Signal for moving over.

- Reduce speed and get into the lane just to the right of the center line well ahead of time.
- Prior to turning, signal your intentions for at least 50 feet and approach the turn with the left side of the vehicle as close to the center line as possible. Failure to signal is dangerous, inconsiderate and illegal. Your signal makes it possible for other cars to complete a turn.
- Look out of your left window for pedestrians and other traffic in your turn path. Yield to any oncoming cars or pedestrians.
- Begin the turn when you enter the intersection. Keep the wheels straight until you can turn; turn just before the imaginary center point in the intersection. Drive just to the right of the center line of the street you're entering and be sure to turn into the first lane past the center line. This avoids conflict with other traffic making either right or left turns. Never turn "wide" into the right lane. The right lane will be used by any oncoming vehicles turning right.
- If the intersection has a lane signed or marked for making left turns, do not make this turn from any other lane. At some intersections, you may make turns from more than

one lane. Signs and pavement markings will tell you if this is allowed. If there are multiple lanes, keep your vehicle in the lane you start from throughout the turn. Be alert for signs that may also PROHIBIT left turns at some intersections.

- Pay close attention to the traffic light cycle. If the light turns yellow while you are waiting for oncoming vehicles to clear the intersection, **DO NOT proceed into the intersection.**

B. From a Two-Way Street on to a One-Way Street
Keep in mind the following differences when turning on one-way streets:

- When making left-hand turns, be alert for "one-way" street signs on traffic lights, posts and stop signs.
- Center lines on two-way streets are yellow.
- Center lines on one-way streets are white.
- In preparing to turn, make the proper "two-way" approach next to the center line.

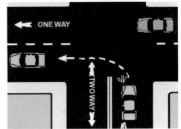

- Turn sharply into the FIRST lane. Remember, you are turning onto a one-way street, so both lanes will be traveling in the same direction. You should turn into the first lane closest to the left curb.

C. From A One-Way Street Onto A One-Way Street

- Make your approach in the traffic lane furthermost to the left curb of the street.
- Turn sharply into the first lane on the left side of the one-way street. DO NOT TURN WIDE.

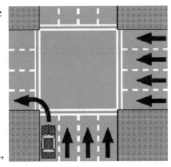

At intersections that are not marked for "No Turns on Red," you may make a left turn on red when turning from a one-way street onto a one-way street. You must come to a complete stop at the light prior to making the turn, the same as right turns on red.

D. From A One-Way Street Onto a Two-Way Street

- Make your approach in the traffic lane furthermost to the left curb of the street.
- Do not start your turn at the crosswalk. Drive into the intersection and then turn sharply into the first lane to the right of the yellow line on the two-way street.
- If the two-way street has multiple lanes, you may move into the right lane ONLY AFTER giving the proper turn signal and checking traffic to your right.
- You CANNOT make this left turn on a red light.

E. Notes on Multiple Turn Lanes

- A vehicle in the second lane can make the same turn as a vehicle in the first lane only when a lane use control sign or marking permits it.

- You will often see white channel lines and arrows on the pavement. These lines help direct you into the correct lane while turning.

F. Right Turns:
Making right turns can be just as dangerous as left turns. Study the diagram below, named HOW TO MAKE A RIGHT TURN, that shows the four basic steps in making right turns.

- On right turns, avoid moving wide to the left before going into the turn or as you make the turn. If you swing wide, the driver behind you may think you are changing lanes or turning left and may try to pass you on the right. If you

HOW TO MAKE A RIGHT TURN
These are four steps in making a right turn. Be careful not to swing to the left before or during the turn.

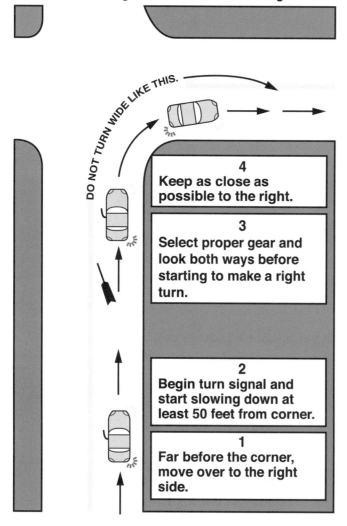

DO NOT TURN WIDE LIKE THIS.

4
Keep as close as possible to the right.

3
Select proper gear and look both ways before starting to make a right turn.

2
Begin turn signal and start slowing down at least 50 feet from corner.

1
Far before the corner, move over to the right side.

swing wide as you complete the turn, drivers who are in the far lane will not expect to see your vehicle in that lane of traffic.

- Well ahead of the turning point, check for traffic behind and beside your vehicle. Get as close as is practical to the right curb or road edge without interfering with pedestrians, bicyclists or parked vehicles.

- Give a signal for a right turn for at least 50 feet.

- Before starting to turn, look to the left and right for cross traffic on the intersecting street and oncoming traffic that may also be turning. Always check for pedestrians and bicyclists before turning. Remember to yield the right-of-way, if necessary.

- Move your vehicle around the corner and into the travel lane closest to the right curb.

A. Turn Warning: Trucks and Buses Turning Right

When driving in city traffic, pay special attention to the turn signals of large trucks and buses. Large trucks and buses MUST make wide turns. Sometimes they must leave an open space to the right just before the turn. To avoid an accident, do not pass a truck on the right if there is a possibility that it might make a right turn.

B. Turns Permitted on Red

Tennessee law allows a right turn on red and left turns on red at certain one-way to one-way intersections, unless otherwise posted.

- When making a right turn at a red light, you must first come to a complete stop before reaching the marked or unmarked crosswalk or stop line. Always yield the right-of-way to oncoming traffic, pedestrians and bicyclists .

- A left turn at a red light or stop signal is permitted at all intersections where a one-way street intersects with another one-way street and the traffic is moving in the same direction into which the left turn would be made. The same rules for complete stops, yielding, and observing signs prohibiting turns must be followed as you would for a right turn on red.

4. Special Turns: Roundabouts and U-Turns

A. Roundabouts: A roundabout is an intersection control device with traffic circulating around a central island. These traffic circles are usually used to discourage drivers from using neighborhood streets for commuting thoroughfares, to slow speeds and to reduce accidents.

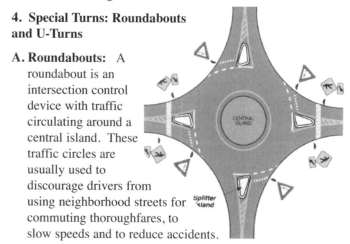

Many Tennessee towns have a form of roundabout that is known as the "town square."

- Always travel around a roundabout to the right, in a counter-clockwise direction.

- On approaching the roundabout, stay in your lane and to the right of the splitter island or yellow pavement markings/curbs directing traffic to the right. These islands are used to prevent vehicles from attempting to travel left around the circle.

- Upon reaching the roundabout, yield to vehicles already within the circulating traffic. Observe the standard right-of-way procedures as with regular intersections controlled by yield signs. Enter the roundabout when there is a gap in traffic and once inside do not stop unless directed to do so by signs, signals or a traffic officer.

- Within the roundabout, proceed at a slower speed (usually posted at 15 to 25 m.p.h.). Exit the roundabout at any street or continue around again if you miss the street on which you wanted to turn.

- In a multi-lane roundabout, do not overtake or pass any vehicles. Remember the roundabout is a low speed traffic control device. Be prepared to yield to vehicles turning in front of you from the inside lane to exit the roundabout.

- Exit the roundabout carefully. Always indicate your exit using your right turn signal. Watch for pedestrians in or approaching the crosswalk on the street you are exiting and yield the right-of-way if necessary.

B. U-Turns: A U-turn is a turn within the road, made in one smooth u-shaped motion, so as to end up with your vehicle traveling in the opposite/reverse direction as before the turn. Some towns and cities do not allow U-turns on streets and roadways under their control. Check with local police to be sure.

You may NOT make a U-turn:

- At any intersection where a traffic light or police officer is controlling the traffic flow.

- At any rural or urban location where you cannot see traffic coming from both directions for at least 500 feet in each direction.

- At any location where U-turns are prohibited by official signs or markings.

- Between intersections in a city. The safest thing to do is drive around the block.

- At or near a curve or the crest of a hill when the driver cannot see 500 feet or more in each direction. Improper turns are a major contributor to traffic crashes.

- It is illegal in Tennessee for any driver to make a U-turn on an interstate highway. Emergency crossovers are for the use of emergency vehicles and highway maintenance crews only. It is extremely dangerous and illegal to use

them to "turn around" in the event you missed an exit or are in a traffic jam. Drive on to the next exit ramp. Do not cut across the median strip, as this maneuver is also illegal.

TRAFFIC LANES AND LANE USAGE

A traffic lane is a part of a roadway wide enough for a car or a single line of vehicles to travel safely. Most lanes on hard-surfaced roads are marked with white or yellow pavement line markings. On dirt or gravel roads, some rural roads, private drives and other roadways (such as parking lot rows and shopping center perimeter roads), the lanes may not be marked, but they are there anyway. When driving on a road without any center line markings, and where vehicles are coming from each direction, drivers must give others going in the opposite direction at least half the road.

1. Overview of Lane Usage: "White on your right, yellow on your left"

This simple statement sums up the principle of "right hand traffic" under which all traffic must move on American roadways. If you ever find yourself driving with the yellow line on to your right, pull over immediately. You are driving on the wrong side of the road!

Always drive on the right side of a two-lane highway except when passing. If the road has four or more lanes with two-way traffic, drive in the right lanes except when passing other vehicles or turning left.

The center lane of a two-way, three-lane or five-lane highway is used only for turning left.

Keeping Right: Drive on the right of the road **except** when:

- Passing another vehicle going in the same direction as your vehicle;

- Driving to the left of center to pass an obstruction in the road. Whenever possible, always drive around obstructions or crashes to the right side to avoid the possibility of becoming involved in a head-on collision;

- A road is marked for one way traffic;

- You are turning left.

Drive in the Proper Lane

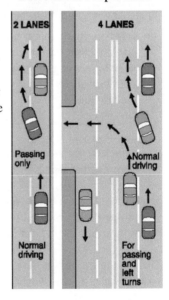

Two Lanes: Two-lane highways have a single broken yellow center line. You should always drive to the right of the center line, except to safely pass another vehicle.

Four Lanes: A four-lane (or more) highway is divided in half by two solid yellow lines in the center. The two lanes on each side are divided by a dashed white line. Drive in the extreme right lane except when passing another vehicle or making a left turn.

One Way: A one-way highway is generally composed of two or more lanes restricted to moving in one direction. There should not be  any vehicles traveling in the opposite direction on these roads.

2. **Divided Highways:** Divided highways have two-way traffic, but the roads for each direction are divided by a median or barrier. Always use the road on the right when driving on a divided highway, such as an interstate, unless  directed to do otherwise. Do not drive within, across or over any median strip or barrier separating these roadways. It is only allowed at an authorized crossover or intersection, or when you are officially directed to do so.

On a divided four-lane highway, when using a designated crossover for a left turn (or a U-turn where permitted), treat the crossover/opening the same as a cross street by keeping to the right side of the crossover paved area.

A. If a vehicle is already in the crossover waiting for traffic to clear, remain stopped in the left most lane of the four-lane highway with your turn signal on until the waiting vehicle has cleared the crossover.

B. DO NOT "swing" into the left side of the crossover or "bunch-up" behind the waiting car. This creates a dangerous situation for any vehicle attempting to use the crossover for a left turn coming from the opposite direction.

- It leaves your vehicle with its rear-end partially sticking out in the left traffic lane. In this position, approaching vehicles coming upon your car are less likely to notice your turn signal than if your vehicle was fully stopped in the left lane.

- It places your car on the wrong side of the road in the crossover and could cause a head-on collision with a vehicle attempting to turn left in the crossover from the opposite direction.

Remember, such a crossover is PERMITTED ONLY at paved openings provided on four-lane highways. There are NO crossovers provided for traffic on interstates.

Driving the wrong way on a one-way road or street is very dangerous and illegal. If you see red reflectors facing you on the lane lines, or red "Wrong Way" and "Do Not Enter" signs, you are on the **wrong** side of  the road. Turn off of a one-way street or get into the proper lane of a two-way street immediately! If you see red reflectors

on the lines on the edge of the road, you are on the wrong interstate or highway ramp. Pull over immediately! Red reflectors always mean you are facing traffic the wrong way and could have a head-on collision.

3. **Dual Use Lanes:** These have both a turn arrow and a straight arrow. You can proceed straight or  make the indicated turn from these lanes as shown by the pavement markings and/or signs found at the intersection. Unless the intersection has a protected arrow for turning, you must follow the standard right-of-way rules.

4. **Shared Center Turn/Two-Way Left Turn Lane:** These center lanes are reserved for vehicles making left turns in either direction from or into the roadway. These lanes cannot be used for passing and cannot be used for travel farther than 300 feet. On the pavement, left turn arrows for traffic in one direction alternate with left turn arrows for traffic coming from the other direction. These lanes are marked on each side by solid yellow and broken yellow lines. Enter the shared lane only when safe to do so.

If a special lane has been provided for making left turns, do not make a left turn from any other lane. Enter the shared center turn lane just before you want to make the turn. If you enter too soon, you may interfere with another driver's use of the lane. Wait in the special lane until traffic clears enough to allow you to complete the desired left turn. **Do NOT** travel in the center turn lane to access a left turn lane at an intersection.

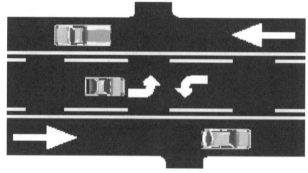

You may turn from a side street or driveway into a shared center turn lane, stop, and wait for traffic to clear before merging into traffic in the lane immediately to the right. Make sure the center turn lane is clear in both directions and then turn into the lane when it is safe.

Be sure to give the proper signal while waiting to move into the right lane and also when moving out of the turn lane back into the right lane of traffic.

If another vehicle is already in the turn lane coming from the other direction, you may NOT enter if it will interfere with the other vehicle's intended turn. When vehicles enter the turn lane from opposite directions, the first vehicle to enter the lane has the right-of-way.

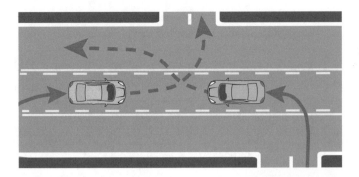

5. Reversible Lanes: Some travel lanes are designed to carry traffic in one direction at certain times and in the opposite direction at other times. These lanes are called "reversible lanes" and are usually marked by double-broken yellow lines. Before driving in them, check to see which lanes you can use for the direction of travel at that time. There may be signs posted by the side of the road or overhead. Special lights are also often used.

- A green arrow means you can drive in the lane beneath it.

- A red "X" means you CANNOT drive in the lane below.

- A flashing yellow "X" means the lane is only for turning.

- A steady yellow "X" means that the use/direction of the lane is changing and you should move out of it as soon as it is safe to do so.

These types of lanes and control devices are usually found in heavily traveled urban areas where there is a high volume of rush hour traffic coming in during the morning and going out during the afternoon.

6. Reserved Lanes: On various roadways, one or more lanes may be reserved for special vehicles. Reserved lanes are marked by signs stating that the lane is reserved for special use, and often have a white diamond posted at the side of the road and/or painted on the pavement surface. **Do NOT** travel in one of these lanes unless operating the type of vehicle indicated, or unless you must turn across the reserved lane in the next half block distance.

- **Transit** or **buses** means the lane is for bus use only.

- **Bikes** means the lane is reserved for bicycles.

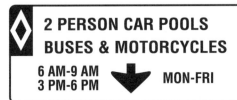

- **HOV:** High Occupancy Vehicle lanes are reserved for car pools and vehicles with more than one person in them. Signs indicate how many people must be in the vehicle, as well as the days and hours to which the reserved use applies. For example, "HOV 2" means there must be at least two people in the vehicle for you to legally drive in that lane.

7. Changing Lanes: Changing lanes on a multi-lane highway or interstate should never be done without thinking and looking. Absent-minded lane changing is extremely dangerous. Common sense, alertness and courtesy are all essential to your safety and the safety of other drivers.

Use the following steps to help you make safe lane changes:

- Pay attention to clearance space ahead and behind your vehicle.

- Check your rear view mirrors.

- Signal your intention to change lanes.

- Look over your shoulder in the direction you will be moving.

- Look behind you to both sides again.

- **Check your blind spots.** As shown above, the driver in front cannot see the motorcycle or other car just by checking his mirrors. He would need to physically turn his head and look over his shoulder in each direction to see those vehicles next to him.

- Change lanes gradually and carefully.

- Do not cruise in the blind spots of any vehicles ahead of you.

When a driver ahead of you (in your lane or the lane next to you) signals a lane change, slow down and leave space for the change. **Do NOT** speed up or change lanes yourself until the other driver has completed his intended movement. Otherwise, you could interfere with his lane change and contribute to a dangerous situation or crash.

PASSING OTHER VEHICLES

Passing another vehicle is a normal part of driving, but it can be very dangerous. Collisions resulting from improper passing are often fatal, since the impact is greater in this type of crash. Before you attempt to pass, be sure you have enough room to complete the maneuver. If you have to cut back to your lane too soon, you risk sideswiping the vehicle you are passing. If you do not cut back to your lane soon enough, you risk a head-on collision.

It is equally important to know when NOT to pass, as well as when to pass. The decision of whether or not to pass is influenced by the knowledge, judgment, attitude and behavior of the driver. BE PATIENT. Study and learn the following passing rules and practice them each time you pass another vehicle.

1. **Passing on the left requires the following safety precautions:**

Know the speed and acceleration ability of your vehicle, and be able to estimate the speed of the vehicle you are passing, as well as that of any oncoming traffic. As a rule, if you see any sign of an oncoming vehicle, it is too close for you to risk a pass. When in doubt, stay in your lane.

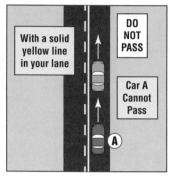 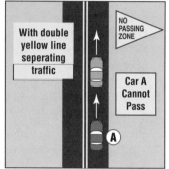

- Stay well behind the vehicle you want to pass to allow yourself a better view of the road ahead. Check well ahead for a NO-PASSING ZONE and on-coming vehicles.

- When overtaking and passing another vehicle traveling in the same direction on a two-lane road in the USA, you should pass only to the left of the vehicle.

- Signal your intended move to the left and check your rearview and side-view mirrors before changing lanes.

- Do NOT swing out across the center line for a look. If you need to do this to see, you are either following too closely or attempting to pass in an area where your sight distance is too limited to pass safely.

- Check your blind spot for any vehicle that may be starting a pass around your vehicle.

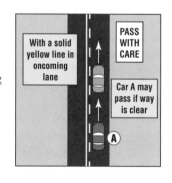

- Move to the left (oncoming traffic lane) ONLY when it is safe to do so. Pass on the left at a safe distance and do not return to the right lane until safely clear of the overtaken vehicle.

- Complete your pass as soon as possible. When you can see the entire vehicle you passed in your rear view mirror,

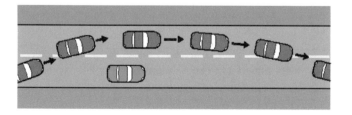

signal right and return to your lane. Be sure to cancel the signal light so that you are not driving with your right turn signal flashing.

- As a general rule, it is NOT SAFE to pass more than one vehicle at a time, although it is not illegal in Tennessee to pass multiple vehicles. It is recommended that you not even consider passing multiple vehicles unless you:

   A. Are on a straight, level roadway where your vision of oncoming traffic is excellent; AND

   B. Can complete the pass of all vehicles and be safely returned to the right lane before coming within 100 feet of the no passing markings (solid yellow line, signs, etc.) and/or any oncoming vehicles approaching from the opposite direction.

- Take extra precautions during inclement weather and twilight hours. Some oncoming vehicles may not be easily visible at these times, especially if they are not using their headlights, as required.

- Whenever possible, try to avoid passing at night, unless you are familiar with the road. It is more difficult at night to see where the passing zone ends. If you are not familiar with the roadway, a slight hill or curve in the road ahead could prove deadly.

2. **Passing on the Right:** The driver may overtake and pass another vehicle on the right only when the conditions permit passing safely. Passing on the right is never permitted by driving off the pavement of the roadway. The driver of a vehicle may overtake and pass upon the right of another vehicle only under the following conditions:

- When the vehicle overtaken has signaled to make or is about to make a left turn. **Never pass on the left of a driver who has signaled a left turn.**

- When the driver is on a street or highway with unobstructed pavement, not occupied by parked vehicles, and such paved roadway is of sufficient width for two or more lanes of moving vehicles in each direction.

- When the driver is on a one-way street which traffic is restricted to one direction of movement, where the roadway is free from obstruction and the road is sufficiently paved for two or more lanes of moving vehicles. Use extra care when you pass on the right. Often drivers do not expect to be passed on the right unless they are traveling on a multi-lane roadway.

- **Do NOT** pass on the right using a bike lane or parking lane at any location, nor in the emergency lane within sight of a traffic light or stop sign. This situation often happens at intersections when vehicles are stopped for a red light.

For example, a vehicle attempts to pass on the right and one of the cars ahead starts to make a right turn when the light changes resulting in a crash. The person passing on the right will be "at fault" because the vehicle turning right was properly traveling within the marked lane of traffic.

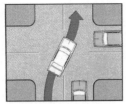

Intersections

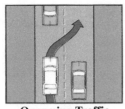

Oncoming Traffic

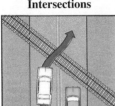

Railroads

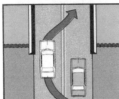

Bridges / Tunnels

3. **No Passing:** It is not always safe to pass. Make certain the way is clear. Give the proper signal before changing lanes. Tap your horn when necessary to avoid surprising the driver ahead. Avoid cutting in too quickly if you must return to your original lane. Remember, you may NOT cross the center line to pass under the following conditions:

- Do not pass when there is an oncoming car.

- Do not pass when approaching any road-way intersection, railroad crossing, narrow bridge, viaduct or tunnel.

- Do not cross the center line to pass another vehicle whenever the solid yellow line is on your side of the center lane marking.

- Do not pass unless the pass may be completed without interfering with the safety of the oncoming vehicle and before the solid yellow line reappears in your traffic lane.

- Do not pass a school bus or church bus when the flashing lights are operating and the stop arm is extended.

- Do not pass when approaching a hill or curve.

- Do not pass a car that has stopped for pedestrians in a marked or unmarked crosswalk. Passing in this type of situation is a frequent cause of death to pedestrians, especially if the passing vehicle is traveling at a high rate of speed.

Safety Tip: When stopping for a crosswalk on a multi-lane road, you should stop about 30 feet before the crosswalk so you do not block visibility of the crossing pedestrians to drivers in the other lane(s).

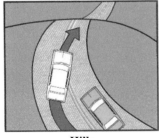

Hills

Curves

- Do not pass on the right shoulder of the highway. Other drivers will not expect you to be there and may pull off the road or turn right without looking.

- The end of a "no-passing zone" does not mean it is safe to pass. It means there is increased visibility ahead. It is still up to YOU to determine if it is safe to pass after considering all the conditions mentioned above.

- The solid yellow line marked on the pavement in a "no-passing zone" indicates that you may NOT cross the center line to pass. You are allowed to turn across the center line if you are making a left turn into or coming out of an alley, intersection, private road or driveway while in the "no-passing zone".

- Do not weave in and out of traffic by repeatedly passing on the left, then back to the right and then passing again on the left. Weaving from lane to lane in an attempt to move faster than the flow of traffic is extremely dangerous.

4. **Being Passed by Another Vehicle:** When another driver tries to pass you, there are many chances for a collision. The other driver may cut in too sharply. You may be changing lanes, or the other driver may be forced back into your lane if he/she has

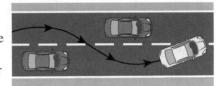

misjudged the distance of oncoming traffic. Keep everyone safe and help the other driver pass you safely by:

- Staying in your lane, and moving to the right if being passed on the left.

- Maintaining your speed. DO NOT speed up to keep the other driver from passing.

- Checking oncoming traffic and adjusting your speed to let the other driver move back into the right lane as soon as possible.

- Slowing down if you observe a car approaching from the other direction while you are being passed. By slowing down, you will allow the passing driver more space to pull back into the right lane in front of you before meeting the oncoming vehicle.

5. **Passing Bicycles**

- When passing and overtaking a bicyclist proceeding in the same direction, do so slowly and leave at least a distance between you and the bicycle of not less than 3 feet. It's the law! Also be sure to maintain this clearance until safely past the overtaken bicycle.

- As a driver you should never attempt passing between a bicyclist and oncoming vehicles on a two-lane road. Slow down and allow vehicles to pass the rider safely.

- NEVER pass a bicycle if the street is too narrow or you would force the bicyclist too close to parked vehicles. Wait until there is enough room to let you pass safely.

6. **Passing Trucks and Buses:** "It amazes me when a car cuts in front of me and then slows down! Don't they realize I

can't stop an 80,000 pound truck the way they can stop a 3,000 pound car?" This statement is heard often from truck and bus drivers regarding the actions of drivers of passenger vehicles passing them on the highway.

In addition to following the guidelines for passing any vehicle, to safely pass a large truck or bus, there are additional rules you must learn:

- Complete your pass as quickly as possible. **DO NOT** stay alongside the truck or bus. This is a common misunderstanding. Staying beside the truck or bus does not let the driver know you are there. Instead, it puts you in the driver's blindspot! If you are traveling alongside a truck or bus and can look over and see any portion of the tractor from the driver/passenger door back to fifth wheel area where the trailer is connected, you are most likely in the driver's blindspot. The driver's blindspots can be seen in the following No-Zone Diagram.

- An excellent point to remember is that **if you cannot see the side mirrors on the truck or bus you are following, then the truck or bus driver CANNOT SEE YOU.** This also means that all you can see are the back doors of the truck or bus, not a good view of the traffic situations on the road ahead. You are following too closely and greatly increasing your chance of being in a rear-end collision with the truck or bus.

- Maintain your speed. NEVER pull in front of a truck or bus (or any type of vehicle) and slow down. This takes away the safety cushion of the driver you have just passed and presents a potentially dangerous situation if you must stop suddenly.

- Keep in mind the terrain you are traveling on when passing. On a level highway, it generally takes longer to pass a truck or bus than a car. On an upgrade, these heavier vehicles often lose speed, making it easier to pass. On a down grade, their momentum will cause them to go faster, so you may need to increase your speed to pass. Remember, it is illegal to exceed the speed posted speed limit even when passing other vehicles.

- There is no need to hesitate passing a truck pulling multiple trailers. Motorists should treat these trucks as they would any other commercial vehicle and follow the same rules for sharing the road.

BACKING AND PARKING

Backing

Never back a vehicle into any travel lane with the exception of backing into a parallel parking space. Drivers do not expect a vehicle to be backing toward them and may not realize what you are doing until it is too late. If you must back your vehicle, look carefully and move slowly.

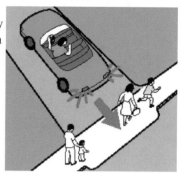

Backing is more difficult for new drivers than traveling forward because the vehicle itself blocks your field of vision. Also, it is harder to control speed and direction. You will need a lot of practice to learn to maintain absolute control of the vehicle. Although it is a small part of the driving skills test, backing is the maneuver that most often causes new drivers to fail that test.

- Backing can be dangerous because it is hard for you to see behind your car. Here are some rules you should follow whenever you have to back your car:

  A. Check behind your vehicle BEFORE you get behind the wheel. Children or small objects are hard to see from the driver's seat.

  B. Before backing, look to the front, both sides and the rear. Place your arm on the back of the seat and turn around so that you can look directly through the rear window. Do not depend solely on your mirrors. Avoid opening the door and sticking your head out to see. This is dangerous.

  C. Back slowly and gradually. Your car is much harder to control and stop while you are backing. Continue to look to all sides of the vehicle for hazards while backing.

- It is illegal to back into an intersection from a driveway. A driver must take care when backing to see that such movements can be done with reasonable safety and are not interfering with other traffic.

- Backing out of a parking space requires special caution and attention by drivers. Be aware of the movements of any cars or pedestrians near or approaching your vehicle. Be sure to look both directions before and during the backing maneuver out of the parking space. Be prepared to stop quickly if any hazard appears.

- If you miss your turn or exit, do NOT back up, but go on to the next turn or exit or where you can safely and legally turn around. It is illegal to back up on the interstate.

- Do not stop in the travel lanes for any reason (lost or confused about directions, vehicle breakdown, or letting out a passenger). Keep moving until you can safely pull your vehicle off the roadway.

Parking

Drivers are responsible for making sure that their vehicles are not hazards when parked. Whenever you park, be sure it is in a place that is far enough from any travel lane to avoid interfering with traffic and is easily visible to vehicles approaching from either direction.

All automobiles are equipped with a secondary braking system commonly called a parking brake (also referred to as an emergency or hand brake). It is good practice to apply the parking brake EVERY time you park a vehicle with a standard or manual transmission. This is particularly important when parked:

- On steep hills or inclines;
- Near a crosswalk where children are present, such as a school or playground;
- Any other area where you feel added security is prudent.

1. Routine Parking Regulations: The following are some routine rules regulating parking vehicles that every driver should know:

- Always park in a designated area if possible.
- When parking adjacent to a roadway outside the city limits, all four wheels must be off the pavement, if possible. No matter what, you must ensure that you leave at least 18 feet of road width for other traffic to pass your parked vehicle. Plus, your vehicle must be visible for at least 200 feet in either direction (200 feet is a little more than the width of a football field).
- Signs or yellow painted curbs usually mark a "NO PARKING ZONE" in cities and towns.
- It is against the law to leave the engine running in a parked unattended vehicle.
- Remove ignition keys from a parked and unattended vehicle. It is a good safety habit to lock the doors of your vehicle when it is left parked and unattended.
- A driver must look, signal and yield the right-of-way when coming out of any type of parking space, including parallel spaces.
- Always set the parking brake when you park. Leave the vehicle in gear if it has a manual transmission, or in park if it has an automatic transmission.
- The "hazard" or four-way flashing directional lights may be displayed during the hours of darkness when a vehicle is disabled or otherwise presents a traffic hazard.
- Double parking is prohibited by law.

2. WHEN PARKING ON A HILL FOLLOW THESE RULES:

- **On a downhill with a curb:** Turn the front wheels toward the curb (right) and set the parking brake. If the car rolls, it will roll into the curb, not the roadway.
- **On an uphill with a curb:** Turn the front wheels away

from curb (left). This way, if the car starts to roll back, it will roll into the curb and stop, instead of rolling into traffic.

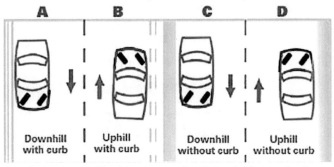

A	B	C	D
Downhill with curb	Uphill with curb	Downhill without curb	Uphill without curb

- **On a downhill without a curb:** Turn the front wheels toward the edge of the roadway (right). Again, this will prevent the vehicle from rolling into traffic if the brake fails.
- **On an uphill without a curb:** Turn the front wheels toward the edge of the roadway (right). This will allow the car to roll away from the center of the road if the brakes fail.

3. NO PARKING ZONES

There are many areas where you cannot park. It is illegal to park:

- In front of a public or private driveway
- On the paved and unpaved portions of the entrance and exit ramps of the interstate highway, except when the vehicle is disabled
- Within an intersection
- Within 15 feet of a fire hydrant
- Within a fire lane
- Within 20 feet of a crosswalk or in the crosswalk marked area
- Within 20 feet of a fire station driveway on the same side of the street or on the other side of the street within 75 feet of the fire station driveway
- Within 30 feet of a traffic signal, stop sign or any other traffic control device
- Within 50 feet of a railroad crossing
- On a sidewalk
- Upon any bridge or within a tunnel
- In a parking space clearly identified by an official sign or pavement markings indicating the space is reserved for use by a physically handicapped person, (unless you are handicapped)
- On the traffic side of another parked vehicle (double parked)
- On the shoulder of any interstate (except for an emergency situation)
- Where official signs prohibit stopping or standing.

Other parking restrictions may be indicated by painted curbs. A painted curb means that you must follow special rules to park there. The colors on the curbs mean:

WHITE
1. Stop only long enough to pick up or drop off passengers.

YELLOW
2. Stop only long enough to load or unload. Stay with your car.

RED
3. Do not stop, stand or park in this space under any condition.

4. PARALLEL PARKING
Your ability to judge distances while controlling the speed of your vehicle is the key to completing this parking maneuver. When parallel parking, be sure to continually check for oncoming traffic conditions.

STEP 1: Check traffic behind you, signal and stop, with your car even with the car in front of the open parallel space in which you are going to park. Your rear bumper should be even with the bumper of the other parked car. Your vehicle should not be any closer than two feet from the other vehicle.

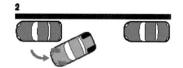

STEP 2: Turn your head to the right and look over your shoulder at the space into which you are going to back. Frequently scan to the front, observing your distance from the other parked car. Begin backing very slowly, turning the steering wheel sharply to the right until the car is at about a 45-degree angle with the street. As the front passenger side door passes the rear bumper of the other car, quickly straighten the front wheels and slowly continue to back straight.

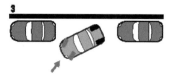

STEP 3: When your front bumper is even with the other car's back bumper, turn the wheels sharply and rapidly to the left as far as necessary. It is extremely important to remember to continually check the space around your vehicle while making this maneuver. Be especially aware of traffic on the road and the distances between your vehicle and the other parked cars.

STEP 4: Turn your steering wheel sharply to the right, and slowly pull forward toward the curb. Continue adjusting slowly and gradually until your car is centered in the parking space.

Upon completion of your parallel parking maneuver, the vehicle should be no farther away from the curb than 18

inches. As you prepare to exit the vehicle, be sure to check the traffic before opening the driver side door. Wait until any traffic has passed, get out quickly and shut the door as soon as you can. Move to the curb or sidewalk quickly for your safety.

5. EMERGENCY PARKING (Disabled Vehicles)
If it becomes necessary to leave your vehicle parked on a highway or street, follow these rules:

- Park the vehicle with all four wheels off the traveled portion of the highway, if possible. Otherwise, pull onto the shoulder of the road as far away from traffic as possible. If there is a curb, pull as close to the curb as possible.

- If you cannot move the vehicle off the highway, raise the hood or tie a handkerchief on the left door handle or antenna to warn other motorists of your stopped vehicle.

- Turn on your car's emergency flasher lights. Set your parking brake, shift into park or leave the vehicle in gear and turn off the engine. Lock the vehicle.

- A stopped car on the interstate (even on the shoulder) is extremely dangerous. Do not stop on an interstate highway except for an emergency.

- Walking on the interstate is both illegal and dangerous. Except for extreme emergency cases, remain in your disabled vehicle until a State Trooper, other police officer, emergency service vehicle or a good Samaritan stops to offer assistance.

6. HANDICAP PARKING SPACES
The handicap parking symbol, which appears on reserved parking signs, placards and license plates, is the international symbol of access for persons with a physical disability. Parking spaces marked with this symbol are only to be used by vehicles displaying a valid placard or license plate with this symbol, and only when transporting the person who was issued the placard or plate.

It is illegal for anyone else to park in these spaces. If you improperly park in these designated spaces, you will be committing a misdemeanor punishable by a $100 dollar fine, and your vehicle could be subject to being towed.

7. PARKING METERS
Many public parking spaces are regulated by coin-fed parking meters. Meter regulations are usually in effect during posted days and hours. In most areas, a maximum time limit for parking in those spaces is also posted. If you exceed the limit or fail to pay the meter fee, you may be issued a parking ticket and your vehicle may be towed.

8. ANGLE PARKING
Angle parking is often used in parking lots, shopping centers and sometimes at curbs.
When you enter an angle parking space on your right:

- Watch for traffic both ahead and behind.

- Signal and begin slowing down.

- Make sure the rear of your car will clear the parked cars.
- Steer sharply into the parking space. Then straighten the wheels, centering your car in the parking space.
- Shift to park or reverse if driving a standard transmission vehicle and apply the parking brake.

Before backing out of an angle parking space:

- Walk around to make sure nothing is in your way.
- Remember that the front of your car will swing opposite to the direction of the turn.
- Move your car back slowly. It is hard to see oncoming traffic. Be sure traffic is clear in the lane where you are backing.
- Maintain a cautious speed so you can yield if necessary to pedestrians or oncoming vehicles.
- When you can see past the tops of cars parked next to you, stop and look again. Look back and to each side for other drivers.
- Back slowly while turning until your left front wheel passes the rear bumper of the car parked on the left.
- Straighten the wheels as your car comes back into the lane for traffic.

Chapter 4B - Chapter Sample Test Questions

Here are some sample test questions. Because these are just study questions to help you review, you may receive a test with completely different questions, in whole or in part. The page number where the correct answer for each question can be found is shown. Also, answers to all the study questions can be found in the back of the book.

10. It is illegal to park:

    A. Within 15 feet of a fire hydrant.

    B. Within 50 feet of a railroad crossing.

    C. Both of the above.

    Page 65

11. The two-second rule for following at a safe distance will hold true at:

    A. Speeds up to 30 m.p.h.

    B. Any speed.

    C. Speeds up to 55 m.p.h.

    Page 48

12. Which lane must you be in before making a left turn from a one-way street?

    A. The lane nearest the left curb.

    B. The lane nearest the center of the street.

    C. The lane nearest the right curb.

    Page 57

13. Motorists are required by law when passing a bicycle traveling in the same direction to allow a minimum distance of:

    A. 1 foot

    B. 3 feet

    C. Safely away from the bicycle.

    Page 63

Interstate Highway Driving Is Different!

Traffic on interstates usually moves more safely and efficiently because access is controlled. There are no stop signs, no railroad crossings and no traffic lights. Interstates usually have few steep hills or sharp curves to limit the view of the road ahead. Limited access or controlled access means that drivers enter or leave the roadway only at entrances and exits, called interchanges, without ever crossing the path of other traffic. Interstates and divided highways have largely removed the chance of head-on collisions.

Interstate driving requires good skills and habits so you can safely get where you are going. Safe use of the interstates demands a complete awareness of a higher speed type of driving and constant alertness by the driver.

Before Driving on the Interstate

Plan the trip in advance so that you know your entrance, direction, and exit. Make sure that your vehicle is in good condition. Check the gas gauge before getting on the interstate. In rural areas, it may be many miles between exits, and you could run out of gas before getting to another gas station. If you cannot or do not wish to drive at or above the minimum speed limit, do not use the interstate.

ENTERING THE INTERSTATE

In most driving situations, you slow down or stop before you enter a busy road, but when entering an interstate, you do the opposite. You must use the merging or acceleration lane to speed up and merge with fast-moving traffic already on the interstate.

Good judgment and good timing are necessary to merge smoothly with fast-moving traffic. Upon entering the interstate on-ramp, stay to the right and increase your speed in the acceleration lane/entrance ramp. Use the ramp to reach interstate speed so you can merge smoothly into the travel lane when the way is clear. Be sure to give the proper left turn signal to indicate your need to enter the traffic lane. Drivers already on the interstate should, for their own safety, make allowance for vehicles attempting to enter. It is your responsibility to yield the right-of-way to other cars on the interstate.

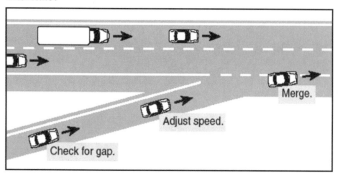

Unnecessary stopping on interstate on-ramps causes many rear-end collisions and also obstructs the even flow of traffic. Do not drive to the end of the ramp and stop, or you will not have enough room to get up to the speed of the interstate traffic. Drivers behind you will not expect you to stop. If they are watching the traffic on the main road for space to merge, you could easily be hit from the rear. If you have to wait for space to enter an interstate, slow down on the ramp so that you will still have some room to speed up before you have to merge. Heavy traffic conditions sometimes create a slowdown at an entrance ramp. Unless it is absolutely unavoidable, it is best to keep your vehicle moving at least at a slow pace.

LANE ADDED   MERGING TRAFFIC

Do you know what the difference in the two signs above is? Both appear to be telling you that traffic is coming into the main road from the right. However, there is an IMPORTANT difference.

- The "lane added" sign means that there is a new right lane added to the interstate/roadway for the incoming traffic. The on-ramp becomes a new lane and the entering traffic does not need to merge immediately. Traffic on the interstate should avoid making lane changes to the right at this location because the entering traffic will not be expecting vehicles to move into their travel path.

- The regular "merge" sign means that the traffic coming from the right is going to need to merge into the existing right hand traffic lane. Drivers on the interstate should be aware and cautious of this incoming traffic.

DRIVING ON THE INTERSTATE

Interstates usually have several lanes of traffic traveling in the same direction. On these roads, leave the extreme left lane for faster traffic. If you drive at an even speed, you will have less need to change lanes. Remember, lane-hopping any time is dangerous, annoys other drivers, increases the risk of a collision, often contributes to "road rage" and very seldom saves the driver any significant amount of travel time.

Keep your vehicle in the middle of your traffic lane. You may change lanes when necessary, but do not weave in and out of traffic. Do not travel alongside other vehicles at the same speed or you risk being in the other drivers' blind spots.

Change speed and/or lanes to avoid these situations. Avoid cars moving in packs and keep a safe space cushion around your vehicle for emergency maneuvers. If you are going to exit the interstate, move to the right lane as early as possible to avoid hasty lane changes, which could result in a dangerous situation or traffic crash.

Stay at least two seconds behind vehicles in front of you, and increase this space to a minimum of four seconds in bad weather, night driving and on higher speed rural sections of the interstate. Scan the roadway ahead and try to watch 15-20 seconds in front of your vehicle for cars braking, entering or exiting. There are times, especially in major cities, when interstates get jammed by heavy traffic or tie-ups, caused by collisions during rush hour traffic. Be alert for any hint that traffic on the interstate ahead is not moving at a normal pace.

For example, when you see cars' brake lights ahead, prepare to slow down. You may have to slam on your brakes to avoid a rear-end crash with the vehicle ahead. If you spot a tie-up causing you to slow down or stop, lightly tap your brake pedal several times to alert drivers behind you.

"Traffic Flow" and Speed Control on the Interstate

Speeds traveled on rural interstates are higher than on other roads. There are fewer stop-and-go situations. Try to keep pace with traffic on the road, but **don't be lured into exceeding the posted speed to "stay with the flow of traffic."**

- Do maintain a constant speed and keep a safe pace with other traffic.

- Do not speed up and slow down unnecessarily.

- Drive the posted speed limit if it is safe to do so.

- Driving too slowly is against the law because it is dangerous. A slowpoke on an interstate can be just as reckless as a speeder.

- Remember, if you drive at a speed below the flow of traffic, you must use the right lane.

- If the minimum speed is too high for your comfort, you should not use the interstate.

- If you are traveling in the left lane and someone comes up behind you at a faster speed, move one lane to your right.

  Left lane is for passing only.
- Courteous and safe driving practices require that drivers in
- any lane, except the right lane used for slower traffic, should be prepared to move to another lane to allow faster traffic to pass.

- Be alert to merging traffic signs.

- Remember, trucks and buses entering the interstate may need extra time to adjust to traffic patterns. Be cooperative and give them extra time and space to adjust to the traffic flow.

High Occupancy Vehicle (HOV) Lanes

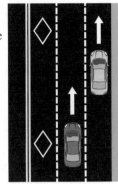

High Occupancy Vehicle (HOV) lanes are specially marked far inside traffic lanes designated for vehicles with two or more occupants. HOV lanes are designed to encourage ridesharing and to reduce the number of vehicles on the Interstate during rush hour, while at the same time moving more people through congested areas.

During high inbound traffic hours (7–9 a.m.) and high outbound traffic (4–6 p.m.), the HOV lane is reserved for the exclusive use of:

- Vehicles with two or more persons. (A baby in a car seat qualifies just like any other passenger.)

- Buses with 2 or more occupants

- Motorcycles occupied by 1 person

- Emergency Vehicles

During these hours of operation, the HOV lane may not be used by:
- Persons driving alone
- Persons driving alone passing vehicles in adjacent lanes

To enter the HOV lane, carefully merge onto the highway as you normally would and safely merge to the far inside lane. If you plan to exit the highway before the HOV lane ends, you must carefully merge over to the exit lane.

HOV lane serves as a general purpose lane on weekends and during non-peak traffic times on weekdays.

Drivers found in violation of the HOV lane are subject to a $50 fine and court costs.

LEAVING/EXITING THE INTERSTATE

Interchanges may be different, and it is important to watch for advance directional signs. Choose the right exit, and be sure you are in the proper lane well before you exit off the interstate. The heavier the traffic, the earlier you should move into the proper lane. Exit signs are usually placed at least one mile ahead of the exit turn-off.

To leave the interstate, signal your intention to change lanes, and move to the lane nearest the exit/off-ramp. Maintain speed until you enter the deceleration lane, which is usually

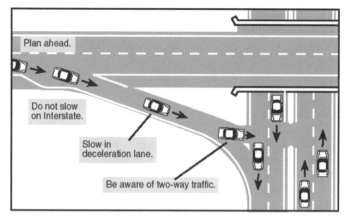

Plan ahead.

Do not slow on Interstate.

Slow in deceleration lane.

Be aware of two-way traffic.

outlined by a series of white reflectors. Reduce your speed to the exit ramp posted speed. Speed should be reduced further on the exit ramp. Your vehicle should be slowed to the posted limit for the roadway you will be entering.

The paved shoulder of the interstate should not be used for vehicular travel except for deceleration when marked for this purpose or for an emergency.

It is illegal to park a motor vehicle, whether attended or unattended upon the paved or unpaved portions of any entrance or exit ramp of any highway unless the vehicle is disabled.

It is also illegal to back up or make a U-turn on interstate highways. If you miss your exit, you must proceed to the next exit. It is illegal to cross the median on the interstate.

Interchanges

It is very important to know how to maneuver on the different types of interchanges. Two common types of interchanges are the diamond and the cloverleaf, which are diagrammed and explained in greater detail in the following paragraphs. There are various other types of interchanges and methods of maneuvering. When approaching any type of interchange, follow the signs telling you how to make the turn you want to make.

Diamond Interchange

Traffic using the interstate may gain access to the intersecting roadway by (1) taking the signed exit ramp, (2) proceeding to the cross roadway and (3) obeying the traffic sign or signal at the intersection. Turns may then be made to the right or left as at any ordinary intersection.

With a diamond interchange, you will always approach the exit ramp before passing over or under the intersecting roadway. Traffic using the cross roadway may enter the interstate by making either a left or right turn onto the appropriate entrance ramp. (1) The **RIGHT TURN** entrance ramp will always be encountered **BEFORE** crossing over or under the interstate. (2) The **LEFT TURN** entrance ramp will always be encountered **AFTER** crossing over or under the interstate.

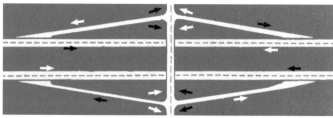

DIAMOND INTERCHANGE

(3) **NEVER MAKE A RIGHT TURN** onto a ramp **AFTER** crossing the interstate lanes. (4) Never make a left turn onto a ramp **BEFORE** crossing the interstate lanes.

Cloverleaf Interchange

At a cloverleaf interchange, all turns are right turns. To turn right, take the right turn before you get to the overpass. To turn left, take the right turn just after the overpass. The road will carry you around to join the crossroad, and you will be going in the same direction as if you had turned left at an ordinary intersection. The advantage of such an interchange is that you do not have to cross the path of traffic to make a turn.

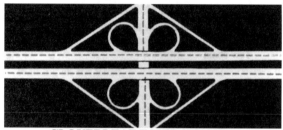

CLOVERLEAF INTERCHANGE

"Weaving" Interchange

One of the most hazardous lane management situations occurs when interstate traffic is both exiting and entering at the same lane. This weaving of vehicles trying to get on or off the highway at the same time requires the complete attention of all drivers and quick reactions for a safe maneuver. A weaving interchange takes maximum cooperation and sensible, courteous action on the part of every driver in order to work. Signs and lane markings do their part. Safe drivers have to do the rest.

You should follow the routine procedures for entering the interstate as those used at normal on-ramps. However, you must be aware that vehicles already on the interstate may be moving right to enter the exit ramp. This will require both you and the other driver to yield and share the interchange in an equal "give and take" manner. If drivers are not paying attention to the directional signs and lane design, the movement of exiting traffic can create the potential for a serious accident. Use extreme caution when using these types of interchanges.

SPECIAL INTERSTATE DRIVING INSTRUCTIONS

1. On the interstate, you may NOT:
   - Drive over or across any dividing section or separation (only emergency vehicles and highway maintenance crews may cross an interstate median).

- Make a left turn or a U-turn except through an opening provided and marked for such turns
- Change lanes without signaling.
- Drive in the blind spot of other drivers. Traveling in a position where the driver ahead of you cannot see your vehicle can be dangerous. Either stay behind or go around. Do NOT follow to the side.
- Drive onto the interstate except through an opening provided for such entrance.
- Park or stop on the interstate except at areas especially provided. Parking on the shoulder of the interstate is prohibited except in cases of emergency. You also cannot park any motor vehicle on the paved and unpaved portions of the entrance and exit ramps, unless the vehicle is disabled.
- Back up if you miss an exit. You must go to the next exit.

2. Always remember these tips for safe interstate driving:
- Drive in a dependable and predictable manner.
- Be a safe and courteous driver.
- Always signal your intentions well in advance.
- Keep your attention constantly on your driving.
- Make frequent traffic checks by looking in your rear view and side-view mirrors often.
- Keep a safe following distance between your car and the vehicle you are following.
- Check instruments often for speed and fuel supply.
- Keep pace with traffic, but don't speed illegally just because other drivers are speeding.
- Stay in the right lane if traveling slower than the other traffic.
- Be alert to merging traffic signs and vehicles entering the interstate.

3. Special situations to be aware of include:
- **Be prepared for the unexpected!** When driving on an interstate highway, look out for pedestrians who may have had a vehicle breakdown, or animals that may be on the roadway.
- **Lane Wandering:** Weaving and wandering are dangerous. Keep to the right unless overtaking or passing. Watch mirrors and signal before changing lanes. Don't cut back until it is safe. Stay aware of surrounding traffic conditions. Watch for drivers driving the wrong direction.
- **Maintain Safe Distance:** Following too closely is the cause of many multiple-car collisions. Higher interstate speeds increase danger and require greater distances between cars.
- **Night Driving:** Darkness increases driving dangers. On the basis of mileage driven, night driving is far more dangerous than day driving. Fatigue and sharply reduced vision are primarily responsible for this greater danger. Also, drinking drivers are more likely to be on the road at night.

Fight Interstate Hypnosis

Continuous interstate driving can become monotonous. A condition of drowsiness or unawareness can be brought about by reduced activity and steady sounds of wind, engine, and tire hum. This is known as interstate hypnosis. All drivers should be aware of its danger and of the methods for fighting it. Use the following tips to help you recognize and avoid this condition:

- Keep shifting your eyes. When driving, look well ahead, but avoid staring. Get into the habit of shifting your eyes left and right and checking your rear view mirror. If you sit and stare straight ahead, you can almost put yourself to sleep.
- Quit driving when you are drowsy. Drowsiness is the first step in falling asleep.
- Keep your car's interior as cool as possible.
- Stop and refresh yourself at regular intervals. Take a break and get out of the car at least every two hours, or every 100 miles or so. Even if you are feeling well, you should stop, get out of your car and walk around, allowing your muscles to relax.
- It is safest for you and others if you do not drive more than eight hours per day.

Dynamic Message Signs

Dynamic Message Signs are along Tennessee interstates in urban areas to provide traffic information to motorists. These

signs are part of the Tennessee Department of Transportation's SmartWay Intelligent Transportation System. The signs provide real-time information to motorists of traffic incidents, weather-related road conditions or road construction ahead, so drivers can consider alternate routes.

The Dynamic Message Signs not only improve driver safety and traffic flow but can also be used for (1) travel time, (2) advance notification of roadwork lane closures, (3) active lane control (4) advance notification of special events that will affect travel either because of added traffic generated or the requirement to close streets or highways, and (5) messages associated with missing child Amber Alerts or other public safety issues. These signs are normally blank when not in use.

DEALING WITH TRAFFIC CONGESTION

Chronic traffic congestion is often the Tennessee commuter's biggest headache. Small changes in driving habits could provide fast relief. Several driving behaviors that sometimes lead to accidents also contribute to traffic congestion include:

- **Rubbernecking** is perhaps the most frustrating of behaviors. Slowing down to look at crashes or virtually anything else out of the ordinary is one of the worst congestion offenders.

- **Tailgating:** Following too closely is common on Tennessee interstates. This accounts for numerous crashes, which in turn clog major routes, often for hours.

- **Unnecessary Lane Changes:** Although it produces virtually NO improvement in arrival or travel times, many motorists insist on weaving in and out of interstate lanes, which at best, slows down all traffic and at worst, causes many crashes.

- **Inattention:** Drivers can be seen eating, grooming in the rear view mirror, talking on wireless phones, text messaging, using the personal digital assistant and even reading newspapers as they drive to work.

Drivers who do not watch the fuel gauge or maintain their vehicles properly can cause traffic congestion. These vehicles can simply run out of gas, malfunction or stall on the interstate or other streets, causing bottlenecks and major slow downs in traffic flow.

If you avoid these "bad behaviors" and keep them from becoming part of your driving habits, you will help keep traffic congestion under control in Tennessee.

MOVE OVER LAW

Tennessee law requires that motorists yield the lane closest to any emergency, maintenance or recovery vehicle that is stopped on the shoulder of the roadway. This applies to interstates and any multi-lane highway (with four or more lanes) that has at least two lanes of traffic traveling in the same direction.

> ### STATE LAW
> **MOVE OVER FOR STOPPED EMERGENCY VEHICLES**
> **$500 MAXIMUM FINE**

When safety and traffic conditions allow, the motorist must yield the right-of-way by making a lane change into a lane that is NOT adjacent to the stationary emergency vehicle. This requirement to move over applies, regardless of whether the emergency vehicle is on the right or left-hand side of the road.

- If the emergency vehicle is stopped on the right shoulder, the motorist merges into the left lane of traffic, freeing the right most lane as a safety barrier.
- If the emergency vehicle is stopped on the left shoulder, the motorist merges into the right lane of traffic, freeing the left most lane as a safety barrier.

ONLY when traffic conditions make it unsafe to make such lane change is the motorist allowed to respond to this situation by simply slowing down and remaining in the same lane.

This law applies to all emergency vehicles, utility service vehicles and maintenance vehicles when the vehicle is stationary and using its flashing lights. They include:

- Police or Highway Patrol vehicles;
- Ambulance or Fire Fighting vehicles;
- Utility vehicles that provide your electric, phone, natural gas and water services as well as solid waste "sanitation" vehicles;
- Tow Trucks or TDOT HELP vehicles;
- TDOT maintenance vehicles or private contractors involved in road construction or repair work.

In addition to above mentioned stationary emergency vehicles with lights flashing, this law now applies to all stationary motor vehicles, such as your car or truck, with their emergency flasher lights on. If you are traveling on a highway having at least four (4) lanes with not less than two (2) lanes proceeding in the same direction as the approaching vehicle and you approach a stationary motor vehicle that is located on the shoulder, emergency lane, or median, and the vehicle is giving a signal by use of flashing lights, you should proceed with due caution. You should yield the right-of-way by making a lane change into a lane not adjacent to that of the motor vehicle if possible, with due regard to safety and traffic conditions.

If changing lanes would be impossible or unsafe, proceed with due caution, reduce the speed of the vehicle and maintain a safe speed for road conditions.

VEHICLE BREAKDOWNS, CRASHES AND EMERGENCY STOPPING

If you have vehicle trouble, move to the right shoulder or emergency stopping area as soon as you can. Turn on your emergency flashers to warn other traffic. If you need help, raise your hood and tie a white cloth to the hood or radio antenna. If possible, it is better to stay in or near your vehicle on the side away from traffic. Walking along the interstate is dangerous. Keep children away from traffic.

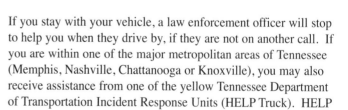

If you stay with your vehicle, a law enforcement officer will stop to help you when they drive by, if they are not on another call. If you are within one of the major metropolitan areas of Tennessee (Memphis, Nashville, Chattanooga or Knoxville), you may also receive assistance from one of the yellow Tennessee Department of Transportation Incident Response Units (HELP Truck). HELP operators have the authority to "remove or cause to be removed" any vehicle that is an "obstruction or hazard to traffic". HELP operators are trained to deal with incident scenes. You should follow their instructions just as you would those of other police or traffic control personnel. **Move It for Safety If you are involved in a traffic crash on the interstate, Tennessee law allows you to move the vehicle to help prevent blocking the traffic flow.** If the vehicle is still drivable and there are NO SERIOUS PERSONAL INJURIES or deaths, you may pull the vehicle(s) to the emergency lane and await the arrival of a trooper or police officer to the crash scene. Never attempt to move a seriously injured crash victim unless directed to do so by proper emergency personnel. Never disturb a crash scene in any manner when a fatality is involved. **Under Tennessee law, you must not leave the scene of any type of crash, and while remaining at the scene, you should not "unnecessarily obstruct traffic."**

*T H P – A Free Cell Phone Call for Help

In the event of a highway emergency, or if you need to report a driver who is violating the rules of the road, you may use your wireless phone at no charge to directly connect with the nearest Tennessee Highway Patrol Dispatch Center. Dial: * T H P (*847) and you will be connected to the nearest Tennessee Highway Patrol Dispatcher for assistance.

The Tennessee Department of Transportation has placed signs along the state's interstate system reminding motorists to move their damaged vehicles to the shoulder if no serious injury has occurred.

> **MOVE DAMAGED VEHICLES TO SHOULDER IF NO SERIOUS INJURIES**

Suggested Safety and Emergency Equipment

The following items should be kept in your car in case of a flat tire, vehicle breakdown or other roadside emergency. These items are important for all travel but especially for interstate driving.

- Spare tire in excellent condition
- Jack and tire iron
- Tire Pressure Gauge
- Can of sealant for small leaks in tire(s)
- Flash light, portable radio and spare batteries
- Car Owner's Manual
- Insurance information and car registration
- Paper, pen or pencil
- Three fuses or reflectors for night-time emergencies

- First Aid Kit
- Fire Extinguisher
- Jumper cables
- Spare bottle of windshield washer fluid
- Empty gas can and an unopened can of motor oil
- Toolbox with screwdrivers, wrenches, small hammer, scissors, duct tape, etc.
- Bottled water and some simple non-perishable snack foods (water is important to carry during the summer)
- Emergency phone numbers of family, friends and auto club or insurance agent
- Cellular phone
- During winter travel, carry a blanket, a small portable heater, window scraper for iced windows, and snow tires or tire chains

Chapter 5B - Chapter Sample Test Questions

Here are some sample test questions. Because these are just study questions to help you review, you may receive a test with completely different questions, in whole or in part. The page number where the correct answer can be located for each question is shown. Also, answers to all the study questions can be found in the back of the book.

14. When entering an interstate highway, you should:
    A. Stop, check for cars and enter when safe.
    B. Check for cars, reduce speed to 25 MPH before entering traffic lane.
    C. Check for cars, increase your speed to match the flow of traffic and merge when the way is clear.
    Page 68

15. Emergency crossovers on the interstate are legal in Tennessee for:
    A. Making a U-Turn when you missed your exit.
    B. Turning around when no others are present.
    C. Emergency vehicles and highway maintenance crews only.
    Page 71

16. Interstate driving demands require the driver to:
    A. Have a complete awareness of higher speed driving
    B. Constant alertness by the driver
    C. Both of the above.
    Page 68

DRIVING AT NIGHT

Night driving presents a serious danger, especially on poorly lighted highways and country roads. The distance that you can see clearly is greatly reduced. Dark colored animals, dark vehicles or objects on the roadside, or people walking or riding bikes and dressed in dark clothing will be harder to see.

The chances of a serious crash are much greater at night, even though traffic is not as heavy as during the day. Drivers who do not adjust to light conditions are part of the night safety problem.

- Many more deaths occur while driving at night, than driving during the day.

- The majority of a driver's reaction time depends on vision. Depth perception, color recognition, and peripheral vision are impaired after dark.

- More fatal crashes take place on Friday and Saturday nights than on any other day.

Drive Slower at Night

The basic rule for safe night driving is this: **NEVER OUTRUN YOUR HEADLIGHTS**. Driving at night is considerably more hazardous and difficult than daytime driving because your range of visibility is limited by your headlights.

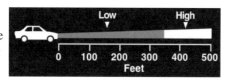

To cope with oncoming traffic during the hours of darkness you should:

a. Make sure your stopping distance is less than your sight distance.

b. Reduce your speed at night and adjust to the road and weather conditions.

c. Adjust your speed so you can stop within the distance you can see.

d. Consider how powerful your lights are and how responsive your brakes are.

e. As soon as you see pedestrians, animals, or objects on the road in front of you, be able to stop before you hit them. If you are overdriving your lights, you will not be able to stop in time.

f. Develop the ability to glance well in front of your headlight beams, looking for dark shapes on the roadway.

g. Glance periodically to the right and left to determine the location of the edge of the pavement and oncoming vehicles

h. Avoid looking directly into oncoming headlights as this

can cause momentary blindness from the glare.

i. Avoid the glare of oncoming lights by watching the right edge of the road and using the white line or road edge as a steering guide.

j. Avoid flashing your high beams to warn the other driver as it might serve as a distraction and interfere with their driving resulting in a collision.

The law requires headlights that will enable you to see clearly any person on the highway at least two hundred (200) feet ahead of your car. Since the effectiveness of headlights diminishes greatly as the distance increases, headlights must be in good order to meet this requirement. They must also be accurately aimed, with clean lenses and a clean windshield inside and out.

Glare and Glare Recovery
The glare from the headlights of oncoming vehicles causes the pupil of the eye to contract. After the vehicle has passed it takes an interval of time for the pupil to readjust to the less intense light. This is called glare recovery time. During this recovery period you are virtually driving blind. Glare recovery time is not based on visual acuity and varies from person to person. The problem is generally more acute in older drivers and those in poor physical condition.

Prepare to Fight Glare: For maximum glare prevention, keep every surface between your eyes and the road as clear as possible – including both sides of your windshield and your eyeglasses. Clean your headlights and the windows (inside and out) at least once a month.

Remember to drive safely and defensively you must adhere to the proper requirements of dimming you lights at night when:
- Meeting or overtaking vehicles within 500 feet.
- Driving in cities and towns always use your low beams
- On curves or turns to the right avoid "blasting" an oncoming car with your high beams.

Aim Your Headlights Correctly:
Your properly aligned headlights will help you see the road better, and will help other drivers to avoid glare. Lights that shine up or out excessively do NOT help you see objects in the roadway. They do however contribute to glare and blinding the vision of drivers in vehicles you are meeting or following. Check you vehicle owner's manual on how to align the lights for your car or have them aligned by a mechanic at a reputable garage or car dealership.

Parking At Night
When parking at night, never leave your headlights on, even if

you plan on being parked for a brief period of time. They are just as likely to blind approaching drivers when your car is stationary as they are when it is moving. They may also confuse approaching drivers as to the exact position of the road. The danger is increased if you are parked on the wrong side of the roadway. Whenever you park on or along a highway at night, leave your emergency and parking lights on. Parking on the shoulder of the interstate is prohibited except in cases of emergency. You also cannot park any motor vehicle on the paved and unpaved portions of the entrance and exit ramps, unless the vehicle is disabled.

DRIVING IN INCLEMENT WEATHER CONDITIONS

Wet pavement can be as treacherous as icy pavement, so always reduce your speed in wet weather. You will need additional distance for stopping, and you may skid on sharp turns.

- Slow down at the first sign of rain on the road.
- The pavement is particularly treacherous when it first begins to rain. Accumulations of dirt and oil will mix with the water, and create a greasy film on the roadway.
- This is when most roads are the most slippery and it will not give your tires the grip they need so you must drive more slowly than on a dry road.

Inclement weather creates vision problems as well as vehicle control problems. Keep your windshield wipers in good condition, and wait a few seconds after rain starts before you turn them on. There should be enough water on the windshield for the wipers to clear it, not smear it with dust and grime.

Use the defroster or air conditioner to keep windows and mirrors clear. If you drive in inclement weather or fog, reduce speed to make up for the reduced visibility.

Use headlights on low beam so the light will be on the road where you need it. In fog or mist, never put your headlights on *high beam because the light will be reflected back into your eyes.*

RAIN: Drivers must change driving habits to adjust to poor driving conditions caused by weather. Rainy weather calls for:
- Slower speed.
- Greater stopping distance.
- Driving with headlights on low beam.
- Use of wipers, defroster as needed for maximum vision.
- An early signal for all turns or lane changes.
- Braking well in advance of a stop to warn following drivers of your intentions.

FOG AND SMOKE: Tennessee experiences forest fires at any time of year, under almost any weather conditions. Where there is fire, there is ultimately smoke, and smoke does not mix well with safe driving. Tennessee also experiences air-ground temperature variances that create fog at any time of the year.

Unforseen changes in weather may create conditions where visibility on roadways is seriously impaired. Under these conditions drivers need to be cautious. The best decision is not to drive in fog or smoke. If you must drive under these conditions, there are actions that every driver should take to protect themselves and their passengers.

The best advice for driving in fog or smoke is "DON'T". If you must travel in fog or smoke you should:

- Drive with your lights on low beam. High beams will impair your visibility. Never drive with just your parking or fog lights on.
- Reduce your speed.
- Avoid crossing traffic unless absolutely necessary.
- Listen for traffic (keep radio off or turned down low and do NOT use cell phone while driving in fog).
- Use wipers and defroster as needed for maximum vision. Have good operating windshield wipers so that they do an effective job.
- Be patient! Stay to the right. Avoid passing.
- Do not stop on any roadway unless absolutely necessary. However, if you can't see the road's edge, pull off as far to the right as possible – well out of the traffic lane – and turn on your emergency flashers.
- If your car stalls or is disabled, move away from the vehicle to avoid personal injury.
- Consider postponing your trip until the fog clears.
- Adhere to warning devices in fog-prone areas.

WHEN DRIVING THROUGH DENSE FOG, HEAVY RAIN OR SNOW DURING THE DAYTIME, TURN ON YOU LOW BEAM HEADLIGHTS.
This gives you better visibility and alerts oncoming cars to your presence, it is also a requirement of Tennessee law.

Slippery When Wet
Some road surfaces are more slippery than others when wet. These roads usually have warning signs. Here are some clues to help you spot slippery roads:

- On cold, wet days, shade from trees or buildings can hide spots of ice. These areas freeze first and dry out last.
- Bridges and overpasses can also hide spots of ice. They tend to freeze before the rest of the road does.
- If it starts to rain on a hot day, pavement can be very slippery for the first few minutes. Heat causes oil in the asphalt to come to the surface and this makes the road extremely slippery until the oil washes off.

- Close to the freezing point, the road is icy and may be more slippery than at colder temperatures.

HYDROPLANING: Slow down when there is a lot of water on the road. In heavy rain, your tires can lose all contact with the roadway due to water or "hydroplaning". A slight change of direction or a gust of wind can cause your car to skid or spin.

a. If you vehicle starts to hydroplane, slow down gradually by letting up on the gas.

b. Don't slam on the brakes.

c. When hydroplaning occurs there is a loss of the traction needed to steer and brake safely.

d. Stopping distances may be tripled and steering control may be reduced or lost.

e. Hydroplaning is more common at higher speeds, although tires can hydroplane under certain conditions at ANY speed. This is one reason you must always be extremely cautious when driving in rainy weather.

Skids: "If Your Wheels Don't Roll - You Don't Have Control"
Skids are caused when the tires can no longer grip the road. Skids are caused by drivers traveling too fast for conditions. If your vehicle begins to skid:

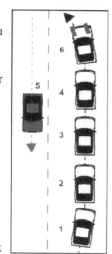

a. Stay off the brake. Until the vehicle slows, your brakes will not work and could cause you to skid more.

b. Steer. *Turn the steering wheel in the direction you want your car to go*. (For example: If rear of vehicle is skidding to the left you want to *steer* to the left to bring the front of the vehicle back "in line" and straighten the direction of motion.)

c. As soon as the vehicle begins to straighten out, turn the steering wheel back the other way. If you do not do so, your vehicle may swing around in the other direction and you could start a new skid.

d. Continue to steer. Continue to correct your steering, left and right, until the vehicle is again moving down the road under your control.

e. The best advice is to do everything you can to avoid ever skidding in the first place. Be aware of weather conditions and slow down well in advance of your stopping point.

Regaining Control of your Vehicle when the wheels have gotten off the paved roadway:

1. Stop feeding the gas. Lift you foot off the gas pedal but do NOT suddenly apply the brake.

2. Maintain a firm grip on the steering wheel, but do NOT jerk the wheel back toward the pavement suddenly.

3. Brake lightly and briefly. Do NOT slam on the brakes or hold the brake pedal down. You want to gradually slow the vehicle.

4. Maintain control of the vehicle. Keep steering the vehicle straight trying to keep the other wheels from getting off the pavement.

5. Do NOT attempt to steer back onto the pavement until there are no cars in your immediate vicinity.

6. Once oncoming traffic is clear and you have slowed the speed of your vehicle you can turn back onto the pavement.

RUMBLE STRIPES

Many of Tennessee's roads and highways are being installed with Rumble Stripes as part of the repaving project. Rumble Stripes are a series of indentations where the edge line is striped overtop the indentations. It has a secondary effect of the vibration and noise, however, its primary function is to improve wet-night visibility of the edge line. The indentations allow water to drain off the markings which improves the visibility of the line markings especially in wet-night conditions.

HIGH WATER AND FLOODING DANGERS

Each year, more deaths occur due to flooding than from any other thunderstorm related hazard. Many of these casualties are a result of careless or unsuspecting motorists who attempt to navigate flooded roads. Most people fail to realize the force and power of water. For example, only six inches of fast-moving-flood water can knock a person off their feet.

Does a heavy vehicle equal safety in flood situations? NO!
Many drivers believe their 3,000 to 5,000 pound vehicle will remain in contact with the road surface...that it is too heavy to float. Think about that for a minute. Aircraft carriers float don't they? Vehicles (and ships) float because of buoyancy.

In fact, most cars can be swept away in 18 to 24 inches of moving water. Trucks and SUVs are not much better with only an additional six to twelve inches of clearance. In moving water, all that is needed is for a vehicle to become buoyant enough to allow the water's force to push it sideways, even while the wheels remain in contact with the pavement.

Once swept downstream, a vehicle will often roll to one side or perhaps flip over entirely. The driver then has only a few seconds to escape. Many drivers panic as soon as the vehicle submerges and are found later with their safety belt intact.

The solution is simple.
TURN AROUND, DON'T DROWN®.

Stay out of the flooded roadway. The water may be much deeper than it appears as the road beds may be washed out.

Also, respect "Road Closed" barriers posted to warn you of the danger. **If a driver knowingly ignores clearly visible and adequate flood warning signs or barricades and drives into a road area that is actually flooded, the driver can be charged with reckless driving. The driver can also be responsible for the restitution of funds for the cost of your rescue.**

Keep the following safety rules in mind when driving in severe weather:

- Avoid flooded areas or those with rapid water flow. Do NOT attempt to cross a flowing stream.

- As little as six to twelve inches of water may cause you to lose control of your vehicle and two feet of water will carry most cars downstream.

- In your vehicle look out for flooding at highway dips, low spots and around bridges.

- Flooded roads could have significant damage hidden by the water. NEVER drive through floodwaters or on flooded roads. If your vehicle stalls, leave it immediately and seek higher ground.

- Do not camp or park your vehicle along streams, particularly when threatening weather conditions exist.

- Be especially cautious at night when it is harder to recognize flood dangers.

More information on flood safety is available through the National Weather Service at: www.noaa.gov/floods.htm.

Severe Thunderstorms or Tornados - listen to your car radio and be alert. If you spot a tornado, DON'T try to outrun it. Get out of the car, find shelter in a ditch or low-lying area and lie face down to protect yourself from flying debris.

Wind - Strong winds, especially crosswinds, can make it more difficult for you to control your vehicle. Wind is very dangerous if you are driving a camper, large recreational vehicle, or if you are towing a trailer. Lightweight vehicles are also more difficult to control in strong winds

a. To gain more control over vehicles in a strong wind, slow down.

b. If you are approaching an open space after driving in a protected area, be alert for crosswinds that can push you to the side or middle of the roadway.

c. If you are pulling a trailer, the wind may cause your vehicle to sway. Be ready to make necessary steering corrections.

d. When you meet large trucks or buses, you may also have to make steering corrections because of the gusts of wind these vehicles create.

○ When a truck or bus is passing you on the left, move as far as possible to the right of your lane and slow down.

○ If you are pulling a trailer, wind currents from these larger vehicles can cause your vehicle to jackknife.

○ As the large vehicle passes, accelerate slowly to keep your trailer pulling in a straight path.

e. If you are driving into a strong head wind (wind blowing toward your vehicle), you may need to accelerate more, and steering will be more difficult.

f. A strong tailwind (wind blowing from behind your vehicle) will increase your speed, so you will have to decelerate and begin braking earlier to stop.

Sun Glare - Bright sunlight in the early morning or late afternoon creates a glare when driving toward the sun. Wearing sunglasses, keeping windows clean and using the vehicle's sun visors, can reduce glare. If the sun is behind you, oncoming drivers may have the glare problem. Be aware that they may not be able to see your turn signals or your car.

Getting Stuck in Mud or Snow – after heavy rains or large snowfalls a driver may find their vehicle stuck if they get off the main paved roadway. Follow these tips when trying to get your vehicle unstuck:

a. Shift to low gear and keep the front wheels straight.

b. Gently step on the gas pedal.

c. Avoid spinning the wheels. Drive forward as far as possible.

d. Shift to reverse and slowly back up as far as possible. Don't spin the wheels.

e. Shift to low gear again and drive forward.

f. Repeat forward - backward rocking until the car rolls free.

g. Put boards or tree branches under the tires in deep mud or snow. Never do this when the tires are spinning or when the driver has the vehicle "in gear".

Most people think of tire chains as a tool only for winter driving. However you may avoid getting stuck if you always carry chains in your vehicle. Drive as far as possible to the right side of the roadway before installing your chains. Put them on the tires before driving in snow OR mud.

DRIVING IN WINTER WEATHER CONDITIONS

The three big errors of most drivers in snow and ice are:

- To over-power and spin the wheels
- To over-brake and slide the wheels
- To over-steer and skid the wheels

Reduced visibility requires that you make every effort to keep the windshield and all glass clear of snow and ice. The heater-defroster should be in good condition. Windshield wiper blades should work particularly well.

a. Carry a high quality ice scraper with a brush for removing snow, frost, and ice from your vehicle's windows, headlights, brake lights, turn signals and outside mirrors.

b. Clear snow, ice or frost from ALL windows **before** driving.

c. A good outside rearview mirror is of great help, particularly if the back window glass tends to fog over.

d. To help others see you, always use headlights when visibility is restricted by atmospheric or other weather conditions.

Inadequate Traction to Go - Overpowering and spinning the wheels reduces the available traction. Start your car slowly and avoid spinning wheels when moving your car on ice or snow.

a. Keep your speed steady and slow – but not too slow.

b. In deeper snow, it's often necessary to use the car's momentum to keep moving.

c. Have good treads on front wheels to improve steering ability. Snow tires are helpful for winter driving.

Reduced Ability to Stop and Loss of Steering - Low traction also makes stopping difficult. When traveling at 20 M.P.H., low traction can increase stopping distance to 200 feet or more.

a. Use brakes cautiously.

b. Abrupt braking can cause brake lock-up, which causes you to lose steering

c. Apply the brakes firmly, to a point just short of lock up, and then easing off the brake pedal slightly (not completely), if the wheels should lock.

d. Re-apply the brakes to a point just short of lock up and hold.

e. Do NOT pump the brake pedal, just apply steady pressure. This will give you the best combination of braking effort and directional control.

Remember: Continuous hard braking on snow and ice can result in the locking of the front brakes causing a loss of steering. Always maintain a safe speed for these conditions to avoid excessive braking.

ABS – Antilock brakes are designed to overcome a loss of steering control. To make antilock brakes work correctly, or work at all, you should apply constant, firm pressure to the pedal. During an emergency stop, push the brake pedal all the way to the floor, if necessary, even in wet or icy conditions.

Ice on Roads and Bridges – Where Not Expected: The sunny side of a hill may be wet, the shady side covered with thin ice. Usually, signs indicate that ice forms on bridges sooner than on the adjoining roads. In such instances, the car ahead of you may have crossed the icy part of the road and stopped. But a long patch of ice behind his car can easily cause you to skid into him.

Ice and Snow Made Slippery by Traffic – On streets and highways where there is considerable stop- and- go traffic, it does not take long after a storm before the snow packs hard and becomes extremely slippery because of many sliding and spinning wheels. To some extent, steering to one side or the

other of the packed section will help avoid the slickest surface. However, great caution should be used when driving on ice and snow.

Hailstorms/Sleet – find shelter by driving under an overpass or bridge.

Chapter 6 - Chapter Sample Test Questions

17. Continuous hard braking on ice and snow often:
    A. Helps you stop faster.
    B. Locks the front wheels causing the loss of steering control.
    C. Keeps the brakes hot and prevents them from freezing.
    Page 78

18. When driving in foggy conditions, do not put your headlights on high beam because:
    A. The light from the fog creates blurry vision on your eyes.
    B. Approaching vehicles won't be able to see your oncoming vehicle.
    C. Low beams provide greater visibility and you can be better seen by other vehicles.
    Page 75

19. Driving at night is:
    A. Safer because of less traffic and less distractions.
    B. More hazardous because your range of visibility is limited by your headlights.
    C. Safer and allows you to increase your speed while adjusting to road conditions.
    Page 74

Section B-7 ALCOHOL, OTHER DRUGS AND DRIVING

PLEASE NOTE: Tennessee is serious about educating the public on the tragedies of driving under the influence of drugs or alcohol. To underscore this, by law, at least 25 percent of the questions on the knowledge test must consist of questions dealing with this topic.

IMPAIRED DRIVING

Alcohol and You
Researchers estimate that between the hours of 10:00 p.m. and 2:00 a.m., 1 of every 10 drivers is intoxicated. More than one-third of these drivers have been drinking at someone else's home. Nearly 50 percent of the drivers arrested for driving under the influence (DUI) are social to moderate drinkers. **Don't think that it won't happen to you.** In your lifetime, there's a high probability that you'll be involved in an alcohol-related crash.

An Overview Of The Effects Of Alcohol
Before you can fully understand why drinking and driving result in fatalities on the highways, you first need a better understanding of the effects of alcohol on the body.

How Does Alcohol Affect the Body?
Alcohol begins to be absorbed into the bloodstream within one to two minutes after an alcoholic beverage is consumed. As you consume alcohol, it accumulates in your blood. Intoxication occurs when you drink alcohol faster than the liver can oxidize it. As the percentage of alcohol in your blood increases, you become more intoxicated.

Once in the bloodstream, the alcohol is distributed to all parts of the body, including the brain and liver. Upon reaching the liver, the alcohol immediately begins to be oxidized. However, the liver can only oxidize about one drink per hour. Contrary to popular belief, this rate cannot be increased by drinking coffee, exercising, taking a cold shower or anything else. **Only time can sober a person who's been drinking. And remember, it is a slow process.**

What Is Blood Alcohol Concentration (BAC)?
Blood Alcohol Concentration (BAC) is a measurement of the percentage of alcohol in the blood. The higher the BAC number, the more impaired a person is. **In most states, including Tennessee, .08 is the level of intoxication which is always illegal.** This means that for every 10,000 drops of blood in a person's body, there are eight drops of alcohol. BAC changes with body weight, time spent drinking, and the amount of alcohol that is consumed.

Amount of Alcohol Consumption
Each drink consumed within an hour increases the BAC level. The more you drink in a fixed amount of time, the higher your BAC will register. This happens no matter what you weigh — or what kind of alcoholic beverage you drink.

Rate of Alcoholic Consumption
Drinking three drinks in one hour will affect you more than drinking three drinks in three hours. Spacing the drinks over a longer period of time will slow the rate at which you become intoxicated and indicates responsible drinking habits.

Body Weight and Fat
The heavier the person, the more alcohol it takes to raise the BAC. Be aware of your size when drinking with others. If you are smaller than your friends and try to drink as much as they do, your judgment and inhibitions will probably be affected sooner.

Body fat also determines how quickly you are affected by alcohol. Alcohol is able to be absorbed in water, not fat. This simply means that people with less body fat have more water in which to dilute the alcohol. So, drink for drink, if people weigh the same, the one with more body fat will show signs of intoxication first.

Amount of Food in the Stomach
All the alcohol consumed eventually gets into the blood whether you have eaten or not. Food in the stomach causes alcohol to be absorbed more slowly, slowing down the rate and the amount of intoxication.

Overall Condition of the Body
Heavy and chronic drinking can harm virtually every organ and system in the body. The liver is particularly vulnerable to alcohol's harmful effects since it oxidizes approximately 90 percent of the alcohol in the body. If the liver is damaged or diseased, the rate of oxidation is reduced, causing the alcohol to stay in the body longer and the BAC to be higher for a longer time. Further, the effects of alcohol on the liver can lead to such diseases as hepatitis and cirrhosis.

RELATIONSHIP OF ALCOHOL TO TRAFFIC CRASHES

Driving after drinking is a widespread problem. It is estimated that two in every five Americans (or 40%) will be involved in an alcohol-related crash at some time in their lives.

Each drink drastically increases your risk of having a traffic crash. Look at the table on Page 80 named Alcohol's Effects on Driving Ability.

With a BAC of .10 percent, you are seven times more likely to cause a crash than if you were sober.

As your BAC increases to .15 percent, your chances of causing a traffic crash increase to 25 times.

At .17 percent BAC, you are 50 times more likely to cause a crash.

Alcohol's Effects on Driving Ability

BAC	Rough Number of Drinks	Risk of Automobile Crash	Comment
.01-.03%	◊ 1 drink within 15 min.	Rises for young adults and others with low tolerance for alcohol	Stiff penalties for BAC as low as .02 if driver under age 21
.04-.07%	◊ 2 drinks within 1/2 hour	Definite for anyone with low tolerance levels	Most people feel high and have some loss of judgment. You may get louder and have some loss of small muscle control, like focusing your eyes.
.08%-above		**LEGAL INTOXICATION*** — Judgment and reasoning powers are severely hampered; cannot do common simple acts. **Definitely unsafe to drive**.	
.10-.12%	◊ 4 drinks within 2 hours	Increases 7 times the normal rate	Judgement loss increases. Many people claim they're not affected anymore, as if they would drink themselves sober when they are actually being affected more.
.13-.15%	◊ 5-7 drinks within 3 hours	25 times the normal rate	You have far less muscle control than normal and feel happy, even though stumbling and acting foolishly.
.16-.25%	◊ 8-12 drinks within 4 hours	50 times the normal rate	You are confused and need help doing things, even standing up. Alcohol-related highway fatalities sharply increase.

*Lower levels are set for younger drivers, commercial drivers, and subsequent offenses, as discussed later in this chapter.

Behavior at each BAC level may differ somewhat with each individual. ALL people at the .10 percent level are definitely too impaired to drive safely. **Research has proven that driving skills, good judgment and vision are greatly impaired at BAC levels as low as .03 and .04 percent, especially for young drinkers.** The above table, named Alcohol's Effects on Driving Ability, describes different levels of intoxication and degree of behavior impairment at each level.

Alcohol's Effects on Driving Ability

Driving involves multiple tasks, and the demands can change continually. To drive safely, you must maintain alertness, make decisions based on ever-changing information present in the environment and execute maneuvers based on these decisions. Drinking alcohol impairs a wide range of skills necessary for carrying out these tasks. Fatal injuries, resulting from alcohol-related traffic crashes, represent a tremendous loss of human life.

The plain and simple fact is that you cannot drive safely when you are impaired by alcohol. The two abilities most important to the driving task are judgment and vision, both of which are affected by small amounts of alcohol. Your ability to judge speed, time and distance are altered after only one drink. Each extra drink greatly affects your driving ability. In addition, your reaction time and coordination begin to deteriorate, while your alertness and concentration fade. All of this adds up to a deadly combination.

Judgment: Ability to Think Clearly and Make Quick Decisions

Good judgment decreases with the use of alcohol. The concern for physical well being also lessens. People under the influence of alcohol take unnecessary and dangerous risks. Examples are driving too fast, passing cars without enough clear distance and speeding around curves. Showing off is another example of impaired judgment.

Vision: Ability to See Clearly Straight Ahead, to the Side and at Night

Alcohol decreases clearness of vision. It reduces the ability to see clearly at night by more than half. Glare vision is poor because of relaxed eye muscles. Glare recovery is also slowed by alcohol. Side vision is reduced by about 30 percent at .05 percent BAC. Judging depth or distance is affected because alcohol causes each eye to get a slightly different picture. These vision impairments greatly increase the chances of a head-on or rear-end collision. Eye muscles are relaxed by alcohol and cannot focus properly. Because the eyes provide almost 90 percent of the information used in driving, any restriction in vision can cause disastrous results.

Reaction Time and Coordination:
This is the ability to react quickly and safely to an emergency or hazardous situation—being able to keep eyes, hands and feet working together.

Reaction and coordination are impaired by alcohol consumption as low as .02 percent BAC. It takes longer to react. Coordination skills to control the car with hands, feet and eyes in response to other vehicles and the road are drastically reduced as alcohol intake increases.

Alertness and Concentration
Being ready to react to changing driving conditions or situations, keeping your mind on driving and paying attention to the task at hand.

Alcohol, in any concentration, is a depressant, not a stimulant. Alcohol slows all nerve impulses and body functions. The false feeling of stimulation that comes with small doses of alcohol is caused by the lessening of inhibitions. That's because the particular portion of the brain controlling this part of behavior is being relaxed. In reality, alcohol has the effect of limiting a driver's ability to be alert and to concentrate.

"Every Day" Drugs
One of the most common and most dangerous instances of drug abuse occurs when people mix alcohol with prescription and over-the-counter drugs. For example, when alcohol is combined with another depressant, like tranquilizers or sedatives, the results are not just added together; they are multiplied. Even some over-the-counter medicines can affect driving. The effects are much stronger, much more dangerous and can affect your driving skills.

If your doctor prescribes a tranquilizer or sedative, make a point to discuss how the drug will affect your ability to drive safely. Just because a drug is prescribed, by law, this is NO defense for driving under the influence of it.

Non-prescription drugs, such as cold tablets, cough syrups, allergy remedies, etc., purchased over-the-counter may contain antihistamines, alcohol, codeine and other compounds that can be especially dangerous for drivers. Read labels and pay attention to warnings (e.g., "may cause drowsiness," "do not operate machinery," "caution against engaging in operations requiring alertness").

If you have questions about a particular drug or combination of drugs, check with your doctor or pharmacist.

DRIVING UNDER THE INFLUENCE OF DRUGS OR ALCOHOL (THE "DUI" LAW)

Studies indicate that marijuana and other drugs also affect judgment and motor functions. This makes driving under the influence of drugs other than alcohol dangerous as well. In Tennessee, it is unlawful for any person to drive or be in physical control of an automobile or other motor-driven vehicle on any public street, highway, road or alley, or while on the premises of any shopping center, trailer park, apartment house complex, or any place frequented by the public while:

1. Under the influence of any intoxicant, marijuana, narcotic drug or drugs producing stimulating effects on the central nervous system; or
2. While the alcohol concentration of the operator's blood or breath is .08 percent or higher.

The defendant's ability to drive when using drugs may be sufficiently impaired to constitute a DUI violation. A driver can register a BAC of .00 percent and still be convicted of a DUI. The level of BAC does not clear a driver when it is below .08 percent. If a law enforcement officer observes things, such as erratic driving behavior, or maintaining an inappropriate speed (too fast or too slow), it would be sufficient cause for stopping the vehicle to investigate. Further sobriety checks could lead to the conclusion that the driver was indeed "Driving Under the Influence" of an intoxicant, narcotic drug or other drug producing stimulating effects on the central nervous system, including prescription drugs. If you have any doubt about your ability to drive, don't get behind the wheel.

Implied Consent Law
By law, when you drive in Tennessee, you have given your consent to be tested to determine the alcohol or drug content of your blood. This test must be administered at the request of a law enforcement officer who has reasonable grounds to believe you have been driving under the influence of an intoxicant or drug.

If you are placed under arrest and a law enforcement officer asks you to take the test and you refuse, it will likely result in the suspension by the court of your driving privileges for twelve (12) months.

No Refusal Law
The No Refusal law was passed in 2012 and allows law enforcement officials to seek search warrants for blood samples in cases involving suspected impaired drivers. The goal is to help law enforcement deter impaired driving while reducing crashes and fatalities on Tennessee roadways.

Consequences of a DUI Arrest
Drinking and driving poses several problems. One is the probability of an accident, and another is being arrested for DUI. The penalties for a DUI arrest are the same whether the driver was drinking alcohol or taking drugs (even prescription or over-the-counter drugs). If you are arrested for DUI, the consequences can be severe.

Penalties Applying to Any DUI Conviction
Regardless of whether the conviction for driving under the influence is a driver's first or not, several other laws apply:

- **IDs with "DUI Offender:"** If a person with a license revoked for DUI applies for a photo identification license to carry during the period before his or her license can be restored, the department is required to indicate on the ID that the person is a DUI offender.

- **Litter Removal:** A DUI conviction also requires as a condition of probation, litter pick-up for three eight-hour shifts. While removing litter, the offender has to wear a vest or other clothing displaying the message, "I am a DRUNK DRIVER." If the offender is a Tennessee resident, the litter pick-up is done in his/her home county.

DUI Penalties

	Jail Time	Fines	License Revocation Period	Vehicle Seizure
1st Conviction	48 hours (7 days if BAC is 0.20% or more)	$350-$1500	1 year	Does not apply
2nd Conviction	45 days – 11 months, 29 days	$600-$3500	2 years	Vehicle is subject to seizure and forfeiture
3rd Conviction	120 days – 11 months, 29 days	$1,100 - $10,000	3 -10 years	Vehicle is subject to seizure and forfeiture
4th or subsequent Conviction (is a Class E felony)	150 days – max allowable for a Class E felony	$3,000-$15,000	5 years [to indefinite]	Vehicle is subject to seizure and forfeiture

- **Vehicle Seizure:** A vehicle can be seized if a driver is charged with driving on a revoked license when his/her driving privileges are already revoked as a result of a DUI conviction (first or subsequent).

- **Vehicular Homicide:** If you are operating a motor vehicle under the influence of a drug or alcohol, and you are involved in a crash resulting in the death of another person(s), you may be charged with vehicular homicide. If convicted, you may be fined and sentenced to prison.

- **Aggravated Assault:** If you are operating a vehicle under the influence of a drug or alcohol, and you are involved in a motor vehicle crash that results in the injury of another person, you may be charged with aggravated assault. If convicted, you may be fined and sentenced to prison.

- **Child Endangerment:** Known as the Drunk Driving Child Protection Act, there are added penalties for people who violate DUI laws when accompanied by a child under 18 years old. There is a mandatory minimum jail sentence of 30 days, and a mandatory minimum fine of $1,000. Both of these child-related penalties are added onto any other incarceration, penalty and fines. If the child suffers serious bodily injury, the violation is a Class D felony, and if the child dies, it is a Class C felony of especially aggravated child endangerment.

Additional DUI Penalties

In addition to the minimum penalties above, the judge will also require the following of the DUI offender:

- To undergo a drug and alcohol treatment assessment and receive treatment, as appropriate, for those who have had a prior DUI in the five years prior to the current DUI.

- Participation in an alcohol safety DUI school program, if available; or

- Participation in a program of alcohol or drug rehabilitation at a treatment facility, if available, for second and subsequent convictions; and

- The payment of restitution to any person

suffering physical injury or personal losses as a result of the DUI, if the offender is economically capable of making restitution.

- The driver's vehicle will be seized if he/she has two DUI convictions within five years **AND** both events happened after January 1997.

Only a motor vehicle equipped with a functioning ignition interlock device (which keeps a car from starting if the driver's BAC is too high). The restriction can be from six months to one year for a first offense, up to three years for a second offense and up to 10 years for third and subsequent offenses

Please note that a person with 2 DUIs in a five year period MUST operate a motor vehicle with the ignition interlock device for six months after reinstatement of driving privileges.

Remember, driving while under the influence of drugs—even prescription drugs—carries the same penalties as for alcohol.

DUI's Are Expensive!
Besides being extremely dangerous and against the law, DUI's are costly. In addition to the fines and court costs, a person charged with DUI can be faced with posting bond to get released from jail, attorney fees, loss of time from work to attend court hearing(s), loss of time from work to serve time in jail, fees for alcohol safety courses and possible treatment, increased insurance premiums, and other expenses. This can add up to several thousand dollars.

YOUNG DRIVER RISKS AND LAWS

Not Just Driving—Riding With Others!
Young people remain especially vulnerable to the threat of alcohol and other drugs. This is not only from their own impaired driving, but also from getting in the car with other drivers who are not sober. **TRAFFIC CRASHES ARE THE LEADING KILLER OF YOUNG PEOPLE, AND NEARLY HALF ARE ALCOHOL RELATED.** In a national survey, nearly half of 10th graders and a third of eighth

graders reported having ridden during the past month with a driver who had used alcohol or other drugs before taking the wheel.

Crash records indicate that young drivers under the influence of small amounts of alcohol appear to have more driving problems than older drivers. Most teenagers are intoxicated at low BAC levels. The young driver's chance of a crash is much greater with BAC between .01-.08 percent than older drivers. This is due to low tolerance of alcohol and limited driving experience.

THE DECISION IS YOURS. BE RESPONSIBLE AND SMART—HELP YOURSELF AND YOUR FRIENDS!

Under 21 Laws

In addition to the standard penalties for driving under the influence of drugs or alcohol discussed previously, there are three special laws that apply to people under the age of 21:

- **18-20 Alcohol Violations:** If you are 18, 19 or 20 years old and are convicted of purchasing, attempting to purchase, or possessing any alcoholic beverage, you will lose your privilege to drive for one year. If it happens a second time you will lose your license for two years. The law applies to any alcohol-related conviction, whether or not you were driving or even in a vehicle.

- **Juvenile Offenders:** If you are between the ages of 13 and 17 and are found to have possessed, consumed or sold either alcohol or drugs, your driving privilege will be suspended for one year or until age 17, whichever is longer. Even if you have never been licensed, you could lose your privilege to drive until you reach age 17. If you have a second conviction, the suspension is for two years or until age 18, whichever is longer.

- **Under 21 BAC:** A person who is at least 16, but is not yet 21 years old, and who is found: (1) driving with a BAC of .02 percent; (2) under the influence of alcohol; or (3) under the influence of any other intoxicant, will be convicted of underage driving while impaired. Penalties for this conviction are: losing your license for one year, a fine of $250 and sometimes, includes public service work.

PREVENTION OF DRINKING AND DRIVING

The best advice, of course, is simply to not drink when you know you are going to drive. One of the most successful programs in recent years has been the designated driver concept, where friends agree ahead of time which person will remain strictly sober. Many night clubs offer the designated driver free non-alcoholic beverages for the evening. Young people, who do not want to drink in the first place, are finding it more socially acceptable to offer to be the designated driver.

Avoiding the Risks

Alcohol-related crashes are not accidents. They can be prevented. If you are planning a night on the town, decide before you start drinking that you are not going to drive. Remember, alcohol affects your judgment. It's a lot more difficult to make the decision not to drive after one or two drinks.

Use the following tips to keep from drinking and driving and still have a good time:

- Drive to social events in groups of two or more and have the driver agree not to drink.

- Arrange to ride with a friend who is not drinking.

- Before you start drinking, give your vehicle keys to someone who isn't drinking and who won't let you drive after drinking.

- If someone offers you a drink and you plan to drive, simply say, "No thanks, I'm driving."

Did You Know?

1. The amount of alcohol in one (12 ounce) bottle of beer is about equal to that in a (1 ounce) shot of whiskey.

2. When alcohol is consumed, it quickly reaches the brain where it short-circuits the parts that control judgment, emotions and confidence.

3. The first thing affected after drinking alcohol is a person's judgment.

4. Reliable research studies show that two or three drinks of alcohol in three hours or less impair the driving ability of most individuals.

5. It takes about one hour to cancel the effects of one drink. It takes about three hours to cancel the intoxicating effects of three drinks.

6. Alcohol-related vehicle crashes are the number one killer of persons under the age of 40.

7. Many drugs, even legal over-the-counter drugs, can impair your ability to drive. If you are taking them for a cold, they make you feel well enough to drive, but they can also affect alertness, judgment, coordination and vision.

8. The combined use of alcohol and other depressant drugs, such as antihistamines, may be more dangerous to health and highway safety than the effects of either the alcohol or drugs alone.

We Are Doing Better

In 2020, 11654 deaths nationwide, (30% of all traffic fatalities) were alcohol-related. 27% of all traffic fatalities (326 deaths) in Tennessee for 2020 were alcohol-related. Of the 326 deaths, 122 also involved a driver who used drugs.

In 2021, the percentage of alcohol-related fatalities was approximately 24%. The percentage of fatalities involving an impaired (drug or alcohol) driver in 2021 was approximately 41%. Only safe driving and adhering to laws that prohibit drinking and impaired driving will reduce the number of traffic fatalities.

Let's get this percentage lower!
NOTE: This chapter was written in consultation with the Tennessee Association of Alcohol, Drug and Other Addiction Services (TAADAS).

For further information on the general subject of drug and alcohol use and abuse, or for referrals for help with such problems, call the toll-free "Redline" at 1-800-889-9789. Or, check the TAADAS web site: www.taadas.org

Chapter 7 - Chapter Sample Test Questions

Here are some sample test questions. Because these are just study questions to help you review, you may receive a test with completely different questions, in whole or in part. Please note that 25 percent of your test questions will be found in this chapter. The page number for where the correct answer can be located for each question is shown.

20. Driving while under the influence of drugs carries:

    A. The same penalty as for alcohol

    B. A lesser penalty than for alcohol.

    C. Absolutely no penalty at all.

    Page 81

21. If you have had three beers in the past hour, about how long will it take for all the alcohol to leave your blood stream?

    A. One hour

    B. Two hours

    C. Three hours

    Page 83

22. As the percentage of alcohol (BAC) in your blood increases, you become:

    A. More intoxicated

    B. More sober

    C. More coordinated

    Page 79

23. Implied Consent Law means:

    A. If asked, you will take a test to determine alcohol or drug content in the blood.

    B. The laws apply even without any signs, markings or signals present at an intersection.

    C. The owner of the vehicle will carry proper insurance.

    Page 81

24. Which of the following driving skills are affected by the use of alcohol and/or drugs?

    A.   Alertness and concentration

    B.   Reaction time and coordination

    C.   All of the above are affected.

    Page 80

Section B-8 DRIVING RESPONSIBILITIES

Problem Driver Pointer System

The Problem Driver Pointer System (PDPS) is used by the Tennessee Department of Safety and Homeland Security to search the National Driver Register before issuance of a driver license. The National Driver Register is a repository of information on problem drivers provided by all 51 U.S. jurisdictions.

Based on information received as a result of the National Driver Register search, PDPS will "point" the Department of Safety Driver License Examiner to the State of Record(s), where an individual's driver status and history information is stored.

If you apply for a Tennessee license — whether it is your first license here, or some other transaction such as a renewal — and you have a problem in another state, we cannot issue you a license until the matter is resolved.

The National Driver Register contains names and limited other identifying information about individuals whose licenses have been canceled, denied, revoked, suspended, or who have been convicted of certain serious traffic violations. If records indicate you have a problem in another state, the examiners will provide you the name of the state reporting the problem and a telephone number you can use to contact that state to clear your record there.

Please Note: To get specific information about what the other state has reported to the PDPS system, you will need to contact the other state. Tennessee does not have this information. We are only provided with the fact that the other state has reported a problem.

LOSING YOUR PRIVILEGE TO DRIVE

In Tennessee, a driver license may be revoked or suspended for the following situations:

1. Driving under the influence of alcohol or drugs, including the failure to submit to a test to determine the blood/alcohol level. (Implied Consent)

2. Allowing unlawful use of a driver license, including fraudulently altering a driver license or allowing another individual to use your license or identification.

3. Mental or physical difficulties that interfere with a driver's ability to safely operate a vehicle (e.g., Alzheimer's disease, seizures and loss of consciousness).

4. Leaving the scene of a personal injury or fatal crash; failure to stop and render aid in a vehicle crash.

5. Perjury, or giving false information on the use or ownership of a vehicle, or for the issuance of a driver license.

6. A felony that involves the use of a vehicle.

7. Evading arrest while operating a motor vehicle.

8. Manslaughter/vehicular homicide involving the operation of a vehicle.

9. Two reckless driving violations within 12 months.

10. Drag racing.

11. Habitual recipients of moving traffic violations.

12. Not complying with the terms of a judgment found against the driver for damages resulting from a motor vehicle crash.

13. Purchasing or possessing any alcoholic beverage, if under 21 years old.

14. Failure to comply with child support requirements.

15. Driving a motor vehicle away from a gas station without paying for dispensed gas or diesel fuel.

16. Failure to show evidence of vehicle insurance/financial responsibility to an officer when involved in a crash or charged with a moving violation.

17. Possession by a driver of five or more grams of methamphetamine in a vehicle.

In addition, persons under the age of 18 may lose their driving privileges for:

- Convictions of any drug or alcohol offense, whether or not the offense occurred while driving;

- Dropping out of school (which is defined as having 10 consecutive or 15 total days in a semester of unexcused absences);

- Failure to make satisfactory progress in school (which, in general, means passing three subjects per grading period); or

- Possession or carrying weapons on school property.

Whenever a driver license is suspended or revoked, it must be turned in to the Department of Safety within 20 days of the suspension or revocation. Any Tennessee Highway Patrol Office or Driver License Service Center can take your license and see that you are given credit for returning it. The license may be mailed to:

**Tennessee Department of Safety and Homeland Security
PO BOX 945
Nashville, Tennessee 37202**

Failure to surrender your license means that you will be fined $75 in addition to any other fines and costs you may owe.

Hearings

Before any license is suspended, revoked or canceled, the department will notify the licensee in writing of the proposed suspension, revocation or cancellation. If your license is about to be suspended, revoked or cancelled, the department will give you an opportunity for a hearing prior to action, except in cases of final judgments and convictions.

IMPORTANT: If you have a new address, you must report it to the Department of Safety within ten (10) days of the change. Although the new address may not appear on your license until you receive a new/renewed/reinstated license, your address must be correct on the official Driver License file. You may make this change:

(a) **by internet—www.tn.gov/safety**

(b) **by letter to: Tennessee Department of Safety and Homeland Security, P.O. Box 945, Nashville, TN 37202,**

(c) **by completing a change-of-address form available at any Driver License Service Center**

Without your correct address, you may not receive important information concerning the status of your driver license.
(Also, you could be "ticketed," if correct address is not on file.)

Non-Resident Violator Compact

Tennessee is a member of the Non-Resident Violator Compact. In a nutshell, this compact means that regardless of where you receive a citation for a traffic violation, you must either appear in court to answer the citation or meet any other requirement the court may set out to satisfy the citation. If you ignore the citation — whether it was issued for a traffic violation here or in another member state, your driving privileges will be suspended, revoked or canceled. The suspension, revocation or cancellation remains in effect until the court notifies the Tennessee Department of Safety and Homeland Security that the citation has been properly disposed of and the proper fees are paid.

Reinstatements

Steps you need to follow to have your driver license reinstated depend on several factors, including why you lost your license and what else is on your record. To clear your record, you must contact:

Tennessee Department of Safety and Homeland Security
Financial Responsibility
P.O. Box 945
Nashville, Tennessee 37202
Phone: (866) 903-7357.
For the Hearing Impaired, TTY USERS SHOULD HAVE THE TENNESSEE RELAY SERVICE CALL (615) 532-2281.
Internet Website: www.tn.gov/safety

DRIVER IMPROVEMENT PROGRAM

The Department of Safety keeps records of traffic violations and crashes for each driver. These records are based on reports forwarded to the department by the courts, and on reports of traffic crashes submitted by investigating officers.

Each traffic violation or crash on a driver's record is given a point value. The assignment of point values for various offenses is designed to impress upon drivers the importance of complying with traffic laws and regulations. If they do not

comply, they may establish a bad driving record leading to suspension of driving privileges.
See chart on page 86 showing points assigned for violations and crashes.

Adult drivers (18 years of age or older) who accumulate **12 or more points** within a 12-month period receive a notice of proposed suspension. To keep adult drivers aware of the possibility of losing their driving privileges, an **advisory letter** is mailed to any licensee having 6 to 11 points on his/her driving record within any 12 months.

Juvenile drivers (less than 18 years of age) who accumulate **6 or more points** within a 12-month period receive a notice of proposed suspension. To keep juvenile drivers aware of the possibility of losing their driving privileges, an **advisory letter** is mailed to any licensee having 1 to 5 points on his/her driving record within any 12 months.

Drivers may choose to attend a Defensive Driving Course to avoid license suspension or to reduce the period of suspension. However, the Defensive Driving Course option is only available once in any five-year period. After a hearing, the department will take whatever action is necessary to correct and improve poor driving habits by education, re-examinations and/or placing necessary restrictions on the licensee and probation. If these steps are unsuccessful, the department will have no other choice than to suspend the person's driving privileges.

Frequent Traffic Violations

Frequent traffic violations and crashes are dangerous and costly. Upon the completion of the suspension time, you must pay the appropriate reinstatement fees and submit proof of liability insurance/financial responsibility (SR-22 insurance is required for adult drivers) with the department before you can get your regular license.

DRIVING WHILE YOUR LICENSE IS SUSPENDED WILL RESULT IN THE EXTENSION OF THE SUSPENSION PERIOD AND COULD ALSO RESULT IN CRIMINAL PROSECUTION.

RESTRICTED DRIVER LICENSES

When a driver license is suspended or revoked, but the driver depends on his or her driving to make a living or to continue schooling, there are certain conditions in which the driver may apply for a restricted driver license. The **restricted license** permits the driver to operate a motor vehicle for very specific purposes that are spelled out when the license is issued. The procedures for applying for a restricted license depend upon the reason the license was taken away in the first place, as summarized below:

1. **DUI:** After conviction for DUI, the trial judge may issue an order for a restricted license to go to and from work, attend college full time, attend religious services at their place of worship, drive as part of employment, a scheduled

POINTS FOR MOVING TRAFFIC VIOLATIONS AND CRASHES

POINTS	SPEEDING	
3	Where speed not indicated	Construction Zone: 4 pts
1	1 thru 5 m.p.h. in excess of speed zone	Construction Zone: 2 pts
3	6 thru 15 m.p.h. in excess of speed zone	Construction Zone: 4 pts
4	16 thru 25 m.p.h. in excess of speed zone	Construction Zone: 5 pts
5	26 thru 35 m.p.h. in excess of speed zone	Construction Zone: 6 pts
6	36 thru 45 m.p.h. in excess of speed zone	Construction Zone: 8 pts
8	46 m.p.h. and above in excess of speed zone	Construction Zone: 8 pts

POINTS	MOVING TRAFFIC VIOLATION FOR NON-COMMERCIAL VEHICLES
3	Speed less than posted minimum
3	Driving too fast for conditions, failure to reduce speed to avoid an accident.
3	Operating at erratic or suddenly changing speeds
8	Reckless endangerment by vehicle-misdemeanor
6	Reckless driving
4	Careless or negligent driving
4	Failure to obey traffic instructions
4	Improper passing
3	Following improperly
3	Following emergency vehicles unlawfully
4	Failing to yield right of way
6	Failure to yield right of way to emergency vehicles. Failure to change land/slow down for authorized vehicles on roadside.
3	Making improper turn
3	Failure to signal direction or to reduce speed suddenly
3	Coasting, operating gears disengaged
3	Improper backing
3	Improper starting, burning rubber, spinning tires, peeling out
3	Driver view or mechanism obstructed
3	Driver mountain highway-control / audible warning
3	Inability to maintain control of vehicle
3	Improper operation of or riding on a motorcycle
3	Improper lane or location, driving on roadways laned for traffic
4	Use of controlled access roadway
3	Inattentive driving, due care, failure to drive in careful manner, unsafe lookout, improper driving
3	Miscellaneous traffic violation; any offense involving the unsafe operation of a Non-Commerical motor vehicle
3	Operating with being licensed or without license required for type of vehicle being operated (under suspension)
4	Cross private property to avoid stop sign or signal
6	Operating vehicle while using cell phone (under 18)
4	Signs and control devices-Failure to obey traffic instructions
4	Improper passing-Passing where prohibited
8	Passing stopped school, church or youth bus taking on or discharging passengers
6	Violation of driver license restrictions, operating contrary to conditions specified on driver license
8	Failure to stop at railroad crossing
5	Leaving the scene of a crash (No revocaton actions)
4	Failure to report a crash
2	Operating without driver license in possession
3	Operating with being licensed or without license required for type of vehicle operated
8	Operating while driver license required for type of vehicle operated is under suspension, revocation or cancellation
8	Fleeing law enforcement officer (misdemeanor)
8	Child Endangerment

POINTS	CRASHES
3	Contributing to a crash resulting in property damage
4	Contributing to a crash resulting in bodily injury
8	Contributing to occurrence of a crash resulting in the death of another person

litter pickup work shift, an outpatient alcohol or drug program, meeting with probation officer, and a scheduled interlock monitoring appointment.

This restricted license is not an option for drivers who have a prior conviction of:

- DUI or adult driving while impaired within 10 years;
- Vehicular Homicide as the latest result of intoxication;
- Aggravated Vehicular Homicide;
- Vehicular Assault.

After the first year of a two-year revocation, drivers may apply for a restricted driver license if they install an ignition interlock device on the motor vehicle for the remaining period of revocation. When applying at the driver license station, these applicants must submit two (2) copies of the court order and proof of car insurance/financial responsibility (SR-22 from their insurance company) and pass appropriate tests and pay the required fees. Required tests will depend on past driving record and frequency of convictions.

2. **Driver Improvement:** Any adult whose driver license has been suspended for frequent traffic violations may obtain this type of license by applying to the Driver Improvement Section of the Tennessee Department of Safety and Homeland Security. Each applicant will be required to submit his/her approval letter, present proof of SR-22 insurance and pass appropriate tests and pay the required fees. Required tests will depend on past driving record and frequency of convictions.

3. **Implied Consent, Drag Racing, Gas Drive-Off:** A person whose license has been suspended by the court for Implied Consent, Drag Racing or Driving away from the Gasoline Pump without paying for the fuel, may apply to the trial judge for a restricted license to operate a motor vehicle for going to and from work, full-time college, scheduled interlock monitoring appointment and working at his or her regular place of employment. At the time of application at the Driver Service Center, two (2) copies of a court order and proof of SR-22 insurance must be submitted along with payment of the required fees.

4. **Juvenile:** A minor who loses his/her license because of drug- or alcohol-related charges may apply to the trial judge for a restricted license to operate a motor vehicle to and from the educational institution or to and from work. Each applicant must bring two (2) copies of the court order to a driver license service center and pass the vision test along with payment of the required fees.

5. **Failure to Satisfy a Citation**: A person who failed to satisfy a citation that resulted in suspension action being taken against their driver license may obtain a certified order from any court in any county where they failed to satisfy a citation. **The order allows the person to drive to and from work only.** The order must show payment of the fines and costs

owed to the particular court or a payment plan for the associated fines and costs along with the date the final payment is to be made. At the time of the application at the Driver Service Center, the person must submit two (2) copies of the court order and pay the required license fees.

PHYSICAL OR MENTAL DISABILITIES

When information is received that an individual's ability to drive is affected by a physical or mental disorder, the driver will be required to submit (within thirty (30) days of notification) a medical report from a medical doctor. This report will provide the effects of the illness or disability on the individual's ability to safely operate a motor vehicle. If the report is unfavorable, the driving privilege will be suspended until the condition improves. Drivers who lose consciousness or control due to epilepsy, cardiac syncope, diabetes or other conditions must be suspended and remain lapse free for a minimum of six (6) months before being eligible for license reinstatement.

Re-Examination of Drivers

If there is information that a driver's ability to safely operate a motor vehicle is questionable, he or she may be directed to report to the nearest Driver Service Center to submit to a complete or partial driver examination. Appropriate corrective action may be required and certain restrictions may be placed on the license.

NOTE: Failure to respond to departmental requests for a medical report or submission to a driver license examination within the prescribed time will result in the suspension of the driving privilege. This suspension lasts until a satisfactory medical report is submitted to the department or until the driver successfully passes the driving tests that are required by the department.

Financial Responsibility

This law is to protect you and the public from financially irresponsible drivers who become involved in crashes. It also provides protection from drivers who have repeated violations and/or obvious disregard for driving laws.

The best way to protect yourself and your driver license is to have adequate insurance to cover death, bodily injury and property damage.

First, a few definitions:

- **Liability insurance** provides coverage for damages you cause to other persons.
- **Collision insurance** provides coverage for damages sustained by your vehicle.
- **Uninsured motorist insurance** provides for coverage for the damages uninsured persons cause.

Although collision insurance is not required by Tennessee law, the Financial Responsibility Law requires drivers to produce evidence of financial responsibility. This is required when charged with any violation or when involved in a motor vehicle crash without regard to apparent or actual fault.

Evidence of financial responsibility can be in the form of:

(1) A declaration page of your insurance policy;

(2) An insurance binder;

(3) An insurance card from an insurance company authorized to do business in Tennessee;

(4) A certificate issued by the Commissioner of the Department of Safety stating that a cash deposit or bond in the amount required by statute has been paid or filed with the Commissioner; or

(5) Proof of qualification as a self-insurer as provided by statute.

REPORTING CRASHES

If a driver is unable to present evidence and is convicted on the charge of failure to show evidence of financial responsibility, his/her driving privileges will be suspended as well as a stop placed on the renewal of vehicle tags and registration. Before reinstatement of driving privileges, evidence of financial responsibility must be presented, along with any other requirements must be submitted.

A crash is any vehicle collision involving another vehicle, person or object. Drivers must immediately notify the local police department if the crash occurs within a municipality, otherwise to the County Sheriff's office or the nearest Tennessee Highway Patrol, of any crash involving death, injury or property damage over fifty dollars ($50). If the driver is physically unable to give immediate notice, and there is a passenger capable of doing so, the passenger shall make or cause notice to be given.

In addition, certain crashes — called "reportable crashes" — must be reported to the Tennessee Department of Safety and Homeland Security. These include any crash within this state in which any person is killed or injured, or in which damage to the property of any one person, including oneself, is in excess of four hundred dollars ($400).

Regardless of who is to blame, the operator and/or owner of a vehicle involved in a reportable crash in this state must file an Owner/Driver Report of the crash to the Tennessee Department of Safety and Homeland Security **within 20 days**. If the driver received an injury and cannot complete the report, it can be filed on behalf of the owner/operator. If the crash involved an unattended vehicle or a domestic animal and you cannot locate the owner, report the crash to the police.

An Owner/Driver report can be obtained 3 different ways. (1) from the Department of Safety's website: www.tn.gov/safety (2) Any Highway Patrol office (3) Any local police station or sheriff's office. Failure to report a crash may result in suspension of driving and registration privileges.

If there is a reasonable possibility of a judgment being filed in Court against you, the owner, operator, or both, and a claim is filed with the Department of Safety by the other party, you are required to do one of these three things:

(1) Show proof that you had liability insurance at the time of the crash;

(2) Obtain notarized releases from all parties who file claims with the department; or

(3) Post cash or corporate surety bond with the department for the amount of damages received by other parties.

If you do not comply with these requirements, your driving and registration privileges will be revoked.

Prior to revocation, you may request an administrative hearing, provided the request is submitted in writing on or before the effective date of the proposed revocation.

If your driving privileges are revoked for failure to establish financial responsibility for a crash, in addition to obtaining notarized releases from all parties who filed claims with the Department or posting cash or corporate surety bond for the amount of claims, you will also be required to pay a reinstatement fee and have a liability insurance carrier file a SR-22 form with the Department of Safety before driving privileges can be reinstated.

Traffic Crashes

If You Are Involved In a Crash — STOP! The law requires drivers of vehicles involved in a crash to stop immediately at the scene, or as close to the scene as possible without obstructing traffic. Turn off the ignition in the damaged vehicle to prevent a fire. If the car is on fire, help the people out and take them away from the vehicle to prevent further injury in case of an explosion.

"Notify the police immediately by calling 911." It is very important to report the crash to the police as quickly as possible. Motor vehicle crashes involving property damage, personal injury or death must be reported to the police. Remain calm and stay at the crash scene.

If you are involved in a traffic crash on the interstate, Tennessee law allows you to move the vehicle to prevent blocking the traffic flow. If the vehicle is still drivable and there are NO SERIOUS PERSONAL INJURIES or deaths, you may pull the vehicle(s) to the emergency lane and await the arrival of a police officer or Tennessee State Trooper to the crash scene.

Do not attempt to move an injured person from a wrecked vehicle unless you have the necessary medical or rescue training or there is an immediate danger such as fire. It is best to wait for emergency fire and rescue personnel to assist injured persons as well as free persons trapped in a vehicle.

Exchange information with other persons involved in the crash as soon as possible. Be sure to get the following information:
- name, address and driver's license number of other drivers;
- license plate numbers of other vehicles;
- name and address of anyone who was injured;
- name and address of each witness;

- name, address and insurance policy number of other vehicle owners.

You should notify your insurance company immediately.

If You Arrive First at a Crash Scene — Notify the police immediately by calling 911.

If you are not professionally trained to render aid, slowly continue on in your vehicle so not to interfere with the arrival of police and emergency medical and fire/rescue services. This will prevent you from being a victim of a secondary collision at the crash scene. These secondary accidents are a result of persons "accident gazing" to satisfy their curiosity, while driving their vehicle near a crash scene.

If you witnessed the crash occur, pull safely off to the side of the road and turn on your vehicle's emergency flashers. Notify the police officer or Tennessee State Trooper that you witnessed the crash.

Do not attempt to move an injured person from a wrecked vehicle unless you have the necessary medical and rescue training or there is an immediate danger such as fire. Unless you are properly trained, it is best to wait for emergency rescue personnel to free persons trapped in a vehicle.

Chapter 8 Chapter Sample Test Questions

Here are some sample test questions. Because these are just study questions to help you review, you may receive a test with completely different questions, in whole or in part. The page number is shown for where the correct answer can be located for each question. Also, answers to all the study questions can be found in the back of the book.

25. If involved in a reportable accident, the operator of the vehicle must file an accident report to the Department of Safety within:

    A. 10 Days

    B. 20 Days

    C. 48 Hours

    Page 88

26. If you are not the first at the scene of accident and your help is not needed, what should you do:

    A. Slow down to calm your nerves.

    B. Stop and look for your own curiosity.

    C. Drive on and do not interfere with procedures.

    Page 89

27. A driver license may be revoked or suspended for:

    A. Frequent convictions of traffic law violations resulting in 12 or more "points" within a 12 month period

    B. Fraudulently altering a driver license

    C. Both of the above

    Page 85 and 87

STUDY QUESTIONS ANSWER KEY

1. B
2. A
3. B
4. C
5. C
6. B
7. A
8. C
9. B
10. C
11. B
12. A
13. B
14. C
15. C
16. C
17. B
18. C
19. B
20. A
21. C
22. A
23. A
24. C
25. B
26. C
27. C

SECTION C

SAFETY TIPS FOR SAFE DRIVING AND SHARING THE ROAD

INTRODUCTION

Staying Safe After the Test

Learning about driving laws and developing safe driving practices is NOT something that ends when you receive your Tennessee driver license. It is your responsibility to always be aware of new laws, rules of the road, and improved safety practices throughout your lifetime as a driver. Remember when you are behind the wheel of a vehicle, you have control over an object that weighs thousands of pounds and your inattention or loss of safe control and operation of such vehicle could result in injury (or death) to yourself and others.

1. **Aim High In Steering:** Look as far down the road as possible to uncover important traffic information to make appropriate decisions.

2. **Get The Big Picture:** Maintain the proper following distance so you can comfortably determine the true hazards around your vehicle. Don't tailgate others.

3. **Keep Your Eyes Moving:** Scan - don't stare. Constantly shift you eyes while driving. Active eyes keep up with changing traffic conditions.

4. **Leave Yourself an Out:** Be prepared. Surround your vehicle with space in front and at least on one side to escape conflict.

5. **Make Sure They See You:** Communicate in traffic with your horn, lights and signals to establish eye contact with motorists and pedestrians. Be reasonably sure of people's intentions.

The information covered in the other sections of this manual provided details on becoming "prepared for the driving task". It takes practice and experience for new drivers to translate these written details into common habits for safe driving. Therefore you should review this manual frequently.

The purpose of Section C of this manual is to provide you valuable information and advice on safety precautions to help you be the best possible driver. This is valuable information that all drivers need to remember and utilize daily as we drive with more vehicles and pedestrians on our streets and highways.

Chapter C-1 DEFENSIVE DRIVING AND OTHER PRECAUTIONS

If every driver always obeyed the rules, and always behaved in a sensible way, driving would be simpler and safer. Unfortunately, this ideal situation does not exist. Instead we frequently encounter drivers who behave unpredictably or recklessly, and other highway users, such as pedestrians and bicyclists, who ignore the rules that apply to them.

> *"Defensive Driving" means being constantly aware of the driving conditions, planning ahead, anticipating dangers and taking the right action so as not to come in contact with any obstacle or other vehicle.*

To protect yourself, you must learn to drive defensively. This means anticipating errors by others and preparing to compensate for their mistakes. In addition, you must always behave in a correct and sensible fashion so that you do not confuse other drivers.

All of us want to avoid collisions that result in personal injury or even death. But, even when there is no personal injury, a collision means inconvenience and auto repair costs. It may also result in a court appearance and fines, as well as increased insurance rates. You have a great financial stake in your own good driving record. *Driving defensively will help protect your life and your driving record.*

> **Courtesy and consideration toward others are the most important driving attitudes you can develop.** *They are the key to safe driving.*

Concentration and Alertness Are Important Elements

Concentration is one of the most important elements of safe and defensive driving. You must develop the habit of keeping your mind on driving. The driver's safety is no place for daydreaming, site-seeing or distracting conversations.

Drive Alert —The defensive driving rules are simple and easy to follow. If you follow them, you should be able to avoid getting yourself into difficult situations. The rules are:

- Use your rearview mirrors. Constantly check the traffic behind you. Always check mirrors before changing lanes.

- Stay out of another driver's blind spot(s) to prevent another vehicle from turning into you.

- Expect the other driver to do the WRONG thing, and have a plan of action prepared to counter his error.

Drive Cautiously

Remember to always use the two-second rule. Periodically test your following distance by picking out a stationary object on the roadway ahead and doing the "1,001, 1,002" count.

Remember if you reach that point before counting to 1,002 you are following too closely. If this is the case, slow down in order to lengthen your following distance. Remember on high-speed interstates, when following large commercial trucks or buses, and in inclement weather or limited visibility conditions, it is safest to increase this following distance to at least 3 to 4 seconds.

Scanning the Road and Traffic for Defensive Reactions

Most of what you do as a defensive driver is in response to what you SEE while driving. When driving, we gather 90% of the information about the road and our surroundings through our eyes. Scanning means looking at the entire scene for anything that might come into your path. As you scan the road, avoid a fixed stare. Keep your eyes moving and learn to read the road. Look ahead, to the sides and behind you.

Scan Ahead – looking ahead will help you see things early and will allow you more time to react. Defensive drivers try to focus their eyes 10 to 15 seconds (about the distance of 1 city block) ahead.

Scan to the Sides – Scan from side to side, checking for directional signs, cars or people that might be in the road by the time you reach them.

Watch for Clues – Look for exhaust smoke, brake or back-up lights and turned wheels on vehicles. Clues like these indicate that the vehicles may pull into your path.

Be Careful in Rural Areas – Watch for hidden intersections and driveways, curves, hills and different road conditions (pavement changing to gravel or dirt road, narrowing road, etc.).

Check Left to Right Before Entering an Intersection – At any intersection, look to the left first, since cars coming from the left will be closer to you. Then look to the right and take one more quick look to the left before you drive through.

Look Behind – Use your rearview mirror to check the traffic behind you frequently, about every 10 seconds. This will alert you if someone is moving up too quickly or tailgating you. Be sure to check the traffic behind you when changing lanes, backing up, slowing down quickly or driving down a long steep hill. But don't keep you eyes off the road ahead for more than a brief look behind.

> **By knowing the speed and position of traffic on all four sides of your vehicle, you will be better able to make decisions quickly and safely in most situations.**

Communicating with other Drivers

Communicating means clearly showing other drivers and pedestrians what you plan to do early enough to avoid a collision. Any time you plan to change directions, use your turn signals – whether you are changing lanes, turning at an intersection, entering an interstate, pulling away from a curb or pulling off to the side of the road. Develop the habit of using your turn signals even when you do not see other vehicles on the road.

> **As a driver you will constantly be making decisions every mile you drive.**

Learn to keep a safe driving space or "safety cushion" around your vehicle

Sharing Space – You must always share the road with others. The more distance you keep between yourself and everyone else, the more time you have to react. This space is like a "safety cushion". The more you have, the safer you will be. This section describes how to make sure you have enough space around you when you drive.

Always drive in such a manner that you are able to control the space between your vehicle and others. At times this may mean slowing or increasing your speed (within lawful limits only). Try to maintain a safety cushion to the front, rear and each side of your vehicle at all times in order to provide an area of escape or prevention should an emergency occur.

1. **SPACE AHEAD:** Rear-end crashes are very common. Rear-end crashes are caused by drivers following too closely (tailgating) to be able to stop before hitting the vehicle ahead when it suddenly slows or stops. The best way to maintain this safety cushion is to follow the basic 2-Second Rule. Also leave extra space when approaching railroad crossings or when stopped behind another vehicle on a hill or curve.

2. **SPACE BEHIND:** It is not always easy to manage the space behind your vehicle. However, you can help keep a driver behind you at a safe distance by keeping a steady speed and using turn signals in advance when you have to slow down or turn. Every now and then you may find yourself being followed too closely or being "tailgated" by another driver. If there is a right lane, move over to the right. If there is no right lane, wait until the road ahead is clear and passing is legal, then slowly reduce your speed. This will encourage the tailgater to drive around you. Never slow down quickly to discourage a tailgater. All that does is increase your risk of being hit from behind.

3. **SPACE TO BOTH SIDES:** You need space on both sides of your vehicle to have room to turn or change lanes. Avoid driving in blind spots of other vehicles. When meeting oncoming vehicles on a two-lane road stay slightly to the right of your lane so as not to "crowd" the centerline. Be courteous and move to the left lane on multi-lane roads when other vehicles are trying to merge into traffic. Keep extra space between your vehicle and parked cars, pedestrians and bicyclists (especially children) on the roadside. Two key rules about space to the side includes:

- "Split the difference" – between two hazards. For example, steer a middle course between oncoming traffic and parked vehicles. However, if one is more dangerous than the other, leave a little more space on the most dangerous side. If the oncoming vehicle is a semi-truck, leave more room on the side that the truck will pass on instead of the side with the parked cars.

- "Take potential hazards one at a time." For example, if you are overtaking a bicyclist and an oncoming vehicle is approaching, slow down, let the vehicle pass first so that you can then safely move to the left to give room to the bicycle.

Other Sharing Space Tips include:

- **MERGING DEFENSIVELY:** A minimum four-second gap is needed whenever you change lanes, enter a roadway or when your lane merges with another traffic lane. If you need to cross several lanes, take them one at a time. NEVER cut across multiple lanes, it can tie up traffic and even cause you to have a collision or create a crash between other vehicles trying to avoid your sudden and unsafe maneuver.

- **HANDLING INTERSECTIONS DEFENSIVELY:** When you cross traffic, you need a large enough gap to get all the way across the road. DO NOT BLOCK INTERSECTIONS or get caught with a portion of your vehicle left in a traffic lane with approaching vehicles. Make sure you can safely complete the cross or entering maneuver before you enter the intersection.

- **START PASS DEFENSIVELY:** Be safe. As a general rule pass only one vehicle at a time. Remember passing does NOT entitle you to exceed the speed limit. At 55 M.P.H. you will need about ten (10) seconds to complete the pass of a single vehicle. That means you need a ten-second gap in oncoming traffic and sight distance to pass. Do NOT pass unless you have enough space to return to the driving lane.

- **FINISH PASS DEFENSIVELY:** Do NOT count on other drivers to make room for you. You will need enough room between your vehicle and the other vehicle ("space behind") to safely return to the driving lane. It's safest not to return to the driving lane until you can see both headlights of the vehicle you just passed in the rearview mirror.

- **HANDLE DANGEROUS SITUATIONS DEFENSIVELY:** Allow space to react to problem drivers or dangerous actions you may encounter including the following.
  - Obstructed vision of yourself or other driver (bushes at intersection, glaring sunlight, pedestrians with umbrellas, etc.)
  - Distractions for pedestrians or drivers (talking on cell phones, roadside attractions, sightseeing tourists, tending to children, etc.)

- Confused drivers or pedestrians (weaving in and out of lanes, looking for road names, reading maps, etc.)

- **HANDLE DRIVER ERRORS DEFENSIVELY:** If another driver makes a mistake, such as a driver who passes you without enough room or in heavy traffic, do not make the situation worse. Take necessary actions to safely avoid an accident.

  - Slow down and allow room for passing drivers to safely return to the driving lane

  - Slow down and allow room for drivers merging suddenly from road hazards, as well as ending lanes or entering/exiting expressways.

  - Slow down and allow room for drivers about to be forced into you lane by another merging vehicle, road construction or emergency vehicles approaching or stopped on the roadside.

If you always drive defensively and follow these traffic space and scanning guidelines you will help keep traffic moving smoothly and safely.

ROAD RAGE

Aggressive driving – tailgating, honking, fist and hand gestures, yelling, speeding, cutting off other drivers, and more frightening, the use of firearms- has become a real danger on America's highways. The National Highway Traffic Safety Administration (NHTSA) says about 66% of all traffic fatalities annually are caused by aggressive driving behaviors, such as passing on the right, running red lights and tailgating. Law enforcement and insurance companies are getting much tougher on aggressive drivers.

Tips to Avoid Road Rage

- Give driving your full attention.

- Obey the law.

- Control emotions so they don't interfere with driving.

- Don't join in the confrontation, even if it is just honking or glaring.

- Don't tailgate

- Drive defensively

- Give an angry driver plenty space.

- Don't take traffic problems personally. Be polite, even when someone else is rude.

- Drive relaxed and within the speed limit, passing only when necessary.

- If a driver follows you, go to a police station or a public place where you can get help. If you are harassed on the road, get the offender's license tag number if possible and report the incident to the authorities.

Because road rage is increasing every year, you must learn to protect yourself against aggressive drivers. If you have a tendency to get irritated and angry behind the wheel, you must learn to change your attitude and your behavior. Otherwise you are an accident looking for a place to happen.

> **YOU CAN'T CONTROL TRAFFIC, BUT YOU CAN CONTROL YOUR REACTION TO IT**

95

Chapter C-2 SPECIAL DRIVING CONDITIONS AND YOUR VEHICLE

Here's a short test: Most accidents happen_____
a.) in clear weather   b.) in snow   c.) in rain   d.) in fog

If you picked anything but (a), you're wrong – pretty days can be deadly too!

While adverse weather conditions certainly create dangerous driving situations, the purpose of this chapter is to provide you with a focus on techniques that will help you to avoid crashes in any weather.

A defensive driver must always be thinking about what the other driver might do and be prepared to respond with proper reactions. However a driver must also be aware of their own actions and how to deal with common driving "obstacles" and vehicle maintenance problems, many of which are covered in this chapter.

AVOIDING COLLISIONS

When it looks like a collision may happen, many drivers panic and fail to act. In some cases they do act, but do something that does not help to reduce the chance of the collision. There almost always is something you can do to avoid the crash, or reduce the results of the crash.

In avoiding a collision, drivers have three options:
1. Stop   2. Turn   3. Speed Up

The following section will give you vital information relating to these three reactions.

1. Stopping Quickly
Many newer vehicles have ABS (Antilock Braking Systems). Be sure to read the vehicle owner's manual on how to use the ABS. An ABS system will allow you to stop without skidding.

With ABS - If you have an antilock braking system and you need to stop quickly:

- Press on the brake pedal as hard as you can and keep pressing on it firmly.

- You might feel the brake pedal pushing back when the ABS is working. Do NOT let up on the brake pedal. The ABS system will only work with the brake pedal pushed down firmly.

Without ABS - If you must stop quickly and you do NOT have an antilock braking system:
Apply the brakes as hard as you can without locking them. You can cause the vehicle to go into a skid if you brake too hard or continuously.

- If the brakes lock-up, you will feel the vehicle start to skid. Quickly let up on the brake pedal.

- As soon as the vehicle stops skidding, push down on the brake pedal again. Keep doing this until the vehicle has stopped.

In emergency or slippery conditions with ABS, wheels don't lock; car remains stable and is steerable.

In emergency or slippery conditions without ABS, all wheels lock; car begins to skid and is not steerable.

In emergency or slippery conditions with ABS, wheels DON'T lock; car remains stable and can be steered around obstacles. In emergency or slippery conditions without ABS, all wheels may LOCK; car begins to skid and can not be steered properly.

2. Turning Quickly
In most cases, you can turn the vehicle quicker than you can stop it. **Evasive steering:** If you are unable to stop in time to avoid a collision, try to steer around the vehicle or object. You should consider turning in order to avoid a collision. <u>Use your brakes only if necessary</u>.

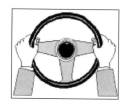

To be able to turn quickly you need to hold the steering wheel correctly. Make sure you have a good grip with both hands on the steering wheel. For most turns, especially quick turns, you must have your hands on opposite sides of the wheel. It is best to have your hands at about the 3 o'clock and 9 o'clock positions. This will keep your wrists and forearms out of the main impact area of the air bag located in the steering wheel should you become involved in a collision.

To make quick evasive turns to the left:

- **Turn the steering wheel to the left as far as necessary to avoid the obstacle or vehicle.** *Hand position = right hand (3 o'clock) swings left toward the 9 o'clock position as far as needed. Left hand moves toward bottom (6 o'clock) to help steady your grip on the wheel.*

- **As you clear the hazard, turn the steering wheel back to the right as far as necessary to get back into your lane.** *Hand position = left hand (9 o'clock) swings right back toward the 3 o'clock position as far as needed. Right hand now moves toward the bottom (6 o'clock) to steady your grip.*

- **As you return to your lane, turn the steering wheel left just enough to straighten the vehicle's path of travel.** Hand position = returning to the basic driving position of left at 9 o'clock and right at 3 o'clock.

To make quick evasive turns to the right, use the same procedures above, except turn the steering wheel in the opposite direction at each step.

Once you have turned the vehicle away from the road hazard or changed lanes, you must be ready to keep the vehicle under control. Some drivers steer away from one collision only to end up in another. ***Always steer in the direction you want the vehicle to go***.

With ABS - **One aspect of having ABS, is that you can turn your vehicle while braking without skidding. (See illustration at right >) This is very helpful if you must turn to swerve, stop or slow down quickly.**

Without ABS - If you do not have ABS, you must use a different procedure to turn quickly.

- As you are braking you will need to let up on the brake pedal and then turn the steering wheel.
- Braking will slow the vehicle some, and it puts more weight on the front tires and this allows for a quicker turn.
- Do not continue braking if you feel the front wheels "lock-up", or turn so sharply that the vehicle can only plow ahead.
- Another consideration is that generally it is better to turn off the road than to crash head-on into another vehicle.

For more information on ABS procedures and safety visit: www.abs-education.org

3. Speeding Up
Sometimes it is best or necessary to speed up to avoid a collision. This may happen when another vehicle is about to hit you from the side or from behind and there is room to the front of your vehicle to get out of danger.

Be sure to slow down once the danger has passed. Also remember to always keep at least a two second (or more) space cushion between your car and the vehicle ahead in order to have an emergency out available.

COLLISIONS WITH ANIMALS

While animal-vehicle collisions can happen any time of the year and with any type of animal (opossum, rabbit, squirrel, dogs, etc.). Fall is the peak season for deer-car crashes. That's mainly because Autumn is both mating season and hunting season, so deer are more active and more likely to roam beyond their normal territory.

Many of these collisions happen at night but they can occur any time of day. Collisions with deer are generally the most dangerous and costly crashes involving animals. No foolproof way has been found to keep deer or other wild animals off highways and away from vehicles.

You can help to avoid an unplanned meeting with a deer or other type animal if you will:

- Be aware of your surroundings. Pay attention to "deer crossing" signs.
- Look well down the road and far off to each side.
- At night, use your high-beam lights if possible to illuminate the road's edges.
- Be especially watchful in areas near woods and water. If you see one deer, there may be several others nearby.
- Be particularly alert at dusk and dawn, when these animals venture out to feed. Scan the sides of the road to watch for the reflection of your vehicle headlights in the eyes of deer.
- If you see a deer, or other animal on or near the roadway and think you have time to avoid hitting it, reduce your speed, tap your brakes to warn other drives, and sound your horn.
- Deer tend to fixate on headlights, so flashing them may cause the animal to freeze in the road.
- If there's no vehicle close behind you, brake hard but don't lock wheels causing a skid.
- If a collision seems inevitable, don't swerve to avoid the animal; your risk of personal injury may be greater if you do. Keep your vehicle under control and on the roadway when you hit the animal.
- Report the crash to the police if it involves a large animal such as a deer or farm animal.
- If the animal is a domestic pet and homes are nearby you should try to notify the pet's owner if possible.
- Always obey the speed limit and wear your safety belt.

Special Info: Learn to Use Your Anti-Lock Brakes!

DO'S AND DON'TS OF ABS

DO: *Stomp.* Slam that brake pedal. Push hard and hold the pedal down. You'll feel the pedal pulsate, and you'll hear noise. Continue to keep you foot firmly on the brake because those are signals the system is working – and that you're in a real emergency situation. The sound and feel often startle people, and their instinct is to let up on the brakes slightly. Don't – that ruins the advantages of ABS.

DON'T: *Pump.* Never pump the brake pedal of a vehicle equipped with ABS, even if the brake pedal is pulsating. The pulsating feeling is simply the ABS system electronically "pumping" the brakes much faster than you could ever do manually.

DO: *Steer.* Use the nonskid feature of ABS to steer around the obstacle that made you slam the brakes on in the first place. Continue steering to a safe place once you're past the obstacle.

DON'T: *Freeze or Jerk.* People sometimes get hurt, or killed, when they jerk the steering wheel suddenly. This can cause them to run into another object or veer off the road risking a rollover. Steer normally to avoid the problem and DON'T freeze at the wheel.

DO: *Practice.* Find a big, empty space, a vacant parking lot such as a deserted/closed shopping center. Be sure the lot is a wide open space without curbs or lots of light poles. Start driving about 20 M.P.H. and slam on the brakes. Steer to prove to yourself that you still can. Keep doing this until it becomes habit to steer when you stomp. When you feel comfortable with this you can set up a cardboard box as a target. Aim for the box as if it were a car suddenly stopped in front of you, hit the brakes and steer around the box and then steer back as you would to steer back into the normal traffic lane after avoiding the obstacle. Practice this in various weather conditions: dry, rain, snow, etc.

DO: *Space.* Keep a safe space between your car and other vehicles. Remember the two second rule for keeping a minimum cushion of space between vehicles. Allow more time/space if conditions are hazardous.

DO: *Read.* Consult the owner's manual for additional driving instructions on the anti-lock brake system your vehicle is equipped with.

DON'T: *Be Aggressive.* Never drive an ABS-equipped vehicle more aggressively than vehicle without ABS. Driving around curves faster, changing lanes abruptly, or performing other aggressive steering maneuvers is neither appropriate nor safe with any vehicle.

DRIVING FACTORS: THE DRIVER, THE VEHICLE AND THE ROAD

Crashes Don't Just Happen, They Are Caused

The majority of accidents relate directly to the driver. A good driver takes interest and pride in the care and operation of his/her vehicle. The driver knows and observes all traffic laws and respects the rights and safety of others. As a result, such drivers have a much better chance of never becoming involved in a serious traffic crash.

The careless driver all too often neither cares for the vehicle he/she drives, seldom observes traffic laws and has little respect for the rights and safety of others. As a result of poor driving habits there are approximately 160,000 crashes reported to the Department of Safety annually.

There are three major components to our highway transportation system that must be considered when driving.

1. **Driver**
2. **Vehicle**
3. **Road**

Neglect or inattention to of any one or more of these three will contribute to most accidents.

Human error is the single most common cause of traffic crashes. The leading factors in crashes are:

- Excessive Speed
- Lack of Concentration
- Improper Evasive Action

Driving safely is not always easy. In fact, it is one of the most complex things that people do and one of the few things we do regularly that can injure or kill us. It is worth the effort to be a careful driver.

Being a safe driver takes a lot of skill and judgment. This task is even more difficult when you are just learning to drive. Every one of the abilities you have can easily be required to drive safely.

1. THE DRIVER: BE IN SHAPE TO DRIVE

Your ability to be a safe driver depends on ability to see clearly, not being overly tired, not driving while on drugs, being generally health and being emotionally fit to drive. In other words, being in "shape" to drive safely.

Your mental and emotional state, as well as your physical condition, affects the way you drive a vehicle. Anger, worry, frustration, fatigue and minor illnesses such as a cold are a few of the temporary conditions that can make you an unsafe driver.

- VISION: Good vision is a must for safe driving. You drive based on what you SEE. If you cannot see clearly, you will have trouble identifying traffic and road conditions, spotting potential trouble or reacting in a timely manner.

  a. Side Vision – You need to use your peripheral vision to see out of the corner of your eyes. This lets you spot vehicle and other potential trouble on either side of you while you look ahead. Because you can't focus on things to the side, you also must use your side mirrors and glance to the side occasionally if necessary.

  b. Night Vision – It is more difficult for everyone to see at night than in the daytime. Some drivers have problems with glare while driving at night, especially with the glare of oncoming headlights. If you have problems seeing at night, don't drive more than is necessary and be very careful when you do drive at night.

c. Judging Distances and Speeds – It takes a lot of practice to be able to judge both distance and speed effectively. It is especially important in knowing how far you are from other vehicles and judging safe gaps between vehicles when merging and when passing on two-lane roads.

d. Have Your Vision Checked Regularly – because seeing well is so important to safe driving, you should have your eyes checked every year or two by an eye specialist.

If you are required to wear glasses or contact lenses, remember to:

- Always wear them when you drive, even on very short trips.

- If your driver license indicates you must wear corrective lenses (Restriction Code 01) you must wear them at all times when driving. You could be fined and receive a ticket if stopped while driving without your glasses or contacts.

- Keep a spare pair of glasses in your vehicle. If your regular glasses are broken or lost, you can use the spare set to drive safely.

- Avoid using dark sunglasses or tinted contact lenses at night, they cut down the light you need to see clearly.

- HEARING: Good hearing is a helpful asset to safe driving. The sound of horns, a siren or screeching tires can warn you of danger. Drivers who have a hearing impairment can adjust and compensate by relying more on their vision to be a safe driver. Statistically the driving records of hearing-impaired drivers are just as good as those drivers with good hearing.

- FATIGUE: You can't drive as safely when you are tired as when you are rested. You do not see as well, nor are you as alert. It takes you more time to make decisions and you do not always make good decisions. When you are tired you could fall asleep behind the wheel and crash injuring or killing yourself or others. Below are some tips to help you avoid fatigue when driving:

a. Try to always get a normal night's sleep

b. Eat lightly. Do not eat a large meal before you begin driving on an extended trip.

c. Do not take any medicine that can make you drowsy.

d. Take breaks. Stop every hour or more often if needed. Walk around, get some fresh air and have some, water, coffee, soda or juice. The few minutes spent on a rest stop can save your life.

e. Try not to drive late at night when you are normally asleep. Your body thinks it is time to go to sleep and will try to do so.

f. Never drive if you are sleepy. It is better to stop and sleep for a few hours than to take a chance on trying to stay awake. If you fail to stay awake it could become a real nightmare.

- HEALTH: Many health problems can affect your driving abilities – a bad cold, infection or virus. Even little problems like a stiff neck, a cough or a sore leg can affect your driving. If you are not feeling well and need to go somewhere, let someone else do the driving. Some serious health conditions can be very dangerous such as:

a. Epilepsy – When this condition is under medical control, epilepsy generally is not an obstacle to driving. In Tennessee, you may drive if you are under the care of a doctor and have been seizure free for a minimum of six months.

b. Diabetes – Diabetics who take insulin should not drive when there is any chance of an insulin reaction, blackout, convulsion or shock. These situations could result from skipping a meal, taking the wrong amount of insulin or when your doctor is adjusting your insulin dosage. *If you have diabetes you also should have your eyes checked regularly for possible night blindness or other vision problems.*

c. Heart Condition – people with heart diseases, high blood pressure or circulation problems or those in danger of a blackout, fainting or a heart attack should not get behind the wheel of a vehicle. If you are being treated by a doctor for a heart condition, ask if the condition could affect your driving.

- EMOTIONS: Your emotions can have a great affect on your driving safely. You may not be able to drive well if you are overly worried, excited, afraid, angry or depressed. If you are angry or excited, give yourself time to cool off and calm down. Try to stay focused on the important task of driving instead of mentally wandering through issues that may have you upset or worried. Taking a short walk or listening to music can be helpful. If you tend to be an impatient person always plan extra time for your driving trips to avoid speeding or other unsafe actions should you encounter heavy traffic or other delays.

- ALCOHOL AND DRUGS: ***Driving should always be a drug and alcohol free zone***! If you drink alcohol, even a little, your chances of being in a collision are much greater than if you did not drink any alcohol (or take any drugs). No one, regardless of their skill or driving experience, can drive safely when "buzzed" or impaired by alcohol or drugs.

2. THE VEHICLE: MAINTENANCE NEED FOR A SAFE VEHICLE

Driving safety starts with the vehicle you are driving. *It is the duty of drivers to make certain that the vehicles they drive are safe to operate.*

A poorly maintained vehicle can break down or cause a collision. If a vehicle is not working well, you might not be able to get out of an emergency situation. A vehicle in good working order can give you an extra safety margin when you need it most.

You should follow the recommendations in your vehicle owner's manual for routine maintenance. However there are some standard equipment and maintenance issues common to all vehicles that every driver should be aware of.

CHECK THE VEHICLE

- **Braking System** – Only your brakes can stop your vehicle. It is very dangerous if they are not working properly. If they do not seem to be working good, are making a lot of noise, smell funny or the brake pedal goes to the floor, have a mechanic check them.

- **Lights** – Make sure that turn signals, brake lights, taillights and headlights are operating properly. These should be checked from the outside of the vehicle.

- **Battery** – Car batteries tend to run down more rapidly in cold or damp weather. A neglected battery may leave you stranded with a vehicle that will not start.

- **Jumper Cables** – In the event your vehicle's battery becomes run down, jumper cables may help get you started. It is a prudent idea to keep a set of cables in your vehicle. See the vehicle manual for proper use to prevent vehicle damage or personal injury.

- **Windshield and Wipers** – Damaged glass in a windshield can easily break in a minor collision or when something hits the windshield. Have a damaged windshield repaired or replaced

   • **_Windshield wipers_ keep the rain and snow off the windshield. Some vehicles also have wipers for rear windows and headlights. Make sure all wipers are in good operation condition. If the blades are not clearing your windshield, replace them.**

   • **_Windshield washer solution_ – Non-freezing windshield washer fluid is essential for cleaning the windshield of debris, salt, and grime when driving in inclement weather. Get in the habit of checking the washer fluid level with each gas fill-up and/or adding more solution with each oil change.**

It is important that you are able to see clearly through the windows, windshield and even your mirrors. The following are things you can do to help:

   • **Keep the windshield clean. Bright sun or headlights on a dirty windshield make it hard to see. _Get in the habit of cleaning the windshield each time you stop to put gas into your vehicle._**

   • **Keep the inside of your windows clean, especially if anyone using the vehicle smokes. Smoking causes a film to build up on the inside of the glass. Carry liquid cleaner and a paper or cloth towel so you can clean you windshield whenever it is necessary.**

- **Heater / Defroster** – A working heater/defroster keeps the vehicle's windows free of fog and ice and helps maintain comfortable driving conditions.

- **Tires** – Worn or bald tires can increase your stopping distance and make turning more difficult especially when the road is wet. Unbalanced tires and low pressure cause faster tire wear, reduce fuel economy and make the vehicle harder to steer and stop. Worn tires can also cause hydroplaning, and increase the chance of a flat tire. Keeping your vehicle steering in alignment will also help reduce tire wear.

- Tread   An easy way to check the tread is with a penny. Stick the penny into the thread head first. If the tread does not come at least to Lincoln's head (2/32 inch), the tire is illegal and unsafe and you need it replaced. Don't forget the spare tire! The spare should also be checked and maintained periodically in case it is needed in an emergency.

Tire pressure is also an important factor when keeping up with maintenance of your vehicle. It's important to have proper tire pressure at all times in order to keep your vehicle safe, save money on fuel and preserve the life of your tires for as long as possible. Check your tire pressure periodically, using a tire gauge. Be sure you are aware of how to find your recommended tire pressure level.

- **Recommended Tire Pressure-** On many newer cars the vehicle's recommended tire pressure is on the sticker in the door jamb. It's usually located on the driver's side front door, and should be visible when the door is open. This tire pressure psi pertains to the vehicle's original tires and should be followed as long as you haven't put aftermarket tires of a different size on the vehicle. If this sticker is not located inside the door jamb, check in other places like the glove box, trunk or back of the sun visor. Do not use the tire pressure psi printed on the tires themselves. This is the maximum recommended pressure for the tire and may not match up with your vehicle's manufacturer specifications, leading to problems with tire wear or safety concerns.

If you cannot find the recommended tire pressure printed anywhere on the vehicle, check in the owner's manual. A tire pressure chart may be present, along with other important information regarding temperature changes, towing and specific driving conditions.

If you have replaced your original tires with an aftermarket brand of a different size or speed rotation, the recommended vehicle manufacturer's tire pressure will no longer apply. In this case, it's important to contact the tire manufacturer or the installer of the tires directly to gain information on the proper tire pressure for that size tire mounted on your year, make and model of vehicle.

- **Steering System** – If the steering is not working properly, it is difficult to control the direction you want to go. If the vehicle is hard to turn or does not turn when the steering wheel is first turned, have the steering checked by a mechanic. Never turn your vehicle's ignition to the "lock" position while the vehicle is in motion. This will cause the steering wheel to lock in place and you will lose control of the vehicle.

- *Suspension System* – Your suspension helps you control your vehicle and provides a comfortable ride over varying road surfaces. If the vehicle continues to bounce after a bump or a stop, or is hard to control, you may need new shocks or other suspension parts. Have a mechanic check the vehicle for suspension problems.

- *Exhaust System* – The exhaust system helps reduce the noise from the engine, cools the hot gases coming from the engine, and moves them to the rear of the vehicle. *Gases from a leaky exhaust can cause death inside a vehicle in a very short time*. If you ever start to notice that you and/or your passengers tend to get a sleepy feeling when driving or riding in your car you may have an exhaust leak that needs to be repaired immediately.

  • When sitting for prolonged periods in a vehicle with the motor running (idling), open a window to provide fresh air. Carbon Monoxide fumes can overcome people in an enclosed vehicle quicker than most people realize. Some exhaust leaks are easily heard but many are not – have the system checked periodically.

  • Never run the motor in a closed garage or other situations where the exhaust (tail) pipe may be obstructed. This includes a car that is stuck in mud or snow.

  • When traveling, if you make an extended stop (rest area, etc.) do not sleep or sit with the car running.

- *Engine* – A poor running engine may lose power that is needed for normal driving and emergencies, may not start, gets poor fuel economy, pollutes the air and could stall when you are on the road causing you and other vehicles a traffic problem. Follow the procedures recommended in the owner's manual for maintenance.

- *Engine Cooling System* – Antifreeze/coolant level should be checked periodically to ensure proper levels as recommended by your vehicle owner's manual. Improperly maintained levels can result in overheating in warm weather or engine freezing during winter. Be careful to check your radiator ONLY when the vehicle is cool, not immediately after operation.

- *Loose Objects* – Make sure that there are no loose objects in the vehicle that could hit someone in the event of a sudden stop or crash. Make sure there are no objects on the floor that could roll under the brake pedal and prevent you from stopping the vehicle. Also check the outside of the vehicle to ensure that there are no loose parts that could come off in traffic and create a safety hazard.

- *Horn* – The horn may not seem like it is important for safety, but as a warning device, it could save your life. ONLY use your horn as a warning to others.

- *Fuel* – Be sure your vehicle always has at least a half tank of gas before starting any trip of significant length. Running out of gas on the roadway can be dangerous and could cause traffic jams or accidents.

3. THE ROAD: UNDERSTANDING ROAD AND TRAFFIC CONDITIONS

A safe and defensive driver never really stops learning "the road". The "road" is a continually evolving portion of the highway transportation system. In order for a driver to develop a thorough understanding of the road you must:

❑ **BE AWARE** of the various road conditions you may encounter when driving. Driving safely means obeying speed limits and adjusting for road conditions. There are various road conditions where you must slow down to be safe. For example, you must slow down for a sharp curve or when the road is rough or damaged. You also must adjust your driving manner in construction zones.

Again the road condition is a topic that you should never expect to stop learning about. In all states, the Department of Transportation is continually improving road designs in attempts to make driving safer. This means that as new ideas are implemented (such as HOV lanes or rumble strips) there will be new conditions regarding the road that drivers will need to become familiar with and understand.

❑ **BE PREPARED** for traffic conditions. Traffic is another factor about the road that is always changing. Chapter C-4 of this manual gives you information on sharing the road with various types of traffic including road construction and maintenance vehicles.

Traffic conditions vary according to many factors:

  • Volume of vehicles (rush hour, mid-day, night, etc.)

  • Types of traffic control devices (signals, signs, channeling devices, etc.)

  • Accidents or work zones

  • Road type (interstate, rural, city, etc.)

  • Weather conditions (rain, wind, snow, ice, etc.)

  • Speed limits and traffic flow – Vehicles moving in the same direction at the same speed cannot hit one another. Collisions involving multiple vehicles often happen when drivers go faster or slower than other traffic.

❑ **BE ALERT** for Traffic Trouble Spots – Wherever people or traffic gather, your room to maneuver is limited. You need to lower your speed to have time to react in a crowded space. **Some situations where you may need to adjust speed for traffic conditions include**:

  • If you see brake lights coming on several vehicles ahead of you.

  • Shopping centers, parking lots and downtown areas – these are busy areas with vehicles and people stopping, starting and moving in different directions quickly and randomly.

  • Rush hours often have heavy traffic and drivers that always seem to be in a hurry.

  • Narrow bridges and tunnels – vehicles approaching each

other are closer together.

- Schools, playgrounds and residential streets – these areas often have children present. Always be alert for children crossing the street, running or riding into the street without looking.
- Railroad crossings – you need to make sure that there are no trains coming and that you have room to cross. Some crossings are bumpy so you need to slow down to safely cross.

❑ **BE "ROAD" EDUCATED**:   Study and learn the rules of the road and periodically "re-learn" them.   Studying this manual is the first step to accomplishing this task. However good drivers don't just study for a driving test and then never pick up a driving manual again. Good drivers periodically review the manual for the newest law changes and safety information and study the manual for any new state they move to whether or not a test is required to transfer their license to that state.

The Road Has Many Users

Our streets and highways are becoming more crowded every day. Whether you are driving your car, truck, SUV, RV, riding your bike, or merely walking, you share the road with other vehicles and drivers. We always need to be aware that we as drivers are not the only users of our streets and highways and other people have certain rights and privileges on the highways of which automobile drivers must be aware and must respect. We share the road with:

- Pedestrians
- Bicyclists
- Motorcyclists and motor-driven bicycles
- Large Trucks and Buses
- Recreational Vehicles (RVs)
- Farm Machinery
- Animals

As responsible drivers we must know and practice the rules for sharing the road safely. You should always be aware of the traffic around you and be prepared for emergency situations. Use common sense and courtesy with other users of our streets and highways.

Your responsibility as a defensive driver includes making allowances for and adapting to the other persons and vehicles on the road. There are skills and techniques you should use for sharing the road. Knowing what to do and how to do it can help you stay alive and avoid damaging your car or someone else's vehicle or causing bodily injury to other highway users.

SHARING THE ROAD WITH PEDESTRIANS

As a driver you must recognize the special safety needs of pedestrians. Any person afoot or using a motorized or non-motorized wheelchair are considered a pedestrian by state law. You should be especially alert for young, elderly, disabled and intoxicated pedestrians. They are the most frequent victims in auto-pedestrian collisions.

Generally, pedestrians have the right-of-way at all intersections. There is a crosswalk at every intersection, even if painted lines and boundaries do not mark the crossing. Crosswalks are intended to encourage people to cross only at certain locations. As you know, some people will cross at locations other than cross walks. As the person controlling the potentially dangerous machine, it's your job to "play it safe" where pedestrians are concerned and protect them when you see they may be in danger. Regardless of the rules of the road or right-of-way, the law specifically requires YOU, as a driver, to exercise great care and extreme caution to avoid striking pedestrians.

Your Role as a Driver

Drivers should not block the crosswalk when stopped at a red light or waiting to make a turn. You also should not stop with a portion of your vehicle over the crosswalk area. Blocking the crosswalk forces pedestrians to go around your vehicle and puts them in a dangerous situation.

- As a driver it is your responsibility to yield the right-of-way, slowing down or stopping if need be to yield to a pedestrian crossing the roadway within a crosswalk when the pedestrian is upon half of the roadway which you are traveling or when the pedestrian is approaching so closely from the opposite half of the roadway as to be in danger.

- When in a marked school zone when a warning flasher or flashers are in operation, as a driver you shall stop to yield the right-of-way to a pedestrian crossing the roadway within a marked crosswalk or at an intersection with no marked crosswalk. You shall remain stopped until the pedestrian has crossed the roadway on which your vehicle is stopped. Remember it's the law!

- Be alert to persons entering the roadway or crosswalks at any location where pedestrian traffic is heavy.

- Be alert to pedestrians to the right of your vehicle and be especially watchful for pedestrians when you are making a right turn.

- You must immediately yield to pedestrians as soon as they step off the curb into the roadway when the pedestrian is on your half of the road or so close to your half of the road that they are in a position of danger.

- Always yield to blind pedestrians carrying a white, metallic, red tipped white cane or using a guide dog.

- Children are often the least predictable pedestrians and the most difficult to see. Take extra care to look out for children in residential areas and at times and places where children are likely to be around. (school zones, school bus stops, playgrounds, parks, near ice cream or snack vendor vehicles /carts).

- Yield to pedestrians walking on the sidewalk when you're entering or leaving a driveway, public parking garage, alley or parking lot and your path of travel crosses the sidewalk.

- Don't honk your horn, rev up your engine or do anything to rush or scare a pedestrian in front of your car, even if you have the legal right-of-way.

Your Role as a Pedestrian

Most of us cross streets and highways every day. We take for granted that we can cross without incident, because most of the time we do. However, sometimes we aren't so fortunate. Each year approximately 7,000 pedestrians die and 100,000 are injured in traffic related accidents. Young children and the elderly are more likely to be killed or injured in a pedestrian related traffic accident.

While it is easy to blame drivers, they are not always responsible for these crashes. All too often, pedestrians are the cause of such accidents. These senseless tragedies don't have to happen. You can avoid potential injuries and even death by reviewing the advice for safe street crossing. You too will be a pedestrian on occasion. So learn and obey the common sense rules when the roles are reversed.

When you are a pedestrian, do all you can to make yourself visible and to help prevent crashes.

Safety Tips for Pedestrians

As a pedestrian, you are at a major disadvantage when crossing streets, intersections and standing on corners. You are not always visible to drivers; especially for large truck and bus drivers and you don't stand a chance if a vehicle hits you. Pedestrians need to be careful of all vehicles and never take chances when they are sharing the road with large vehicles, like trucks and buses. Here are some safety tips that can keep you safe when walking from one destination to another.

WALKING

Pedestrians must walk along sidewalks when available. It is unlawful for pedestrians to walk in the road where there are sidewalks.

When there are no sidewalks, always walk on the left side of the road facing traffic (traffic should be coming toward you), this allows you to see any sudden dangers coming at you. Two or more pedestrians should walk in single file and never side by side of each other.

BE ALERT

Be alert and ready to move out of the way in case a driver cannot see you. It is not a good idea to walk or jog along busy roadways while wearing audio headphones or listening to portable audio devices. You may not hear the important traffic sounds that would help you avoid potential dangers.

WATCH YOUR WALKWAYS

Walk on sidewalks and in crosswalks whenever possible. It is important to pay attention to walk signals and keep a safe distance when standing on street corners. Trucks and buses make wide right turns and occasionally run up onto the corner of the sidewalk. It is important for you to be alert and to move back. Most likely, the truck driver will not see you or may be distracted and you could be seriously injured or killed if hit.

KNOW YOUR NO-ZONES

Be careful of the blind spots, or No-Zones, around cars, trucks, and buses when walking near or around them. Always assume the driver does not know that you are there. Because of a truck's large blind spots, a driver may not see, so it is up to you to avoid a crash. Never walk behind a truck when it is backing up; truck drivers cannot see directly behind the truck and could seriously injure you.

STOPPING DISTANCES

Use caution when crossing intersections and streets. You may think vehicles will stop for you, but they may not see you or even be able to stop. Remember, trucks, cars, motorcycles and bicyclists, all have different stopping capabilities. In fact, trucks can take much more space to stop than passenger vehicles. Never take a chance with a truck, even if the driver sees you he may not be able to stop.

MAKE YOURSELF VISIBLE

Wear bright or reflective clothing, especially when walking at night. Dressing to be seen will make it safer for you and drivers. Professional drivers do a lot of driving at night, and there's a good chance a truck driver will not see you if you don't make yourself visible. Carrying a flashlight is your safest bet for being seen at night.

WATCH OUT FOR WIDE LOADS

Trucks with wide loads have very limited visibility as well as difficulty maneuvering. Wide loads are much heavier and take up lots of room on the road. You need to be aware when walking near a truck with a wide load, because the driver may not see you. Trucks with wide loads make even wider right turns, require more space, and take even longer to stop than other trucks on the road. Remember to keep your distance when walking around these large trucks.

Crossing

Before crossing, stop at the curb, edge of the road, or corner before proceeding.

Look left-right-left, and if it's clear, begin crossing, look over your shoulder for turning vehicles.

Continue to check for approaching traffic while crossing.

At intersections with traffic lights and pedestrian signals, it's important to follow the signals carefully. Pedestrians may cross on green traffic signal or when you see the WALK Signal, following the basic rules for crossing.

If you are in the middle of the street and the DON"T WALK signal starts flashing, continue walking. You will have time to complete the crossing.

Pedestrians may NOT cross on a red or yellow traffic light, or on a red-green combines light unless facing a WALK signal. (This is red for turn(s) while green is for straight traffic or vice versa).

On a green arrow, whether alone or accompanied by a steady red or yellow, you may enter the road ONLY if you can do so safely without interfering with vehicle traffic.

The WALK signal and the green traffic light indicate that it's your turn to cross the street, but they do NOT mean it is SAFE to cross. The WALK signal, the GREEN light means LOOK and then IF it's safe, proceed to cross.

Although drivers must yield to pedestrians crossing the roadway, pedestrians must not suddenly leave a curb or other safe waiting place and walk into the path of vehicle traffic if it so close that it is an immediate hazard. Vehicles cannot stop at once!

SHARING THE ROAD WITH BICYCLES

On most roadways, bicyclists have the same rights and responsibilities as other roadway users and in most cases, they must share the lane. Bicyclists are prohibited on limited-access highways, expressways and certain other marked roadways. Bicyclists are required to travel on the right hand side of the road and travel in the same direction as vehicles. They must ride as close to the right side of the road as practical, while avoiding road hazards that could cause them to swerve into traffic. When you are sharing the road with bicyclists, you should always expect the rider to make sudden moves. Trash, minor oil slicks, a pothole, or crack in the concrete, a barking dog, a parked car or a car door opening as well as other surprises can force a bicycle rider to swerve suddenly in front of you.

Similarly, when cyclists are traveling past parked cars, they tend to move away from the cars, toward the center of the lane. This is to avoid injuring or being injured by persons getting out of those cars. In such cases, the bicyclist is operating the bicycle properly. If possible, give the cyclist the entire lane. When road conditions prevent this, pass the cyclist with extreme caution. Cyclists who are not on the extreme right hand side of the lane are not being careless, but are in fact attempting to account for traffic conditions and/or preparing to make a left turn.

Bicycles are hard to see. The riders are exposed and easily injured in a collision. Oncoming bicycle traffic is often overlooked or its speed misjudged.

When following bicyclists, give them plenty of room and be prepared to stop quickly. Use extra caution during rainy and icy weather. At night, do not use high beams when you see an oncoming bicycle rider.

Safety Tips for Drivers:
- When passing and overtaking a bicyclist proceeding in the same direction, do so slowly and leave at least a distance between you and the bicycle of not less than 3 feet. It's the law in Tennessee! Also be sure to maintain this clearance until safely past the overtaken bicycle.
- A driver should never attempt passing between a bicyclist and oncoming vehicles on a two-lane road. Slow down and allow vehicles to pass the rider safely.
- NEVER pass a bicycle if the street is too narrow or you would force the bicyclist too close to parked vehicles. Wait until there is enough room to let you pass safely.
- If you are about to pass a bicycle on a narrow road and you think the rider doesn't know your coming, tap your horn gently and briefly as a signal that you're going to pass. Don't blast your horn or otherwise startle or try to intimidate the bicyclist.

- The most common causes of collisions are drivers turning left in front of an oncoming bicycle or turning right, across the path of the bicycle.
- When your vehicle is turning left and there is a bicyclist entering the intersection from the opposite direction, you should wait for the bicyclist to pass before making the turn. Also, if your vehicle is sharing the left turn lane with a bicyclist, stay behind them until they have safely completed their turn.
- If your vehicle is turning right and a bicyclist is approaching on the right, let the bicyclist go through the intersection first before making a right turn. Remember to always signal your turns.
- Merge with bicycle traffic when preparing for a right turn. Don't turn directly across the path of the bicyclist.
- Drivers often fail to pick the bicyclist out of the traffic scene, or inaccurately judge the speed of cyclists making a left turn.
- Watch for bicycle riders turning in front of you without looking or signaling, especially if the rider is a child.
- Most bicyclists maintain eye contact with drivers of vehicles around them, particularly when the cyclist or vehicle is making a turn. Before turning, a driver should attempt to gain and maintain eye contact with the bicyclist to ensure a safer turn.

HAND SIGNALS

So far, you may have only been a passenger or pedestrian, but it is important to let other drivers know if you are stopping or turning. Now that you are driving your first vehicle (your bicycle), it's time to learn some of the rules of the road for communicating with other road users. While drivers of motorized vehicles use their blinkers or backup lights to communicate, as a driver of a bicycle, you will do this with hand signals.

Left Turn
Extend your left arm out sideways with all fingers extended or use your index finger to point left.

Right Turn
Extend your left arm out sideways bent at a 90-degree angle at the elbow joint, hand pointing upward and the palm of hand facing forward.

Alternative Right Turn
Extend your right arm out straight with all fingers extended or use your index finger to point right.

Stopping or Slowing
Extend your left arm or right arm sideways and bend your arm at a 90-degree angle at the elbow joint, hand pointing downwards and the palm of your hand facing backwards.

Residential Areas are Danger Zones for Bicycles
Bicyclists may ride in the middle of the street and disregard stop signs and traffic signals. BE CAREFUL in all neighborhood areas where children and teenagers might be riding.

Children riding bicycles create special problems for drivers. Children are not capable of proper judgment in determining traffic conditions, therefore drivers should be alert to the possibility of erratic movement and sudden changes in direction when children on bicycles are present.

Watch out for bikes coming out of driveways or from behind parked cars or other obstructions.

Bicyclists riding at night present visibility problems for drivers. At night, watch the side of the road for bicyclists. Bicyclists are required to have proper illumination, a front and rear deflector, but drivers should be aware that bicyclists are not easily seen. Lights from approaching traffic may make them even harder to see at night.

If you see a bicyclist with a red or orange pennant flag on the antennae attached to the bike, slow down: this is a common symbol to indicate the rider has impaired hearing.

Lane Positions for Bicycles
Bicyclists are required to ride as far right in the lane as possible only when a car and a bicycle, side by side, can safely share the lane. Even then, there are certain times when a bicycle can take the full lane.

A bicyclist should be allowed full use of the lane when:

- The rider is overtaking and passing another vehicle going in the same direction.
- If the lane is marked and signed (as shown at right) for bicycle use only, drivers must NEVER use this lane as a turning lane, passing lane or for parking.
- There are unsafe conditions in the roadway, such as parked cares, moving vehicles or machinery, fixed obstacles, pedestrians, animals, potholes or debris.
- The lane is too narrow for both a vehicle and a bicycle to safely share the lane. In this case it is safest to let the bicycle take the full lane.

Safety Tips for Bicyclists
Bicycles are the most vulnerable of all vehicles on the road. As a bicyclist riding in traffic or on the sidewalk, you should take extra precautions to protect yourself. Vehicles on the road, especially large trucks and buses, may not see you on your bike. Crossing the street or making a turn can be dangerous in traffic if others do not see you or your signals. The tips below can help keep you riding safely.

PROPER LIGHTING
Tennessee law requires that a bicycle used at night must be equipped with a lamp on the front that emits a white light visible from a distance of at least 500 feet to the front and either a red reflector or lamp emitting a red light that is visible from distance of 500 feet to the rear when directly in front of lawful upper beams of head lamps on a motor vehicle.

Consideration should also be given to placing reflective material on the frame of the bicycle to provide additional side and front visibility of the bicycle in low-light conditions. Riders are also encouraged to wear bright clothing with reflective material on both the helmet and clothing.

WEAR YOUR HELMET
Before you get on your bike, put on a helmet. It is the best thing you can do to be safe. Bikes offer no protection in case of a crash, so you need to wear your protection. Wearing your helmet may save your life if you are hit by or run into a large truck or bus. Remember, riding into a truck is equivalent to hitting a steel wall. Your helmet is your life.

BIKERS BEWARE
Always be aware of the traffic around you. This is especially important when riding in traffic with large trucks and buses. Trucks and buses make wide right turns. Never sneak in between a truck or bus and the curb or you could get crushed. Never assume that all drivers see your hand signals or will yield for you. Assume you are invisible to other road users and ride defensively.

CHECK YOUR BRAKES
Always check your brakes so that you are prepared to stop. Also remember that a truck requires more space to stop than you do on your bike. Never assume that a truck will be able to stop quickly if you get in the way. You may have to get out of the way to save your own life.

RIDE WITH TRAFFIC
Avoiding a crash is the safest way to ride. Ride on the right side, with the flow of traffic. Riding against traffic may cause you to miss traffic control devices, such as traffic signs and stop lights. Be especially careful when riding near or around trucks and buses. Use caution and pay attention to trucks. Watch for their signals because the driver may not see you or be able to stop soon enough in an emergency situation. However, you should to be prepared in case the truck's signals don't work or the driver doesn't use them. That is why you, as the bicyclist, need to watch out for yourself. For a bike rider, the safest bet is to always be aware of the traffic around you.

BEWARE OF THE NO-ZONE
Beware of riding too closely to a large truck. Large trucks have blind spots in the front, back and on the sides, which make it difficult for the driver to see around them. If you ride in these blind spots, truck drivers cannot see you and your chance for a crash are greatly increased.

To learn more specifics on bicycle riding and safety contact:
The League of American Bicyclists
1612 K Street NW, Suite 800
Washington, DC 20006

SHARING THE ROAD WITH MOTORCYCLES

Research shows that two-thirds of car-motorcycle collisions are caused, not by the motorcyclist, but by the driver who turned in front of the motorcycle. The drivers didn't see the motorcycles at all or didn't see them until it was too late to avoid the collision.

Why Drivers Don't Always See Motorcyclists

Drivers tend to look for other cars and trucks, not for motorcycles. The profile of a motorcycle is narrow and the body is short, making it harder to see and making it harder for a driver to estimate the cycle's distance and speed.

Motorcycle riding requires frequent lane movements to adjust to changing road and traffic conditions.

Motorcycles have the right to the use of the full lane. Riders need the lane's full width to respond to and handle hazards such as potholes, shifting traffic blocking them from being seen or strong winds or blasts of air from passing vehicles. You must never try to share a lane with a motorcycle, and you should always respect the cycle's space and position in traffic.

Driver Tips for Sharing the Road with Motorcycles:

- **Passing -** Pass as you would pass a car, and don't pass too close or too fast as the blast of air can blow a motorcycle out of control.
- **Left turns -** Always signal your intention to turn. Watch for oncoming motorcycles.
- **Following Distance -** Allow at least a two-second following distance, so the motorcycle rider has enough time to maneuver or stop in an emergency. Both cyclists and drivers are more likely to make bad decisions if there is not enough stopping distance or time to see and react to conditions.
- **Check Your Blind Spots When Changing Lanes -** Motorcyclists riding alongside a lane of cars are often out of view of the driver. An unsuspecting driver may change lanes and clip or hit a motorcycle.
- **Anticipate Motorcyclists' Maneuvers -** A cyclists will change lane position to prepare for upcoming traffic conditions. Expect and allow room for the rider to adjust to road hazards that you can't see. At intersections, where most collisions and injuries occur, wait until the rider's intentions are absolutely clear (turning or going straight) before you move into the path of travel. Be even more careful in difficult driving conditions- rain, wet roads, ice and heavy winds- when the motorcyclist's braking and handling abilities are impaired.
- **Pay Extra Attention at Night -** You can easily misjudge distance because the single headlight or single tail light of a motorcycle can blend into the lights of other vehicles. Always dim your headlights as you would for other cars and trucks.
- **Drive Aware -** Whenever you are on the road or at an intersection with a motorcycle, use extra caution and care. Learn to watch for the narrow profile.

Hazards that can affect Motorcyclists' Maneuvers:

Special conditions and situations may cause problems for motorcyclists which drivers need to anticipate. Drivers should be aware of these problems, so they can help share the road safely with motorcyclists. Here are a few examples:

- Bad weather and slippery surfaces cause greater problems for motorcyclists than for cars. The conditions create stability problems for all vehicles. Allow more following distance for cyclists when the road surface is wet and slippery. Also be alert to the problem of glare that rain and wet surfaces create, especially at night.
- Strong cross winds can move a cycle out of its lane of travel. Areas where this can happen are wide open, long stretches of highways and bridges. Large, fast-moving trucks sometimes create wind blasts which under certain conditions, can move the cyclists out of their path of travel.
- Railroad grade crossings are a particular hazard to cyclists, and will usually cause them to slow down and possibly zigzag to cross the tracks.
- Metal or grated bridges cause a cycle to wobble much more than a car. An experienced cyclist slows down and moves to the center of the lane to allow room for handling the uneven surface. An inexperienced cyclist may become startled and try to quickly change direction. Be prepared for either reaction.
- Being aware of these situations and consciously looking out for motorcyclists can help you share the road safely.

Safety Tips for Motorcycles

Among all motor vehicles, motorcycles are the most vulnerable on the road. Because motorcycles do not have safety belts, you can be thrown off your seat in a crash, which can result in serious injury or even death. Imagine your chance for survival if a truck strikes you, or if you strike it. Hitting a truck is like hitting a steel wall. However, your chance for survival will be increased if you wear a helmet and follow the safety tips below when riding your motorcycle.

WATCH THE NO-ZONES

Never hang out in a truck's blind spot or "No-Zone." Trucks have large No-Zones on both sides, the front and behind the truck. Truck drivers cannot see you when you ride in these blind spots, which allows for a greater chance of a crash. The front blind spot is particularly dangerous if you need to stop quickly. Because of their lightweight and braking system, motorcycles can stop much faster than trucks. A truck may not be able to stop as quickly as you do, so you need to take special precautions to avoid crashes before they happen.

ALWAYS WEAR A HELMET

Make sure to always wear a helmet. Beware of helmets that do not meet U.S. Department of Transportation (DOT) standards. Check for the DOT label inside your helmet. Helmets are the most important piece of equipment you can wear when riding your motorcycle. A helmet could be your only source of protection in a serious crash.

DRIVE TO SURVIVE

Motorcycles are the smallest vehicles on the road. Unfortunately they provide virtually no protection in a crash. Other drivers may not see you on your motorcycle, so you must be aware of everything on the road. Be extra cautious, paying attention to the signals and brake lights of other vehicles, especially trucks. However, you still need to be prepared in the event their signals or lights don't work. Ride with caution and drive defensively. Even though your motorcycle may be small, you must adhere to the laws of the road. Never ride in between lanes in traffic or share a lane with another vehicle. Don't instigate aggressive driving with other motorists; you will only increase your chance of a crash.

CHECK YOURSELF AND YOUR BIKE

Conduct a safety inspection of your motorcycle before each ride, and wear protective clothing including gloves, boots and a jacket. Proper maintenance and protective clothing will help reduce your chance of an crash or the severity of injury if you are involved in a crash, especially with a large truck or bus.

WATCH YOUR SPEED

Of all vehicles, motorcycles accelerate the fastest, while trucks and buses are the slowest. Please watch your speed around trucks, especially in bad weather or at night. Colliding with the back of a car or truck will end your riding days.

To learn more about motorcycle safety, pick up a copy of the Tennessee Motorcycle Operator Manual at any Driver License Service Center. Additional information and an electronic copy of this manual is available online at www.tn.gov/safety

SAFETY TIPS FOR CAR DRIVERS

When driving on the highway you are at a serious disadvantage if involved in a crash with a larger vehicle. In crashes involving large trucks, the occupants of a car, usually the driver, sustain 78 percent of fatalities. In order to keep you and your family safe when driving around large trucks and buses, you should be extra cautious. Sharing the road with larger vehicles can be dangerous if you are not aware of their limitations. Here are a few tips to help you drive safer to prevent an accident and minimize injuries and fatalities if one does occur.

CUTTING IN FRONT CAN CUT YOUR LIFE SHORT

If you cut in front of another vehicle, you may create an emergency-braking situation for the vehicles around you, especially in heavy traffic. Trucks and buses take much longer to stop in comparison to cars. If you force a larger vehicle to stop quickly this could cause a serious, even fatal accident. When passing, look for the front of the truck in your rear-view mirror before pulling in front and avoid braking situations!

BUCKLE YOUR BELTS

Always buckle your safety belt. Safety belts are your best protection in case of a crash, especially if you get into an accident with a large vehicle such as a truck. Trucks require a greater stopping distance and can seriously hurt you if your car is struck from behind. However, your safety belt will keep you from striking the steering wheel or windshield, being thrown around, and from being ejected from the car. Wearing a safety belt is the single most important thing you can do to save your life, especially in a crash with a large truck.

WATCH YOUR BLIND SPOTS – THE "NO-ZONES"

Large trucks have blind spots, or No-Zones, around the front, back and sides of the truck. Watch out! A truck could even turn into you, because these No-Zones make it difficult for the driver to see. So, don't hang out in the No-Zones, and remember, if you can't see the truck driver in the truck's mirror, the truck driver can't see you.

INATTENTIVE DRIVERS

Inattentive drivers do not pay attention to driving or what is going on around them. They can be just as dangerous as aggressive drivers when they drive slowly in the passing lane, ignore trucks brake lights or signals, and create an emergency braking situation. They also create dangerous situations when they attempt to do other things while driving, such as using cell phones. When you are driving, please focus only on the road. If you need to attend to another matter while driving, safely pull over in a parking lot or rest stop.

AGGRESSIVE DRIVERS

Aggressive drivers can be dangerous drivers. They put themselves and others at risk with their unsafe driving. Speeding, running red lights and stop signs, pulling in front of trucks too quickly when passing, and making frequent lane changes, especially in the blind spots of trucks, can create dangerous and potentially fatal situations on the road. These situations can lead to road rage not only for the aggressive driver, but also for others sharing the road.

AVOID SQUEEZE PLAY

Be careful of trucks making wide right turns. If you try to get in between the truck and the curb, you'll be caught in a "squeeze" and can suffer a serious accident. Truck drivers sometimes need to swing wide to the left in order to safely negotiate a right turn especially in urban areas. They can't see cars directly behind or beside them. Cutting in between the truck and the curb increases the possibility of a crash. So pay attention to truck signals, and give them lots of room to maneuver.

NEVER DRINK AND DRIVE

Drinking and driving don't mix. Alcohol affects a person's ability to make crucial driving decisions, such as braking, steering, or changing lanes. Remember, you are not the only one in danger when you decide to drink and then drive. You are sharing the road with everyone including large vehicles and your chances of getting into an accident are greatly increased. If you get into an accident with a truck, you're out of luck. The odds of surviving a serious accident with a large truck are too low. However, if you do live through it without serious injury, think of your higher insurance rates, your large legal fees, and other social and professional setbacks it will cause you. So think before you drink.

SHARING THE ROAD WITH LARGE TRUCKS AND BUSES

You will always be sharing the road with trucks because they haul more freight more miles than any other form of transportation. Trucks are the sole method of delivery and pickup for approximately seventy-seven percent (77%) of America's communities.

A typical tractor-trailer combination, a loaded semi-trailer hinged and being pulled by tractor unit may weigh up to 80,000 pounds or 40 tons. Depending on the trailer length, the total length of the combination may exceed 70 feet.

In 2015, 4,311 large trucks and buses were involved in fatal crashes.

Many truck-car crashes could be avoided if drivers know about truck (and bus) limitations and how to steer clear of unsafe situations involving large vehicles. Seems obvious, doesn't it? But the fact is that while most people realize it is more difficult to drive a truck than a car, many don't know exactly what a truck's limitations are in terms of maneuverability, stopping distances, and blind-spots. Remember: Large trucks, recreational vehicles and buses are not simply big cars. The bigger they are:

1. The bigger their blind spots. Trucks have deep blind spots in front, behind and on both sides. Make sure you position your vehicle so that the driver of the truck can see you in the side mirrors of his truck.
2. The longer it takes trucks to stop. A car traveling at 55 MPH can stop in 240 feet however a truck traveling at the same speed of 55 MPH, takes about 450+ feet to stop.
3. The more room they need to maneuver, such as making right turns. Trucks must swing wide to the left to safely negotiate a right turn. They cannot see motorcycles or cars behind or beside them.
4. The longer it takes an automobile or motorcycle to pass them.
5. As stated above, the more likely you are to be the "loser" in a collision.

Truck drivers are always watching for automobiles and smaller vehicles and working to avoid collisions. There are some techniques that you can use to help them and yourself share the road safely and reduce the likelihood of a collision with a large vehicle.

Do NOT enter a roadway in front of a large vehicle. A truck or bus cannot slow down or stop as quickly as an automobile. By pulling out in front of these vehicles, you could easily cause a rear-end collision.

Do NOT drive directly behind a truck or bus. Keep a reasonable distance between your vehicle and the large vehicle ahead. This gives you a better view of the road to anticipate problems, and you will give yourself room for an emergency "out".

Do NOT cut abruptly in front of a large vehicle. If you are exiting, it will only take a few extra seconds to slow down and exit behind the truck. Cutting off a large vehicle on the interstate is particularly dangerous because of the high speeds being traveled.

When passing a large vehicle, do NOT pull back over into the lane in front of the truck unless you can see the whole front of the vehicle in your rearview mirror. Complete your pass as quickly as possible and don't stay alongside the truck. Do NOT slow down once you are in front of the truck.

Position your vehicle so you are outside the truck driver's "blind spots", and be sure the truck driver can see YOU in the side rearview mirror. **If you can't see the truck's mirror, the driver cannot see YOU.** A truck's blind spots are immediate in front, on either side of the car and up to 200 feet in the rear. A trucker may not be able to see the road directly in front of the cab. If the tractor has a long hood, the trucker may not be able to see the first 10-20 feet in front of the bumper, plenty of room for a motorcycle or car to slip unnoticed into a dangerous position.

If you are stopped behind a truck on an uphill grade, stay to the left in your lane so the driver can see you. When stopped in a traffic lane, leave extra space in front of your car in case the truck rolls back when it starts to move.

Pay close attention to the large vehicle's turn signals. Trucks make wide right turns that require them to swing to the left before turning right. Always make sure you know which way the vehicle is turning before trying to pass.

Do not linger beside a large vehicle because you may not be visible to the driver in the wide area the truck needs for maneuvering a turn.

When you are near a Commercial Vehicle Weigh Station, avoid driving in the right lane so slow-moving trucks can easily merge back onto the roadway.

Dim your lights at night. Bright lights reflected in the mirrors can blind the driver.

Never underestimate the size and speed of approaching trucks and buses. Because of their large size they often appear to be traveling more slowly than their actual speed.

Risky Situations with Large Vehicles

Passing a Large Vehicle: A tractor-trailer or other combination vehicles take a longer time and requires more space to get around than a car.

- On a two-way road, leave yourself more time and space when passing these large vehicles. Check to your front and rear and move into the passing lane only if it is clear and you are in a legal passing zone.
- If the truck or bus driver blink their vehicle headlights after you pass, it's a signal that you are cleared to pull back in front of their vehicle. Move back only when you can see the front of the truck in your rearview mirror.
- Remember that on an upgrade or steep hill, a large vehicle usually loses speed.
- Because of their weight, trucks travel faster downhill and you may have to increase your speed to pass a truck on a downhill grade. Complete your pass as quickly as possible and don't stay alongside the truck. After you

pass, maintain your speed. Don't pass a truck, then slow down, making the truck driver brake while traveling downhill.

- When a truck passes you, you can help the driver by keeping to the far side of your lane and reducing your speed slightly. NEVER SPEED UP AS A TRUCK OR BUS IS PASSING.

- When you meet a truck/bus coming from the opposite direction, keep as far as possible to the right of the road to avoid being sideswiped and to reduce wind turbulence between vehicles. The turbulence PUSHES vehicles APART. It does NOT suck them together.

The "Right Turn Squeeze": Trucks make wide right turns and often must leave an open space on the right side. Do NOT move into that space or try to pass a truck if it might be making a right turn. If you are between the truck and the curb, the driver may not be able to see you and your car can be crunched or sideswiped by the truck's trailer.

A Truck Backing Up: When a truck is trying to back into a loading dock, there may be no choice except to block the roadway for a short time. Never try to cross behind a truck when it is preparing to back up. This is a high-collision situation because you will be in the driver's blind spots. Give the driver plenty of room and wait patiently for the few minutes it takes to complete the maneuver.

Maintaining a Safety Cushion with Large Vehicles: As stated previously, trucks and buses need more maneuvering room and stopping distance than small vehicles. A good safety strategy is to leave plenty of space between your vehicle and the larger vehicle, especially in these situations:

If you are driving in front of a truck, keep your speed up so you maintain a safe distance in front of the truck. Always indicate your intention to turn or change lanes early enough for the driver of the truck or bus to prepare for your maneuver. Avoid sudden moves, slow downs or stops.

Don't cut in front of a truck or bus. You can remove the driver's cushion of safety.

When following a truck or bus, it is a good idea to add more following distance.

If rain or water is standing on the road, spray from a truck passing you, or the truck you are trying to pass, will seriously reduce your vision. You should move as far away from the truck as you can, while staying in your lane.

Don't drive too close to trucks that are transporting hazardous materials, since they make frequent stops, such as railroad crossings.

Hills or Mountain Roads: Beware of dangers caused by slower moving trucks or buses on steep hills, inclines, or

mountain roads. Watch for slow moving trucks or buses going both up and down hills. Heavy vehicles cannot maintain speed when climbing hills and must go slowly down hills to stay under control. Watch for trucks or buses that might be in trouble. Smoking wheels or a high speed can be a sign of brake loss. If you encounter this situation, fall back and DO NOT pass.

Runaway Truck Ramps: These ramps are designed to stop out-of-control trucks or buses going down step downgrades. Vehicles should never stop or park in these areas.

Learn the "NO-ZONES" for large vehicles:
Many motorists falsely assume that trucks and buses can see the road better because they sit twice as high as the driver of a small vehicle. While trucks and buses do enjoy a better forward view and have bigger mirrors, they have serious blind spots into which a small vehicle can disappear from view.

The NO-ZONE represents danger areas around trucks and buses where crashes are more likely to occur.

1. The area approximately up to 20 feet directly in front of a large vehicle is considered a NO-ZONE. When small vehicles cut in too soon after passing or changing lanes, then abruptly slow down, trucks and buses are forced to compensate with very little room or time to spare.

2. Unlike small vehicles, trucks and buses have deep blind spots directly behind them. Avoid following too closely in this NO-ZONE. If you stay in the rear blind spot of a large vehicle, you increase the possibility of a traffic crash. The driver of the bus or truck cannot see your motorcycle or car and your view of the traffic ahead will be severely reduced.

3. Large vehicles have much larger blind spots on both sides than cars do. When you drive in these blind spots for any length of time, the vehicle's driver cannot see you. When passing, even if the vehicle's driver knows you are there, remaining alongside a large vehicle too long makes it impossible for the driver to take evasive action if an obstacle appears in the roadway ahead.

4. Truck and bus drivers often cannot see vehicles directly behind or beside them when they are attempting to safely negotiate a right turn. If you cut in between the truck or bus and the curb or shoulder to the right, it greatly increases the possibility of a crash in this "right turn squeeze'.

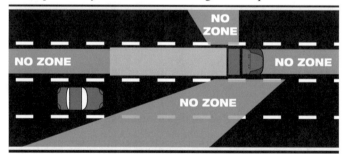

OVERHEAD VIEW OF "NO-ZONE" AREAS

School buses are one of the safest forms of transportation in the nation-nearly 2,000 times safer than the family car.

Crashes are rare because school systems and the school bus contractors work hard to train drivers to avoid crashes.

The reality of school bus safety is that more children are hurt outside a bus than inside one. ***Children are at greatest risk when they are getting on or off the school bus.*** Most of the children killed in bus related crashes are pedestrians, five to seven years old; they are hit by the bus or by motorists illegally passing a stopped school bus. In fact pedestrian fatalities while loading and unloading school buses account for nearly three out of every four fatalities. The child who bends over to retrieve a dropped school paper, or who walks too close to the bus while crossing the street, needs to be aware that every school bus is surrounded by a danger zone.

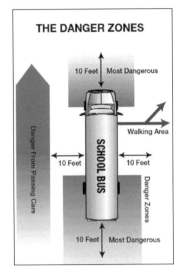

THE DANGER ZONES

This Danger Zone is the area on all sides of the bus where children are in the most danger of being hit. Children should stay ten feet away from the school bus and NEVER go behind the bus.

In many of our school systems, children are taught to escape that zone by taking five giant steps as soon as they exit the bus. If they must cross the street after exiting the bus, they are taught to cross at least five giant steps in front of the bus-and to be sure they're able to be seen by the school bus driver and can maintain eye contact with the driver.

Perhaps the most difficult thing to teach children, especially young children, is not to go back to pick up items they've dropped near the bus, or left on the bus.

Parents and other adults must also do their part. For instance, most drivers need to learn to share the road with school buses and stop when the bus stops to take on or let off passengers. If we all do our part- if drivers heed school bus warning lights, bus drivers drive defensively, parents help their children learn to ride safely and children learn to avoid the bus' danger zone- it can be safer still to ride to and from school in that yellow bus.

Safety Tips for Drivers

Drivers must be familiar with the Danger Zone. Since children are taught to take the "five giant steps" from the school bus for safety, drivers must ensure that they stop far enough from the bus to allow for this needed safety space. Certain slow-moving farm vehicles, construction equipment and vehicles drawn by animals may share our roadways. Use

caution and prepare to slow down when approaching and passing slow-moving vehicles from the rear.

Be alert for slow-moving vehicles, especially in rural areas. Driving on empty rural highways can be just as dangerous as driving in heavy city traffic. It is easy to relax your attention… and suddenly come upon a dangerous surprise. Animals in the road, farm equipment moving from one field to another, horse drawn vehicles just over the crest of a hill, or a low spot covered with water are not unusual hazards in rural driving.

Stay alert, watch for warning signs, and slow down when approaching curves or hills that block your view of the roadway ahead. The "slow moving vehicle" emblem, a fluorescent or reflective orange triangle, must be displayed on the rear of vehicles drawn by animals, and most farm vehicles and construction equipment.

Farm Machinery: Watch for tractors, combines, and other farm equipment moving across the road and traveling on state highways in rural areas. This type of equipment can be very large and wide enough to take up more than one traffic lane. Farm machinery usually does not have turn signals and to make a right turn, operators of farm machinery may first pull wide to the left, then turn to the right. In most cases, these vehicles will be traveling at less than 25 M.P.H. Coming over the top of a hill at 55 M.P.H. to find a large slow-moving tractor in front of you is a frightening and dangerous experience. Expect the unexpected and be prepared to protect yourself and your passengers.

Horse Drawn Carriages: In some areas of Tennessee you may be sharing the road with animal-drawn vehicles. They have the same rights to use the road as a motor vehicle and must follow the same rules of the road. They are subject to heavy damage and injury to the occupants if hit by a car. Warning signs will be posted in areas where you are likely to find animal-drawn vehicles. **Be Alert!**

Horseback Riders: Horseback riders are subject to, and protected by, the rules of the road. They also must ride single file near the right curb or road edge, or on a usable right shoulder, lane or path. The law requires you to exercise due care when approaching a horse being ridden or led along a road. Areas where horseback riding is common will usually be marked with an advisory sign. You must drive at a reasonable speed, and at a reasonable distance away from the horse. Do NOT sound your horn or "rev" your engine loudly when approaching or passing a horse.

Closing Speeds

Normal speeds for slow-moving vehicles may range from 5 to 20 mph. When a vehicle traveling at normal highway speed approaches a slow-moving vehicle from the rear, the speed deferential will dramatically shorten the time it takes to reach the slow-moving vehicle.

Turns and Passing

Slow-moving vehicles may make wide turns and may turn right or left at any time into unmarked entrances. When approaching from the rear, stay a safe distance behind the vehicle until it is safe to pass, then be certain the driver has seen you and is aware of your intent to pass before you begin.

When lights are required for these slow moving vehicles, a self-luminous red lamp on the rear of the vehicle is normally visible for 500 feet to the rear. Other devices to identify slow-moving vehicles may include slow moving emblem reflectors, as well as rotating or oscillating red or amber lights. You may see this on slow-moving vehicles such as farm tractors, machinery, construction equipment or horse-drawn vehicles.

Lane Usage

Slower traffic must drive in the right-hand lane. The left lane is for passing and turning. Slow-moving vehicles may be wider than the lane width. It may be necessary for these wide vehicles to temporarily move into an adjoining lane to avoid roadside obstructions.

SHARING THE ROAD WITH HIGHWAY WORK ZONES

Work Zone Safety: It's Everybody's Business

Work zones on U.S. highways have become increasingly dangerous places for both workers and travelers, with the death rate approaching two per day. Approximately 40,000 people per year are injured as a result of crashes in work zones. With more than 70,000 work zones in place across America on a given day, highway agencies are realizing that it is not enough to focus on improving the devices used in the work zone areas, but that they must also reach out to the public in order to change the behavior of drivers so that crashes can be prevented.

What is a Work Zone? A work zone is any type of road work that may impede traffic conditions. Many work zones involve lane closures. They may also be on the shoulder or in the median. Moving work zones such as sweepers, line painting trucks, or mowing equipment and workers are also quite common.

Highway work zones are set up according to the type of road and the work to be done on the road. There are a number of events that make up a work zone. They can be long-term projects of short term actions. A work zone can also exist at anytime of the year. The common theme among work zones is the color orange. Work zone materials such as cones, barrels, signs, large vehicles, or orange vests on workers give you an indication that you are either approaching a work zone or are already in a work zone. In these work zones, workers will normally be wearing bright yellow-green apparel such as shirts, vests or hardhats to ensure they are highly visible.

What do you do when approaching a Work Zone? Watch for the color orange – it always means: "road work—slow down". All temporary signs in work zones have an orange background and black letters or symbols. These signs will be found on the right side of the road, or on both left and right sides when the roadway is a divided highway, and they will tell you what (one lane traffic, uneven lanes, etc.) and how soon (miles or feet ahead) you will encounter the work zone. Most work zones also have signs alerting you to reductions in the speed limit through the work zone.

These speed reductions are necessary for the safety of the workers and motorists. The reduced speed limits are clearly posted within the work zone and if there are no reduced speed limit postings, drivers should obey the normal posted speed limit. Under Tennessee law, speed violations that occur in the work zones where the speed has been reduced and where employees of the Department of Transportation as well as other construction workers are present, will result in a fine up to a maximum of $500 dollars. What should you do when driving through Work Zones? Signing, traffic control devices, roadway markings, flaggers, and law enforcement officers are used to protect highway workers and to direct drivers safely through work zones or along carefully marked detours. As a driver you should learn and abide by the following safety tips for driving in work zones:

Slow down and pay full attention to the driving situation! Drive within the posted speed limits, which are usually reduced in work zones. If you don't, you'll pay the price. A car traveling 60 M.P.H. travels 88 feet per second. If you see a sign that says "Road Work 1500 Feet", you'll be in that construction zone in 17 seconds!

Obey the posted speed limits which are usually reduced in work zones. Workers could be present just a few feet away. If you don't, you'll pay the price.

Merge as soon as possible. Motorists can help maintain traffic flow and posted speeds by moving to the appropriate lane at first notice of an approaching work zone. You can be ticketed and the cause of an accident for being a last chance merger.

Use total concentration when driving through work zones. Pay attention to your surroundings. This is not the time to use the cellular phone, look for a new CD, change the radio station, read the paper, apply make-up, shave, eat or drink or fill out the expense report.

Keep your ears open! Do not wear earphones while driving. Turn your lights on before you enter the zone! Turn on your vehicle's headlights to become more visible to workers and other motorists.

Follow the instructions on the road work zone warning signs and those given by flaggers. Follow their signals, and don't change lanes within the work zone unless instructed to do so. *Expect the unexpected! Avoid complacency.* Work zones change constantly. Don't become oblivious to work zone signs when the work is long term or widespread.

Use extreme caution when driving through a work zone at night whether workers are present or not.

Calm down. Work zones aren't there to personally inconvenience you. They're there to improve the roads for everyone and improve your future ride.

Watch the traffic around you, and be prepared to react to what the traffic is doing. Check the taillights/brake lights of vehicles ahead of you for indications of what is happening on the road ahead. Be ready to respond quickly.

Adjust your lane position away from where the side workers and equipment are located when possible.

Keep a safe distance between your vehicle and traffic barriers, trucks, construction equipment and workers. **Don't tailgate!** Most work zone accidents are caused by rear-end collisions.

Some work zones – like line painting, road patching and mowing – are mobile. Just because you don't see the workers immediately after you see the warning signs doesn't mean they're not out there. Observe the posted signs until you see the one that says "End Road Work".

Expect delays; plan for them and leave early to reach your destination on time.

Avoid road work zones altogether by using alternate routes, when you can.

SHARING THE ROAD WITH TRAINS

Actually, you don't share the road with trains-you stop and let them have the right-of-way! You can stop your car suddenly but a train can't. **Drivers must ALWAYS yield the right of way to trains because IT'S THE LAW.**

The average car weighs 3,000 pounds and the average loaded train weighs 12 million pounds!

A train traveling at 55 miles per hour takes a full mile to stop. You are 30 times more likely to die in a collision with a train than with a car or even a large truck or bus.

Over half of the train collisions with cars in America happen at crossroads with lights, bells, or gates and two-thirds of the crashes happen in full daylight.
Why?

Impatience - Drivers don't want to wait the 30 seconds to 2 minutes average time it takes for the train to pass through the intersection. They try to beat the train.
Negligence - When drivers see a railroad crossing sign or warning, they don't respect the potential for danger; they cross the tracks without looking, listening, or stopping. Most of the collisions occur within 25 miles of the driver's home,

suggesting that drivers KNEW the tracks were there and they were in the habit of crossing without looking.

If you are on a collision course with a train, only you can avoid the collision. The train cannot stop in time or swerve to avoid you.

Stopping for Railroad Crossings
Countless people lose their lives or suffer tragic injuries due to train/vehicle collisions. Invariably, the cause of these collisions is the disregard, and often willful evasion, of railroad crossing warnings by drivers.

Railroad Crossing Warning Signs: Railroad crossing signs signal a driver to slow down, look, listen and be prepared to stop for a train. These signs include the round yellow railroad ahead crossing sign, the railroad cross-buck sign, pavement markings and at crossings with significant vehicular traffic, red flashing

ALWAYS EXPECT A TRAIN
lights and crossing gates.

Railroad Crossing Stop Signs: If you approach a railroad crossing at which a stop sign is posted, you must come to a complete stop and proceed across the tracks only after looking both ways to make sure a train is not approaching. Never assume the track is not used or a train is not approaching.

Safety Guidelines for Railroad Crossings:
Obey the Warning Signs: Look both ways and **LISTEN**, because you may have to stop. Expect a train on any track at any time. Don't trust a "schedule" because trains can cross at any time of the day or night. Due to the size of trains, the actual speed of a train can be very deceiving.

Don't Attempt to "Beat the Train": Under no circumstances attempt to race a train to a crossing. If you lose, you will never race again.

Don't Try to "Evade the Gates": Never drive around a crossing gate that has extended down. If the gates are down, stop and stay in place. It's against the law to drive through lowered gates. Don't cross the tracks until the gates are fully raised and the lights have stopped flashing.

When Approaching a Railroad Crossing: Slow down far enough ahead of the crossing to be certain that you can stop when you reach the point where a train could first be seen. Railroad crossings equipped with electric or mechanical signal devices require the operator to bring the vehicle to a complete stop within 50 feet, and no closer than 15 feet from the nearest rail and shall not proceed until it is safe.

Avoid Stopping on the Railroad Tracks: Never proceed to cross the tracks unless you can legally clear all tracks without stopping. If you are crossing the tracks and the warning lights begin flashing or the gates start coming down, don't stop. **KEEP MOVING!** The warning signals will allow enough time for you to finish driving through the crossing before the train arrives. The gate on the far side of the tracks will not block you in. **DO NOT EVER TRY TO BACK UP**.

If your vehicle stalls on the tracks, all occupants should exit the vehicle immediately and get away from the tracks even if you do not see a train. Locate the Emergency Notification System (ENS) sign and call the emergency number provided telling them about the stalled vehicle and give them the DOT crossing number found on the sign. If you cannot locate the ENS sign call 911 to notify local law enforcement.

If a train is approaching, run toward the train at a 45 degree angle. This allows you to be away from and behind the point of impact, to prevent injury. If you run in the same direction a train is traveling you could be injured by flying debris! (*See illustration below*)

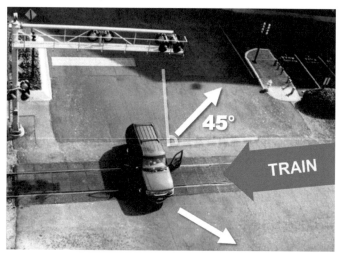

The Emergency Notification System (ENS) sign, normally blue in color and may be located on the crossbuck post or signal post. (See Illustration below)

Your vehicle is replaceable. You are not! No Vehicle is worth a human life.

REPORT PROBLEM OR EMERGENCY 1-800-555-5555 X-ING 836 597 H XYZ RAILROAD

Watch for Additional Trains:
Where there is more than one track, a driver waiting for one train to pass must make sure another train is not approaching from the opposite direction. Once the first train has cleared the tracks, caution should be taken that a second train is NOT proceeding in the opposite direction. Don't go across the tracks until you are sure that no other trains are coming on another track from either direction.

Watch for Vehicles that Must Stop at Highway-Railway Crossings: School Buses, Passenger Buses and Trucks carrying hazardous materials must stop at all crossings whether signals are activated to not. Never attempt to pass these stopped vehicles on a two-way road. For safety's sake

do NOT pass such stopped vehicles on a multi-lane roadway unless the crossing is clearly marked with signal lights and/or gates that are NOT activated. Otherwise the stopped vehicle in the right lane may block your clear view of the tracks.

Intersection Warning Signs; Some variation of the sign shown on the right will be posted prior to intersections or crossroads where railroad tracks cross one of the roadways. Always be alert and pay attention to these signs as they give you advance warning that you may encounter a train if turning onto the road indicated in the sign.
For more information on Railroad Crossing Safety contact:
Operation Lifesaver of Tennessee
9208 Apache Trail
Brentwood, TN 37027
www.tnol.org
or
Federal Railroad Administration
Office of Public Affairs (Stop 5)
1120 Vermont Ave., NW
Washington, DC 20590
www.fra.dot.gov

SAFETY TIPS FOR 15-PASSENGER VANS

The following safety tips will help prevent crashes, including rollover crashes in 15-passenger vans, as well as protect you in case an unavoidable crash does occur.

Safety Restraints
All occupants in 15-passenger vans must wear safety belts at all times. This is the law in Tennessee, as well as many other states. As stated previously, NHTSA estimates that 80 percent of 15-passenger van fatalities were not properly restrained at the time of the crash. Our research shows that 195 people were killed in 15-passenger vans in Tennessee between 1994 and 2007, and of the 181 people with known restraint usage, 138 (76%) were not restrained. With this proportion, we can estimate that 105 lives may have been saved if everyone had been properly restrained.

Tire Pressure
Tires need to be inspected and tire pressure checked every time the van is used. Excessively worn or improperly inflated tires can lead to a loss of control situation and rollover. Tread should be checked to insure there is enough grip, and to make sure there are no signs of tread separation. Also important to note is that many of these vans have extremely different tire pressure recommendations for front versus rear tires. Under-inflation of the rear tires (especially the left rear) is a major cause of tread separation.

Driver
Anyone who operates a 15-passenger van should be trained and experienced, since these machines react much differently

than passenger cars. There are no special endorsements or licenses needed to operate a 15-passenger van in the State of Tennessee. Just as important as experience, is attention. Drivers should be well-rested and should not use cell phones or other handheld devices, so they maintain focus on the road. These vehicles require longer stopping distances and do not turn as easily as passenger cars. As with all vehicles, drugs and alcohol should not be used by the driver. Since these vans are bigger and it is often more difficult to see other traffic, it may be a good idea to use an occupant as a spotter. Nearly 70% of the fatal 15-passenger van crashes in Tennessee involved two or more vehicles.

Check the Load

Have passengers sit as far towards the front of the vehicle as possible. With most 15-passenger vans, the rear seat is located behind the rear axle. This causes an uneven weight distribution, pushing the center of gravity (CG) further back. Do not tow any trailers or put cargo on the roof of the van. These actions also impact the CG, increasing chances of rollover.

Avoid Conditions that Lead to Loss of Control

This is even more important in 15-passenger vans than any other vehicle. Most rollovers occur at high speeds as a result of sudden steering maneuvers. Caution should be used on interstates and state highways to avoid running off the road. If the van's tires should drop off the roadway, gradually slow down and steer back on to the roadway when it is safe to do so.

SAFETY TIPS FOR RECREATIONAL VEHICLES (RVs)

Recreational vehicles (RVs) can be a great way to travel across the country. However, to be safe you need to know about safe operation and maintenance. RVs are very different from cars and because of their size; they handle more like a large truck. This also means RVs have some real limitations. In order to keep your friends and family safe on your next trip, make sure to read these tips below, and enjoy the view.

WATCH YOUR BLIND SPOTS - THE "NO-ZONES"

RVs are large and have many blind spots. Learning to use your mirrors and signals properly can help prevent serious accidents. Your mirrors are very important, but they do not allow you to see everything on the road, so always be aware. In addition, trucks have even larger blind spots, and may not see you; be ready to respond defensively to dangerous situations.

PREPARE TO STOP

RVs are similar to trucks in that they are heavier than cars, and require a longer stopping distance. Pay attention to traffic and to other vehicle's brake lights. Always keep enough room between your RV and the vehicle in front of you. This will help prevent accidents in case of an emergency braking situation. Driving at a safe speed will also ensure your safety in the event of any sudden stops.

CHECK YOUR TIRES

Maintaining proper tire pressure, inspecting tires regularly, avoiding excess loading, and driving at a safe speed, can help prevent tire problems. Before each trip, make sure you check to see if your tires are properly inflated. Maintaining the correct air pressure and tread depth will ensure their longevity and your safety.

WATCH YOUR WEIGHT

Weight distribution is very important in maintaining the proper center of gravity in a RV. Be sure to secure all heavy items. They can shift during travel and may affect handling, ride quality and braking. Distributing the weight closer to the ground and equal on both sides keeps the center of gravity low and will provide better handling of your RV.

WEAR YOUR SAFETY BELT

Always wear your safety belt. Make sure all passengers in your RV wear safety belts whenever the vehicle is in motion. In case of an accident or sudden stop, passengers who are not buckled in may be thrown around and seriously injured.

Chapter C-4 HELPING TEENS AND NEW DRIVERS LEARN TO DRIVE

If you are trying to teach someone how to drive, the most important thing you can do is to drive safely yourself. Though it sounds trite, it is true. Your friend or family member is now watching more carefully than you can ever dream. How do we know? Examiners quite often hear, "Well, that's how my dad/mom does it." Sometimes the young driver is saying this to defend such things as "rolling stops". Luckily, it is also often said with pride, when the applicant is giving a parent credit for their safe driving habits.

Getting a driver license is often referred to as the modern equivalent of a rite of passage to adulthood for the young, new driver – and it's certainly a dangerous one. The driving world they enter is far too intense to tackle without serious preparation.

As a parent (or concerned mentor) you are the one who cares most about your teenager's driving ability and safety. This chapter will help give you some hints and ideas on ways to participate in the process of educating your teenager (or inexperienced adult) behind the wheel.

Which Comes First, the Book or the Road?
You both will find it helpful to review this chapter, and any other materials you can find before actually letting the new driver get behind the wheel. People under the age of eighteen (18) must have a learner permit for 180 days and qualify under the GDL program before they can be road tested. This requirement involves "book learning" before getting on the road and a minimum amount of "supervised on the road learning" before getting a license to drive solo. This is a good principle for people of any age who are just learning to drive.

A SAFE Attitude for Driving and Learning
Attitude determines how the knowledge and skills your teen or new driver have learned will be used. It determines whether a driver will be cooperative or competitive in traffic, whether he or she will accept a high level of risk or put into practice the concepts of defensive driving.

Your biggest contribution to your new driver's safety and effectiveness behind the wheel will be the examples you set. Patience, courtesy, and a willingness to improve will be your best assets. Now is the time to review your own driving habits and offer your teen or new driver the example of courtesy and consideration for other road users. This may do more than anything else to ensure your teen's driving safety.

Verbal Teaching in the "Moving Classroom"
A second helpful thing you can do is to talk out loud while you are driving. Rather than overload the new driver with information and advice while he or she is also trying to simply learn the mechanics of driving, take advantage of teaching opportunities while you are behind the wheel. These are truly "teachable moments". For example, you can:

- Point out tricky road signs, and ask what they mean.
- When a light turns yellow, talk about how you knew whether it was safe to stop, or safer to continue through the intersection.
- Ask the teen/new driver questions about the traffic behind you or beside you – make them aware that you have to pay attention to traffic all around you, not just in front of you.
- Practice the "two-second" rule by explaining out loud the steps you are taking to gauge your following distance.

Once you start doing this, you will be surprised at all of the wisdom you already have. You may also be surprised when it opens the door for your pupil to offer friendly and constructive criticism of your own driving habits! Since most of us have room for improvement, you will, hopefully, be able to accept with humor any good criticism they have.

Planning Safe and Informative Practice Sessions
It's important to plan practice sessions. Always decide where to go and what you are going to do before setting out. Random driving around during practice sessions can be dangerous. It is all too easy for the novice driver to get into trouble particularly in the early stages. Before venturing into traffic for practice driving, be sure that your teen / new driver has good coordination with hands and feet. Until the novice is sure of the pedals, the danger of hitting the wrong pedal in a panic situation is always present. Nothing substitutes for actual experience on the road. However you will want to have your first lessons concentrate on simply gaining control of the vehicle. Later lessons can build on this, getting increasingly more challenging. Listed below is some ideas for one approach you might choose to follow:

Phase One: Have the new driver practice controlling the car itself. Find someplace safe and away from traffic. A large deserted parking lot is ideal for these initial sessions because it allows the beginner to concentrate fully on the feel of the controls and the response of the car. Start by practicing these basic skills:

- Buckling up, adjusting the seat and mirrors so that all necessary controls are within easy reach.
- Operating the gearshift (and clutch if manual transmission), gas and brake pedals.
- Backing and pulling the car forward. Right and Left turns while driving in the parking lot.
- Staying within an imaginary lane.

Phase Two: Take the driver to a quiet residential area and let your new driver practice not only the above skills, but also add:

- Pulling into traffic and navigating simple intersections

- Keeping proper lane position and allowing safe
  (2- second) following distances.

- Easy lane changes.

Phase Three: After you are satisfied that the basic controls are fairly well mastered, you are now ready to take the new driver into heavier traffic. Again, you will practice all of the above, and add:

- Parallel parking and up / down hill parking

- Navigating multiple turn lane intersections

- U-turns and quick stops (simulating emergency)

Phase Four: When you have confidence the new driver can handle greater challenges, you should guide him or her to practice all the above in the following conditions:

- On high-speed multi-lane highways or interstates

- In various weather conditions

- At night in good weather and bad weather

- City driving or heavy traffic areas

Additional hints to help you as a teacher / mentor:

Stay Alert: Anticipate problems and always be ready to react to help avoid accidents or other unsafe situations.

Communicate Clearly: Give directions well in advance and try to always use the same terms (don't say accelerator one time and gas pedal the next, for example).

Don't hit the beginner with everything at once: rather than taking the new driver to a multi-lane intersection for their first left turn do this in a calmer traffic area. Remember even a simple right turn involves several steps (checking mirrors, signaling, lane use, braking, turning, etc.) To expect a beginner to follow all of these correctly during the early sessions is asking too much.

Don't get excited during practice sessions: calmly respond to errors as needed. Don't "yell and fuss" over every mistake. This can quickly erode the new driver's confidence and make performance difficult.

Don't overload or distract: Remember everything you say is also a distraction for the drive. Be sparing in your comments and, above all, try to avoid letting the beginner get into a situation he or she isn't ready to handle.

Stop and Discuss: Stop as soon as you can, while a major mistake is still fresh in the new driver's memory. Then take time to discuss what happened and what the safest response should be.

Two Reference Tools to Consider

Driving Log: Safety researchers have found that the more supervised miles new drivers have before driving on their own, the fewer accidents they have. This seems like common sense, but is there a magic number of miles you should ride with your student? The University of Michigan's Transportation

Research Institute recommends 3,000 miles.

Each new driver is different, of course, and yours may not need that many miles to be a confident, competent driver. Tennessee's GDL program requires a specific number of hours (50) be driven by minors prior to being eligible to move up to the Intermediate license level. To keep track of these hours we suggest either getting a simple spiral ring notebook to keep in the glove compartment to record your practice sessions – or – you may choose to make copies of the sample log on page 118.

Driving Contracts: The first year of driving is a high-risk period for the beginner. Inexperience combined with a lack of skill means that one in five male 16-year old drivers and about one in ten female 16-year olds will have a crash during their first year of driving. Some of the worst accidents occur at night and with a group of young people in the car. If alcohol or any other kind of impairment is involved the risk in this situation is magnified several times. This is one of the reasons that Tennessee's GDL program places restrictions on these two areas for new teen drivers.

As it gets closer to the time when your new driver will be applying for the Intermediate Driver License, some parents find it helpful to sit down and spell out just what they expect when they turn the car over to their teen. It is up to you whether you would want to have this "contract" written and signed, or just discussed as a family, but areas you could consider covering in your agreement include:

✓ Where they may drive (miles, road types, etc.)

✓ What hours of the day they may drive

✓ The condition the car should be returned (gas in tank, clean, etc.) and the consequences if this is neglected.

✓ Who pays for the car's gas and maintenance

✓ What amount they will contribute toward auto insurance

✓ Responsibility for parking tickets or vehicle damage

✓ Consequences for moving violations, including speeding

Safe driving is very much a matter of seeing what needs to be seen and making good decisions, but this is not simple to achieve. Experience and training play a major role in ensuring that a driver's eyes will look in the right places at the right time and that their knowledge of safe and defensive driving will help them make the proper response to the situation.

Being a good defensive driver means more than just being cautious; and mere experience isn't enough either! The good defensive driver has to work at developing good driving techniques. And this work does not end with passing the driver license examination. The novice driver's biggest enemy is the complacency that comes from early success at learning driving basics. As parents or mentors your role is to help the teen overcome that complacency and continue to build driving skills after licensing.

Helping Non-English Speaking Beginners

If you have shouldered the task of teaching someone to learn to drive, whose first language is not English, two areas in particular deserve special attention. First, make every effort to ensure that the driver studies the material on traffic signs and signals thoroughly, and help him or her to "translate" these while you are out driving together. Second, put yourself in the role of an examiner, and let the driver practice following simple instructions in English (for example: "Turn left"; "Slow down"; "Go straight at the next intersection";, etc.). All applicants must understand and speak enough English to safely communicate with the examiner before a road test can be administered.

A Special Final Word to Parents

Remember – a driver license examiner spends less than 30 minutes driving with your child. Just by virtue of the fact that it is an examination, this is a special trip. Most applicants will perform at their very best level during the examination. Just because they perform at the passing level does not necessarily mean they will always use those safe driving procedures after the examiner is no longer in the car.

The driver license examiner can evaluate a driver's competence, but the responsibility of education and teaching that child to drive rests with the parents or concerned mentor. This means that it is wise to continue to monitor your teen's driving performance even after they have been issued a driver license.

GRADUATED DRIVER LICENSE DRIVING EXPERIENCE LOG

Tennessee's Graduated Driver License law requires the parent, guardian or certified driving instructor to sign a certificate (Form SF-1256) confirming that the teen driver has accumulated a minimum of fifty (50) hours of behind the wheel driving experience while holding a valid learner permit. This experience must include a minimum of ten (10) hours of night-time driving. The driving log below is provided as a tool to assist the teen and parent in tracking this experience. *This log is NOT required to be submitted to the Driver License Office prior to road testing. It is simply provided as a convenience.*

Driving Date & Time (Hours and Minutes) D = Daytime N = Nighttime				Driving Environment (residential, city, rural, interstate, mixed, etc.)	Driving Skills Practiced*	Driving Conditions (sunny, raining, snowing / paved, gravel, dry, wet, icy, etc.)		Miles Driven		Mentor P = Parent PD = Parent Designee I = Qualified Instructor	Mentor Initials
Date	Hrs.	Mins.	D	N			Weather	Roadway	Beginning	Ending		
Totals												

*Examples: yielding-of-way/courtesy; maintaining driving focus/attention; vehicle control/handling; speed control; safe braking; space management; 2 second rule; safe/proper backing; maintaining lane position; passing; turns/intersections; pre-driving habits (seat belts, mirrors, etc.); traffic controls (RR signals, traffic lights, etc.).

UNDERSTANDING TENNESSEE'S DRIVER LICENSE PROGRAM

CAREFULLY READ ALL THREE (3) SECTIONS OF THIS COMPREHENSIVE MANUAL

SECTION A:
  DIFFERENT TYPES OF LICENSES
  WHAT DOCUMENTS ARE NEEDED TO APPLY
  INFORMATION FOR APPLICANTS UNDER AGE 18
  DESCRIPTION OF REQUIRED DRIVER LICENSE TESTS

SECTION B:
  GOOD DRIVING PRACTICES
  RULES OF THE ROAD
  TRAFFIC SIGNS AND SIGNALS
  STATE DRIVING LAWS AND PENALTIES
  IMPORTANT CONTENT USED IN KNOWLEDGE AND SKILLS TESTING

SECTION C:
  SAFETY TIPS
  DEFENSIVE DRIVING
  SHARING THE ROAD SAFELY
  HELPING TEENS AND NEW DRIVERS LEARN TO DRIVE

Tips to Help with Your Visit to the Driver Service Center
This manual includes:
- Types of Driver Licenses and Identification Licenses
- Steps to make application for and renew your Tennessee Driver License
- What Necessary Documents you will need to bring
- What Your Fees Will Be

VISIT THE DRIVER SERVICE CENTER MOST CONVENIENT TO YOU
To get location information, days and hours of operation, as well as scheduling your road skills test appointment, go online at: www.tn.gov/safety or by calling toll-free 1-866-849-3548.

Our Driver Service Centers will typically have an increased volume of customers when we reopen after being closed for a holiday, so please plan your visit accordingly. You may also wish to consider using our website at: www.tn.gov/safety to check your eligibility to renew online.

TDD (Telecommunications Device for the Deaf) (615)-532-2281

Made in the USA
Columbia, SC
07 December 2024